P9-CKT-240

ONE SHOT AT FOREVER

THE 1971 MACON IRONMEN

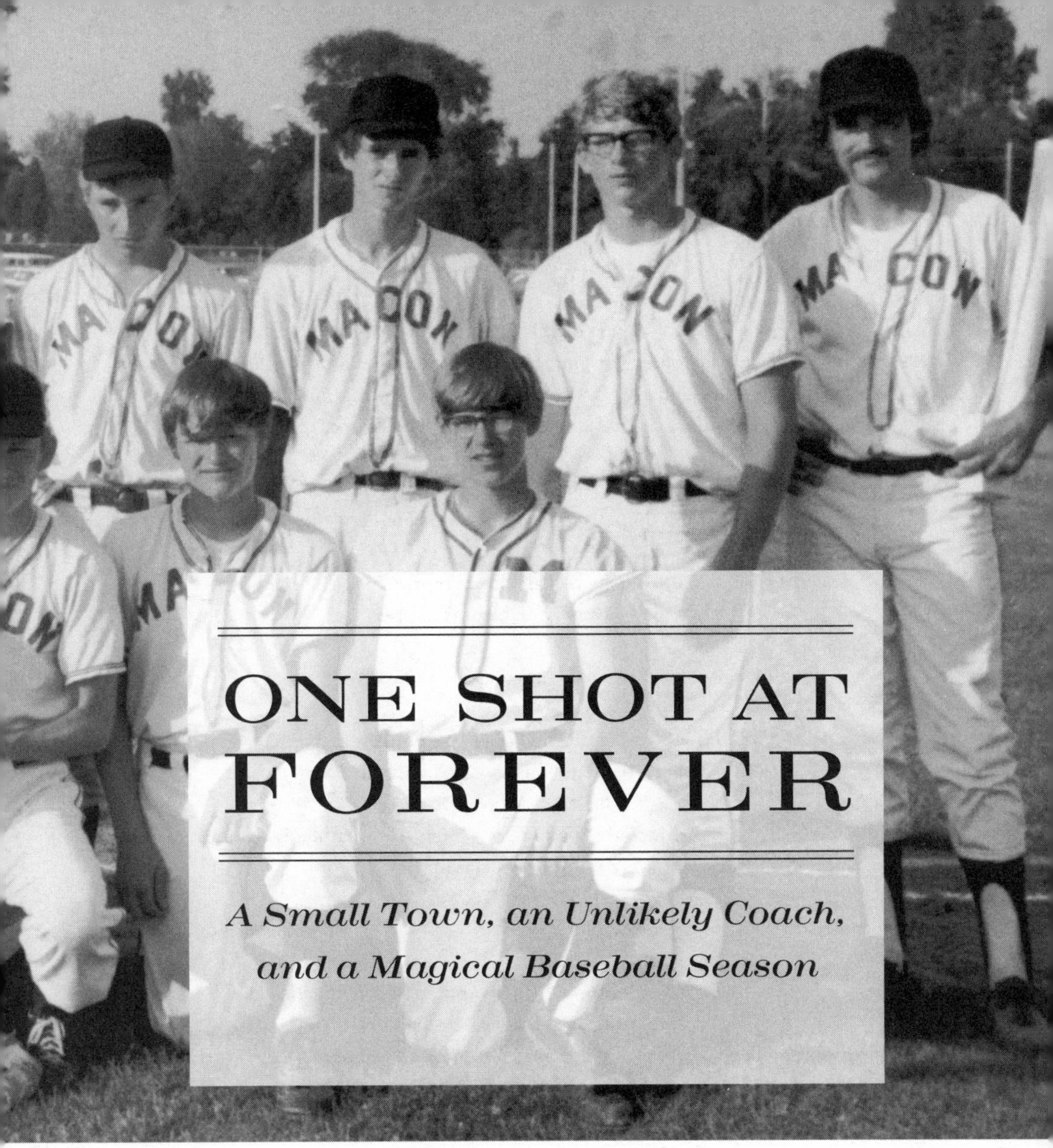

ONE SHOT AT FOREVER

A Small Town, an Unlikely Coach, and a Magical Baseball Season

Chris Ballard

HYPERION
NEW YORK

Printed in the United States of America. For information address Hyperion, 114 Fifth Avenue, New York, New York, 10011.

Photo on pp. ii–iii courtesy of Dale Otta.
Map on p. xi courtesy of Chris Heine.

Excerpt from *A False Spring* by Pat Jordan reprinted with permission of the University of Nebraska Press.

Library of Congress Cataloging-in-Publication Data
Ballard, Chris.
One shot at forever: a small town, an unlikely coach, and a magical baseball season/Chris Ballard. p. cm.
ISBN 978-1-4013-2438-4
1. Baseball—Illinois—Macon—History. 2. High school athletes—Illinois—Macon—History. 3. Macon (Ill.) —Social life and customs. I. Title.
GV863.I2.M332B35 2012
796.357'6209773582—dc23 2011042752

Portions of this book originally appeared in *Sports Illustrated*.

Hyperion books are available for special promotions and premiums. For details contact the HarperCollins Special Markets Department in the New York office at 212-207-7528, fax 212-207-7222, or email spsales@harpercollins.com.

Book design by Fearn Cutler de Vicq

FIRST EDITION

1 3 5 7 9 10 8 6 4 2

THIS LABEL APPLIES TO TEXT STOCK

To Alexandra, Callie, and Eliza,

who make this all worthwhile

Contents

Part Two
The Forever Season

Part Three
Ghosts

ONE SHOT AT FOREVER

ILLINOIS

Waukegan
Chicago
Peoria
Champaign
Springfield
Decatur
Mt. Zion
Macon

Prologue

Macon, Illinois, Spring 2010

Out in the corn country of central Illinois the clouds stretch forever, thick and soft, as if painted onto the sky of an old-time movie set. Below them lies Route 51, two lanes that'll take you to Chicago in three hours or St. Louis in two if you really gun it. Years ago you had no choice but to drive through each of the rural outposts along the highway, but now the road has bypasses, so the towns wash past, invisible but for a water tower, maybe a church spire. Moweaqua. Radford. Dunkel. They're just names on turnoff signs.

Macon appears no different. It flashes by in less than a minute, marked only by an exit and a sign that reads A CITY OF PROGRESS BUILT ON PRIDE, EST. 1869. A glance down the streets, beyond the town marker that reads POPULATION 1,200, suggests progress has slowed of late. The Macon Motel, hard by the highway, is a run-down, one-story building with a plastic billboard that, in listing the amenities, reads only PHONE. A bit farther down the road, the battered façade of the Whit's End, the town's only restaurant, is visible, promising CARRY-OUT BEER.

It's worth pulling over here, though, just off the exit at Andrews Street. Head into the P&V Quickstop, the one next to the Dollar General store, and look past the tank-topped blonde at the cash register, the one with the sad eyes who's working her gum as if she needs it to last the whole afternoon. Keep going, above the dusty disposable cameras and the COPENHAGEN sign, and you'll see it, up on the highest shelf, scuffed and dulled, its miniature batter frozen in midswing.

The cashier doesn't even know the trophy is there, just shrugs and chews when it's pointed out. Then again, she's never heard the story of the Macon High Ironmen of 1971, knows nothing about their unlikely coach and the most improbable, magical season in the history of Illinois high school baseball. Plenty of people around here don't.

After all, a lot's changed in Macon since then. Many of the family farms have been bought up by big business. Commuters moved in from Decatur, twenty minutes to the north. Schools consolidated. When Macon High became Meridian High in 1994—the same brick buildings just with new signs slapped on them—the basements and trophy cases were emptied of memorabilia.

Now the story of the Ironmen must live on in other ways. Through the white-haired man down at the Whit's End, the one with stacks of old news clips. Through the stooped newspaper reporter up in Decatur. Through the third base coach in the dugout of the Atlanta Braves, the one who still listens to the team's old fight song on the drive to spring training every year. And most of all, through the quiet, hazel-eyed man, his hair now gray, his hips rickety, who sometimes stops by the P&V late at night to steal a glance up at the piece of his life that remains on that shelf.

Standing there, peering up, the man sometimes wonders how one long-forgotten season can hold so much power. How its memory can lift up some men but haunt others. How it can continue to change so many lives.

Part One

Welcome to Macon

HERB SLODOUNIK, *DECATUR HERALD*

The grain elevator in downtown Macon, the "skyline" of the town

Prelude

Bob Fallstrom had to read the sheet twice, and still he didn't believe it. Was this some sort of joke? The work of a smartass kid?

By 1971 Fallstrom had been at the Decatur *Herald & Review* for twenty-two years and had spent the bulk of that time covering small-town high school sports in central Illinois. Over the years he'd seen plenty. He'd covered future major leaguers like Bill Madlock and farm boys who'd never seen a curveball. He'd dealt with coaches who were autocrats, coaches who were assholes, coaches who didn't know their own players' names, and, once, a married coach who skipped town on the day of a big game with the school nurse. But he'd never seen anything like this.

In his hand, Fallstrom held a rumpled survey returned by L. C. Sweet, the baseball coach at Macon High, a tiny school twenty minutes south of Decatur that had enjoyed surprising success the previous season. For Fallstrom, who was both the sports editor and lead columnist at the *Herald & Review*, the survey was a way to avoid spending weeks calling the coaches at the fifty-odd schools his paper covered. The form included lines for batting order and schedule, the coach's lifetime record, and then, at the bottom, a few questions about team strengths and weaknesses. It was boilerplate stuff, and by now Fallstrom knew what to expect: coaches talking up their players and, when possible, inflating their own credentials. And who could blame them? Everyone wanted to look good in the *Herald & Review*, which was the only daily paper for dozens of small towns and held tremendous sway in central Illinois. As the saying went in the newsroom, "If it's in the *Herald & Review* sports section, it must be true."

This was different though. Fallstrom called over Joe Cook, his right-hand man in the sports department.

"What do you make of this?" Fallstrom said, handing over the sheet. "Make sure to read the whole thing, down to the bottom."

Cook scanned the answers, then broke out laughing. There, at the end of the survey, under the heading of "Team Weaknesses," Sweet had written the following word: "Coaching."

1

Beginnings

Lynn Sweet never set out to be a baseball coach, and he certainly never dreamed he'd live in a place like Macon. In fact, when he got the call from Macon principal Roger Britton in the fall of 1965 inviting him to interview for a job teaching English, the first thing Sweet did was ask where, exactly, the town was.

A week later, Sweet threw on a coat and tie, hopped into his brown '58, six-cylinder Ford Customline and hit the road, heading south from Chicago. As he drove, the city faded away, replaced by endless miles of denuded cornfields, the splintered stalks poking out of the hard earth like blond stubble. Every once in a while, Sweet breezed through a town, but mostly it was just him and that big blue sky. To pass the time he rolled down the windows, letting the cool air fly through his hair, and hummed a song about a Tambourine Man. He wasn't quite sure where he was going, but that was fine. He rarely was.

At twenty-four, Sweet was a dreamer and something of an idealist. The son of a hard-driving Army sergeant, he had, as he put it, "broken the other way." Sweet was against the war, fond of bucking convention, and convinced the world was full of good people who occasionally had bad ideas. From his mother, he'd inherited a love of the arts, books, and ideas, while his father had given him not only his name—Lynn Junior often went by his initials "L. C." to differentiate himself from his father—but also the ability to relate to most any man. Later, he would come to look, as one opposing player put it, "like Frank Zappa had decided to coach baseball," but for now he was still clean-cut, with short dark hair that framed a wide face, hazel eyes, thick eyebrows, and long eyelashes. Darkly handsome, he was both funny and a good listener, a combination women tended to find irresistible.

By the time he drove south to meet Britton, Sweet had come to a crossroads of sorts, forced to confront his future after years of giving it the slip. He'd dropped out of college twice and worked as a roofer, a painter, and, briefly, on the Kraft Foods factory line, a soul-deadening experience he hoped to never repeat. As far back as he could remember, he'd disliked school but loved reading. His mother read to him frequently when he was young and pushed him to make his own discoveries. He tackled Orwell in the fourth grade, later fell for Aldous Huxley, and wrestled with Joyce.

Though an indifferent student, Sweet was beloved by his teachers. On his seventh grade report card, one Cora Johnson of Hopewell Elementary School, in Hopewell, Virginia, had deemed the boy a "dreamer" and a "time-waster" who could "just about exasperate one at times." Yet she went on to write that she "just loved the boy and thoroughly enjoyed having him in [her] class," calling him "cooperative, helpful (in his own way)" and possessed of "a good mind."

In other words, Sweet had many of the makings of a good teacher. So, when faced with a choice between following his father into the military and entering a profession that would provide a draft exemption, Sweet told his father, "Sorry, this cat's not going," and majored in English at Southern Illinois University, with the intention of becoming a teacher. He was two months into a student teaching assignment in Chicago when Britton happened upon his name on a list of prospective teachers.

Sweet immediately intrigued Britton, who was a conservative principal in every respect but one: the hiring of teachers. Believing students should be exposed to a variety of influences and approaches, he'd set out to surround himself with the most interesting people possible after rejoining the Macon School District in 1965. During his first few years Britton hired, among others: a hard-ass former Marine to teach industrial arts; a foul-mouthed six-foot-two, two-hundred-and-forty-pound Southern good ol' boy to coach football and teach chemistry; and a statistical whiz from the nearby Caterpillar factory's quality control division to teach math. Once, upon being impressed with a barmaid at the Lone Oak Tavern in Decatur named LaVonne Jones, Britton brought the entire school board to the bar to meet her, then hired her on the spot.

In Sweet, however, Britton recognized a rare commodity: an English teacher who was young and male. From the look of his file, Sweet was also well educated (that SIU degree) and worldly (that Army brat background), at least by Macon's standards. That he had only a couple months of experience didn't bother Britton. He was more worried about how to convince the young man to move to a place like Macon.

Macon was indeed an unlikely destination for Sweet, who had grown up in a series of midsize cities in Virginia and Arizona before his father got a job teaching ROTC at the University of Illinois, allowing the Sweets to settle in Champaign. Now Sweet was living at the Ravenswood YMCA in Chicago and embracing the burgeoning counterculture of the '60s. He listened to the Rolling Stones, hung out at poetry readings with kids in berets, smoked his share of grass, and stayed up late debating politics and religion.

Now here he was, driving through a sea of cornfields and mulling a job offer in a town so small he was unaware of its existence only a week earlier. Just when Sweet began to wonder if he'd overshot Macon, or taken the wrong road, he saw a grain elevator rising like an iron redwood over the flat plains. It was easily the tallest building for miles. He had arrived.

As Sweet rolled into Macon, past the barber shop, the feed store, and Cole's Arrowhead Tavern, he felt like he was going back in time, and in some respects he was. Though only two hundred miles from Chicago, Macon was, in 1965, still stuck in the Eisenhower era. Men had short hair; women wore long skirts; and the ideological shifts sweeping other parts of the country had yet to make their way this far into the heartland. Here, the greatest generation still held sway. Even though tens of thousands of war protesters had picketed the White House and marched on the Washington Monument only a month earlier, in Macon the United States was still viewed as infallible. The idea that anyone would want to stand up and shout about going to war was absurd. If Sweet was representative of where the country was headed, then Macon symbolized where it had been.

It was also, in the truest sense of the word, a community, the kind of town where kids were sent to the post office each morning to bring back the mail and the local paper, the weekly *Macon News*, ran the grade school menus on the front page of every issue (goulash and meat loaf were big). The paper's slogan was "We print everything but dollar bills," and that wasn't far off the mark. The *News* contained a regular feature called "Two Minutes with the Bible," and breaking news stories included headlines such as "Local Cemetery Board Hires Custodian"; "Win Places [Boy] on State Vegetable Judging Team"; and "Evening Woman's Club Meets in Kyle Home," a story that included the following dispatch: "Howard Brown, County Supt. of Schools, gave a very interesting report on 'Squares.' He says we should all start being square and stand up for what we think is right."

If the town felt frozen in time, it was due in part to its location. When the Illinois Central Railroad crews set up a freight and depot stop south of Decatur in 1845, creating the settlement that would later become Macon, they just as easily could have chosen any other patch of flat grass in the surrounding prairie lands, which stretched for miles in every direction. With no reason for the town's existence—no river, hilltop, or swath of ideal topography—there was no compelling reason for people to settle there. As a result, Macon remained an outpost, an hour from the nearest midsize city, be it Champaign or Springfield, and twenty minutes from the closest small one, Decatur. By the time Sweet arrived in 1965, Macon was a largely self-sufficient town of twelve hundred, boasting one bank, two grocery stores, two barber shops, a post office, and enough jobs and farmland that residents didn't have to look elsewhere for their needs. It was possible to go months, if not years, without ever leaving the town, and many people did.

Of course, Sweet didn't know any of this as he pulled into the Macon High parking lot. He just knew he was a long way from the schools of Chicago. Certainly, Macon High wasn't much to look at: a one-story brick building that, on its north end, became the junior high. Out back, a rutty baseball diamond shared real estate with the football field. A sign out front read WELCOME TO THE HOME OF THE IRONMEN.

Strolling into the front office, Sweet was greeted by a skinny, neat woman with a brown bob haircut. It was Roger Britton's wife, Vera. Presently, Roger himself appeared. Tall and still possessed of the athletic build that made him an elite high-jumper and hurdler as a teenager, he had neatly parted, gray-flecked hair and a long, sharp nose. He struck Sweet as an easy man to get along with, and most of the time he was. What Sweet didn't know was that Britton was both a powerful, persuasive speaker and a savvy salesman, naturally attuned to the ever-changing angles of leverage in any situation. He was the kind of man who, during contract negotiations with the Macon School Board, once brought a phone into the meeting. While discussing a pay raise, the phone rang. Britton picked it up, spoke for a moment, and then placed the receiver off to the side. "Well, this is the other school," he announced, looking around the room. "They want an answer right now." Scared of losing a young, talented principal, the board OK'd his pay raise on the spot. It's a shame none of the men thought to pick up the call. If they had they'd have discovered Vera Britton on the other end.

At the moment, however, Britton was focusing his considerable talents of persuasion on luring Sweet to Macon, and he thought he knew how to do it. Walking down the white-tiled linoleum halls, past the tiny cafeteria and the chemistry and typing classrooms, Britton emphasized how, with 250 students and nineteen teachers, Macon High offered the kind of intimate, personal environment where a young teacher could have an impact. He mentioned that he was a former English professor and, upon learning that Sweet was a Cubs fans, casually mentioned that not only was he a Cardinals man himself, but if an employee were to, say, sneak off for an afternoon ball game, it wouldn't be viewed as the worst offense in the world. Finally, Britton came to a stop in a small, white-walled classroom at the southwest corner of the building. A row of large windows looked out upon empty cornfields and two dozen individual desks were arranged in rows. Blackboards covered two of the walls.

"Here's your desk, your textbooks, and your grade books," Britton said, pointing to a stack of materials on an old wooden desk. "We play poker on Wednesday nights."

Sweet stared at him. "That's it? I got the job?"

Britton nodded. He hadn't said a word about what he expected of Sweet or his curriculum, and this was by design. Britton had taught in three schools, had a master's in education from Millikin University in nearby Decatur, and was pursuing an advanced degree from Eastern Illinois University. He'd been around a lot of teachers of all inclinations and Sweet struck him as a man who valued autonomy, who perhaps harbored grand ideas about teaching. He was a man to be encouraged, not reined in.

"But I haven't accepted it yet," Sweet said.

"True, but we'd like you to," said Britton.

Sweet stood there considering the offer, and the friendly but assertive man in front of him, and he began to warm to both. *It's not like I have to live in Macon the rest of my days*, he thought. Life was full of opportunities; if he didn't like this one, he'd move on to the next. Besides, he was only an hour from friends and family in Champaign and, best he could tell, Britton was offering him carte blanche as a teacher. Plus, he did like poker.

Ah hell, Sweet thought, *why not?* He extended his hand and smiled.

Britton smiled back. "Welcome to Macon," he said. He turned to leave, took one step, and then paused. "One more thing," Britton said. "There are three taverns in the town and as teachers we don't drink at them. To set a good example, you understand."

Sweet nodded and gave Britton a look that said, *Of course I understand.*

A few minutes later, when the paperwork was in place, Sweet walked out to his Ford. He turned on the ignition, pulled out of the parking lot, and promptly drove down to Cole's Tavern, where he drank a beer with the locals and talked about the Chicago Bears. He then proceeded across the street to Claire's Place for another beer before dropping in at the Nite Owl on Wall Street, where he shared a Pabst with the afternoon crew, at which point Sweet felt safe in his determination that all three were fine establishments.

It wasn't Champaign or Chicago, but Macon would do.

2

Shark

Three years later and five miles up the road, a fourteen-year-old boy who would become very important to both Lynn Sweet and the town of Macon found himself in a bit of a jam. From his hiding place, he could hear sirens, could hear police yelling at him to "COME DOWN RIGHT NOW STEVE SHARTZER." He appraised his options and thought about making a run for it.

The trouble began a few months earlier, when Steve was biking through his hometown of Elwin one afternoon looking for something to do, an endeavor that usually proved futile. If Macon was a dot on the map, Elwin was a pencil point. Just off County Highway 30, Elwin harbored ninety-odd people, one gas station, one motel, and one runty grain elevator. Really, it was more of a four-way stop sign than a town. Steve's parents had moved to Elwin from Decatur when he was in the second grade to provide their two children with a quiet environment. However, it proved far too quiet for Steve's tastes, and in the intervening seven years he'd gone to great lengths to entertain himself. More often than not, this meant turning even the most mundane activity into a game.

Steve was a pure, obsessive, born competitor. When he was one, his father learned that if he rolled a small rubber ball to his son, Steve would reach up and roll it back. Not once. Not twice, but for five, ten, fifteen minutes at a time. By the time he was three, Steve could swing a bat and catch a baseball. Not allowed to leave the block, he'd sit at its end, where it abutted Fairview Park, and stare down at the expanse of grass below, watching the older boys play pickup games of baseball. Inch by inch, he'd scoot farther down that hill until, finally, he was close to enough to really watch. Always, he hoped they would ask him to play. They never did.

By four, Steve was hitting balls in the family's tiny back lot in Decatur, which was separated by a wooden fence from an alley, which in turn bordered a synagogue. One afternoon, he sent a ball soaring over the alley and crashing through one of the ornate windows of the synagogue, a mammoth blast for a child his size. The rabbis were not impressed. Neither was his father, Bob. At least not that he let on.

From an early age, Steve learned one abiding lesson from his dad: losing hurts. Bob Shartzer was a veteran of World War II and the Korean War who worked for the railroad on the St. Louis to Chicago line. He was a big man who spoke rarely, drank hard, and was not to be messed with. He saw in his son a boy with loads of talent who nonetheless needed to learn early on that life handed you nothing. So whenever he played a game with Steve, whether it was Old Maid or checkers, Bob refused to let the boy win. After each loss, Steve yelled. Then, when that proved fruitless, he began crying, sometimes for minutes on end.

"Can't you let him win, just once?" Georgianna Shartzer said to her husband.

"He'll win some day," Bob replied.

When, as a six-year-old, Steve begged his dad to erect a basketball hoop in their backyard, his father complied. Only, instead of a full set, he installed only an iron pole with a bracket at the top gripping a naked rim. "When you can make it on this I'll get you one with a backboard," Bob Shartzer said. Steve hated his dad for this, but he had no choice. So he practiced incessantly. He had one bald rubber ball and his "court" consisted of a ten-foot patch of dirt, which made dribbling problematic and, when it rained, impossible. Still, Steve made the best of it, looping in one jumper after another from most every spot in the yard. By the time, many years later, that Bob Shartzer deemed his son worthy of a backboard, Steve was accurate from anywhere inside twenty-five feet. On principle, he considered refusing it.

That backyard in Elwin was Steve's world growing up. A good half acre in size, it bordered on a cornfield and, beyond that, groves of wild elm trees. Stuck in a town with only a few boys his age, Steve collected rocks and, when he couldn't find those, stole pieces of gravel from the driveway so he could swat them with a broomstick. He fired football after football through a tire attached to a rope swing. He sat rapt in front of *Jim Thorpe—All-American* on the family's small color TV, then went outside and tore around the house until he threw up, believing that doing so would make him the best athlete the world had ever seen.

There was no pursuit Steve didn't think he could master. When he saw an older kid throwing the discus, he thought, *Hell, I can do that.* So he trudged out to the backyard lugging a high school discus and stood there, at the back of the lot, heaving the iron plate out into the cornfield, time and again. After each throw, he marked the landing spot with a cornstalk, then walked back to do it again, just trying to move that stalk. By the time he was at Macon High, where all the kids from Elwin commuted for high school, he could throw the discus more than 160 feet, a distance that would qualify him to compete at the state finals.

Baseball was his first love, though. By the time Steve was six he was playing with the eight-year-olds in Little League. By ten, when everyone had taken to simply calling him "Shark," both because of his name and his demeanor, he was bruising other boys' hands with his throws. When a kid named Stuart Arnold came out for the Elwin team, small for his age and intent on being a catcher, Steve knocked him over the first day with his fastball.

As he got older, Steve began to wonder whether there were other uses for his arm. Which was how, as a cocky, wiry eighth grader with a short brown burr haircut that invariably cow-licked in the front, he came to stop his bike outside the general store, having spied, parked off to the side, an unmanned produce truck. Peering in the back, Shartzer saw a sea of tomatoes—boxes and boxes of fat, round, red tomatoes. Each one, he noticed, was roughly the size of a baseball.

Half an hour later, Steve and a buddy were lugging a crate through town like a couple of scrawny sherpas, looking for a suitable launching spot. There weren't many options; only a few buildings in Elwin were more than one story. The grain elevator at the intersection of 51 and County Road 30, however—now that was forty feet tall. So up they scrambled, higher and higher above the two-lane road known as the Mt. Zion blacktop. There, perched on metal scaffolding, they could see many things. Including, it turned out, cars approaching from a good three miles away.

Steve informed his buddy of his intention: to hit every car not once but at least twice.

"But how are we going to do that from way up here?" his buddy said.

"I'll show you," Steve said. And with that, he took a tomato and, gauging the speed of an oncoming car, lobbed it up into the air. Then, while the tomato arced toward the asphalt, Steve reloaded and pumped two more overhand shots at the hood of the approaching sedan.

The first shot, the lob, missed. The other two did not.

It's worth considering for a moment the physics of the situation. The cars on the highway were going 60 mph, Shartzer was fifty feet away, and the tomatoes were of varying weight and size. In essence, his task was akin to a quarterback trying to properly lead a wide receiver, only the receiver happens to be standing in the open door of a passing train. Yet, again and again, Steve torched those cars. *Splat. Splat. Splat.* Tomato guts shot into the air; seeds sprayed across windshields.

Some of the drivers kept right on going. Others screeched to a halt, then leapt out and looked around angrily for a culprit. They never thought to look up. Even if they had, Shartzer was hidden from view.

For months, Shartzer wreaked havoc from on high. He loved the sense of danger, the power of the moment, and, most of all, the challenge. Every time he hit one of those cars, it was proof of his talent, testimony to the future that awaited him. Sometimes friends joined him; other times he chose a different launching spot. No one, it seemed, was the wiser. Down in Macon, farmers spent their afternoons muttering about how crates of tomatoes kept mysteriously disappearing from their trucks.

Eventually, however, Steve tired of tomatoes. As he saw it, they had two flaws: They were soft and they didn't always carry well.

You know what carried well? Apples.

And that's how Steve found himself jammed above the axle of a big soybean truck on the night of the Macon High prom, sirens screeching outside.

Earlier in the evening, accompanied by a kid named Waldo Ross, Shartzer had once again ascended the grain elevator. He and Waldo were having a grand time flinging fruit, detonating one shot so artfully that pulp smattered the dress of a prom-bound girl like apple shrapnel. And then they did it: Steve hit an Illinois state trooper. Not once, or twice, but with the elusive triple.

"Oh SHIT!" said Waldo, suddenly very scared.

"GodDAMN!" said Steve, suddenly very proud.

Then the cop car stopped, turned around, and came roaring back—right toward the grain elevator. With the same quickness that served him so well in so many sports, Steve scrambled through a busted-out window in the elevator and climbed atop the wheel well of one of the towering bean trucks, wedged under the motor some ten feet off the ground and prepared to hide for as long as was necessary. Until Waldo, who was neither as quick nor as creative as his friend, tried to wedge in next to him.

"Get out of here. There ain't room for both of us," Steve hissed.

But the boy kept pushing and pushing until he had all but one leg in that crevice. Moments later, the cop yanked on that leg and down came Waldo. Steve was still hidden, though. For what felt like an hour, but couldn't have been more than five minutes, Steve huddled there, scared shitless in a way only fourteen-year-old boys who've suddenly realized they're not indestructible can be. Finally, he heard Waldo's voice.

"Shark, come out. We're caught."

By this time, two more troopers had arrived, though it seemed like ten to Steve when he walked out to see all those twirling lights. What's more, the cops had their hands on their guns. Steve thought about running, but before he could move he was thrown to the ground and handcuffed.

A few hours later, Bob Shartzer showed up at the police station in Decatur to retrieve his son. After a brief lecture from a tired officer about the dangers of throwing fruit, Steve was released into the night.

In a town the size of Macon, the Shartzer incident naturally created a bit of a stir. In the teacher's lounge a few weeks later, Sweet was pouring a cup of coffee when Carl Poelker, the math teacher, ambled over.

"You hear about the kid up in Elwin last month?" Poelker asked.

Sweet said he hadn't. But as he listened to the story of how an eighth-grader had taken out a cop car going full speed from the top of a grain elevator, he had a very different reaction than most of the other teachers.

Now that, Sweet thought, *is one helluva arm.*

3

Write Your Own Obituary

Steve Shartzer arrived for his first day of English class during his sophomore year at Macon High to find a strange-looking teacher at the front of the room, back turned to the class, reading a newspaper. By now, Lynn Sweet bore little resemblance to the clean-cut young man who'd first moved to Macon nearly four years earlier. A thick Fu Manchu mustache curled over the corners of his lips; a pair of bushy sideburns dipped down his cheeks; and dark hair flopped across his forehead. He looked like an unkempt Beatle, one who in this case happened to be wearing an outlandish green corduroy blazer with a rainbow ribbon tacked to it.

Shartzer looked around for a desk but all he saw were four large, round tables, so he joined some of the two dozen other students at one of them. Behind him, the walls were plastered with posters: Mick Jagger in midserpent dance, Grace Slick in eyeliner, and a Ray-Banned Bob Dylan. In the corner stood two rows of bookshelves. One teemed with an eclectic collection of novels and short stories, many of which were rarely seen in a town like Macon. The other overflowed with magazines and comic books, everything from *Popular Mechanics* to *Spider-Man*. Conspicuously absent, either on Sweet's desk or the tables, were grammar textbooks.

Once everyone was seated, Sweet turned around.

"I'd like to start class with an exercise," he said, brandishing the *Herald & Review* from the previous Sunday. "Who can tell me what the most interesting part of the paper is?"

Hands shot up.

"Sports?"

"Comics!"

Sweet shook his head. "Nope. It's the obituaries."

There were puzzled looks. Sweet paused. "You know why? Because each one tells a life's story, right there in one column of the paper."

And then Sweet began to read. He read about farmers who'd lived through World War I and women who'd raised nine children during the Depression. He talked about the scope of each life, about all the crazy, interesting things these people had done, of how much they'd *lived.*

When he was finished, he gave the class its assignment. "Now I want you to write your own obituary."

There were giggles, but Sweet was serious. He told them to take out paper and a pencil.

A boy behind Shartzer raised his hand. "But Mr. Sweet," he said. "How are we supposed to know how we're going to die?"

"You're not," said Sweet. "How you die is the one thing you *don't* have control over. What you do have control over is the rest of your life. Write about how you want to live." He paused, then smiled. "Have fun with it."

And so they did. It was neither the first nor the last unconventional assignment Sweet would give the class. Over the weeks and months that followed, Sweet never produced a grammar text or taught a traditional lesson. He did, however, quiz the students on the funnies page, to make sure they "at least picked up the newspaper," and required them to memorize ten esoteric vocabulary words every Monday, upon which he tested them on Friday. Forty years later, many of the students would still be able to recall the words: *banal, xenophobic, hirsute.*

Every so often, Sweet announced a class-wide, collaborative project. One time, he told the students they would be creating their own magazine and could choose any subject they wanted. As a joke, one of the boys suggested it be all about carp, the ugly, tasteless fish that always seemed to bite first in the local waterways. When Sweet embraced the idea, the kids thought this hilarious and fantastic—a whole magazine about carp!—and spent long hours working on it. A month later *Carpmaster Magazine* was published, complete with tongue-in-cheek reviews, letters to the editor, cartoons, how-to's, fake ads, essays (including "The Carp, America's Noblest Gamefish"), and recipes. (For example, "Carp Stew" called for "3 freezer-burned carp, 1 lb. of spoiled cheese, 2 strips of bacon, and 2 lbs. of spoiled hamburger.")

Even mundane tasks became exercises in creativity. Sweet required students to add a third line in the upper left-hand corner of their assignments, below their name and class, listing their future profession. Thus papers would read:

Jane Metzger
English IV
P.E. Teacher

In Shartzer's opinion, though, hands-down the best part of Sweet's class was his reading policy, or lack thereof. Rather than a set list, freshmen and sophomores were often allowed to read whatever they wanted, a freedom that blew their minds. Instead of the *Odyssey*, they could choose to read about rebuilding a motor in *Popular Mechanics*. The only requirement was that they finish the story and understand it, then write a properly prepared report.

When Sweet did assign class-wide books, they were often ones the students had never heard of, like Aldous Huxley's *Brave New World*, which was considered radical at the time in a town like Macon. Sweet had a way of explaining the novels that made sense, though. When the class read *Lord of the Flies*, he took all the students out behind Macon High to a creek and had them reenact parts of the book, forcing them to choose sides and role-play. When they read a classic such as *Macbeth*, he asked them to read it again if he felt they didn't understand it the first time. When they did, the students were surprised to find that they enjoyed it more the second time. As Sweet explained, "The more you give to a great piece of literature, the more it gives back."

Most of the students had never experienced a teacher like Sweet. Some had grown up on farms that lacked hot water. Others had gone the first fifteen years of their lives without reading anything much longer than a comic book. Yet as a freshman named David Wells later put it, with Sweet, "I was learning without even realizing it."

In Shartzer's case, it was in spite of his best efforts. Steve was one of those boys who'd avoided books the best he could, preferring to spend his time playing sports. He was bright enough, but had often put that intellect to use finding ways to avoid doing work, whether it was charming a teacher or enlisting his older sister Pat's help on a book report. Yet even Shartzer didn't mind Sweet's class. By the end of the semester, the strange-looking man in the corduroy jacket had become his favorite teacher. He was by no means alone. Had you polled the Macon High population, there's a good chance a majority of the students would have agreed.

The local parents, however, were not as enamored. Not only did they find Sweet's curriculum unusual and the lack of grammar troubling, but he kept sending their kids home with strange, seemingly dangerous books. Not just *Brave New World* and *Heart of Darkness* but *Lord Jim* and, worst of all, "that play," *Inherit the Wind*, which struck many in the deeply religious town as blasphemous.

Had Sweet's teaching methods been the extent of his transgressions, the parents might have let it slide. They were not.

The whispers had started within weeks of Sweet's arrival in Macon in January of 1966. They began in the halls of the high school and spread through the town like so much pollen drifting in the wind, from the taverns to the Methodist Church off Route 51 to the fake-wood tabletops in dozens of kitchens. Did you hear about that new teacher? Did you hear what he has those kids reading? Did you see that new Mustang he's driving? Did you know he's not going to church, *any* church? Did you see that girl he had with him last week, the one from Champaign?

Even if Sweet had wanted to stay under the radar in Macon it would have been impossible. New hires at the high school were announced on the front page of the *Macon News*, accompanied by a home address. If he forgot to pay his taxes it was a matter of public record, his name included in the *News'* annual Delinquent Personal Property Tax List, which listed all sums, ranging from the paltry ($1.93 for one Ms. Elsie Damery in 1965) to the truly scandalous (a town-high $171.95 for Mr. J. T. Hogan).

Other information could be ferreted out without much trouble. With limited telephone service, houses in Macon had what were known as party lines where scores of farmhouses might share one telephone line. To distinguish between each, different rings were used. Thus a *riiiiing-riiiiing* might signal that someone was calling for you while a *ring-ring* meant it was for your neighbor. This was all well and good, except that anyone on the loop could, if they were adept, pick up the phone and listen in to anyone else's conversation. Some women in Macon, it was said, spent a good amount of time doing this. They were the same ones who could be seen huddled together at tables or in the vinyl booths at the local diner the next day.

These whisperers held an unusual amount of power in a town as small as Macon. Technically, there was an official town government, but the city council met only once a month, for an hour and a half or so, in a small building under the water tower. None of the councilmen were professional politicians, to say the least. The mayor at the time was a good-natured man with white hair named Wayne Jones; his day job was as the janitor at Macon High.

More problematic for Sweet, most everyone in town cared what went on at the high school. Because Macon was so small and had an unusual number of large families—the Jesses numbered fifteen, the Tomlinsons fourteen—just about every adult in town could claim children, nieces, nephews, or grandchildren who attended Macon High. And thus most everybody had a stake in what went on there. If the town's power structure was loose, the school's was the opposite. The principal answered to the superintendent, who in turn answered to the school board, which consisted of seven elected men—and they were always men—who were usually parents or important local citizens.

Men like these had usually come of age during World War II, then settled down to raise large, God-fearing families. To them, teachers were expected to instill discipline and emphasize that there was a right way and a wrong way to do things in life. The sooner you learned to do the former, the sooner you'd have your own large, God-fearing family.

Sweet, it became apparent to the board and many others in town, wasn't much interested in any of that. What they needed was someone to keep him in line, because Britton didn't seem inclined to do so. When Britton was elevated to superintendent, hope arrived in the form of a new principal by the name of Bill McClard.

When he moved to Macon at the age of thirty-two, Bill McClard was, without a doubt, a man on the rise. Armed with a bachelor's from Illinois State and a master's from Eastern Illinois University, he'd worked at two high schools, first as a teacher and then as principal. The son of a Navy man, McClard was short and thick, with a boxer's nose and a soft chin. A heavy smoker, he'd developed a bit of a paunch in his thirties and, due to a bad back, tended to hunch forward as he walked, giving the impression that he was carrying a heavy load that he was in a great hurry to deliver. A reserved, proud man, he'd been deeply influenced by his time in the Army.

As a result, McClard saw school as an extension of the military, a hierarchical system in which teachers were the lieutenants and students were the foot soldiers. Like many teachers at Macon High, he kept a wooden, cobblestone-sized paddle on his wall. These paddles were treasured items. Some teachers named them ("Board of Education" was popular) while others whittled holes in the wood, the better to approach maximum smacking velocity before making contact with a young man's backside. When students got into trouble, especially male ones, McClard sent them to the gym. To a call of "Line up the miscreants!" the boys turned and bent over so that a cadre of teachers could take turns doling out blows. Sometimes the teachers wound up and halted just short of making contact, just to see the boys jump.

Needless to say, McClard found a welcoming community in Macon. Britton had hired him because he was talented and came highly recommended but also because he knew the school needed someone to play the role of bad cop. Needless to say, McClard's zealous embrace of this role went over well with the school board. Meanwhile, the other teachers—an inclusive, collegial bunch—invited him to play cards, drink beer, and, on the weekends, attend raucous pig roasts. His wife, Viola, a pretty and gregarious brunette who went by "Vi," quickly became a fixture on the social scene, attending the women's club meetings and, to many, serving as better company than her husband. The couple was happy in Macon, and McClard saw the job as an ideal stepping-stone to bigger and better things. An ambitious, intelligent man, he had visions of larger school districts, maybe eventually a job at the state board of education in Springfield. He had only one problem. Its name was Lynn Sweet.

By the time McClard was established in Macon, Sweet had settled in quite nicely, or so he believed. He'd become friendly with a group of teachers, was beloved at the taverns, and knew the best spots to go fishing and hunting. Still blazingly single, he used his $450 monthly take-home check to rent a tiny month-to-month apartment over the Laundromat on Front Street that, while spare, suited him just fine, even if it didn't allow him to be much of a host. When one of his teaching buddies came over one night with dinner, Sweet looked around for plates only to realize he didn't have any. Instead, they ate right off the table.

Sweet had expected some blowback to his unconventional teaching methods. Even so, he found he'd underestimated just how traditional Macon High was. All it took for a reminder was a walk down the hall to the class of Jack Stringer, a bowtie-wearing ex-Marine who had the bottom of his ear shot off in combat. Early in Stringer's tenure, a tall, petulant student made the mistake of talking out of turn during class. Stringer strode over to the boy, picked him up by the shirt collar, and threw him up against the wall. Then he stared the student in the eye and yelled: "BIG BOY, IF YOU EVEN THINK ABOUT TALKING AGAIN WHILE I'M TALKING, I WILL COME RIGHT BACK HERE AND ME AND YOU ARE GOING TO GO ROUND AND ROUND." When the boy started talking again minutes later, Stringer threw down his chalk, took four quick steps, and put the student to the ground, using a knee to pin him. "I TOLD YOU I'D BE BACK, BIG BOY. REMEMBER, I KILLED MEN BETTER THAN YOU IN KOREA. JUST GO AHEAD, JUST TRY IT AGAIN." And that was all it took. Stringer became so feared at Macon High that one time, when he had to leave school at noon feeling sick, his next class of students arrived and sat in absolute silence for forty-five minutes awaiting his return, lest Stringer come back and find them talking.

Sweet, however, refused to engage in corporal punishment or intimidation. As he liked to say, "If you do it right, you don't need the hammer."

If the students had balked at Sweet's methods, or overrun his classroom, it would have been easy for McClard to rein him in, but the opposite was the case. The students adored Sweet, whom they saw as young, interesting, and suffused with big-city cool. Other teachers expected to be addressed as "Mister" or, on the field of play, "Coach." Sweet instructed his kids to call him only "Sweet." So they did.

Carl Poelker, the young, blond math teacher hired away from Caterpillar, at first wondered if there was a trick to Sweet's methods. Then he watched how Sweet played cards with the kids during lunch and invited them to bring meat to grill on the barbecue he stashed outside his classroom, the smell of burgers and dogs wafting into the nearby parking lot. He noticed how Sweet hung out with students after school, how he took them on hunting trips, and asked about their parents. And then it hit Poelker: *He just really cares about the kids as people, so they don't want to let him down.* If Sweet bucked the system, or didn't adhere to school regulations, Poelker noticed he usually did so on principle. If a rule didn't make sense, Sweet saw no reason to follow it.

McClard, however, didn't care how anyone *felt* about the rules. They existed for a reason and were to be respected and obeyed on principle. And Sweet not only flouted the school's rules—*McClard's* rules—but refused to demonstrate the proper respect for a principal's authority.

From the start, the two men clashed over small matters: grading policy, how Sweet chose to spend his class time, and of course the junior class play, which Sweet thought would be more entertaining if he "modernized" parts, like making the lead male in *Just Ducky* a recovering alcoholic who suffered from hemorrhoids.

It must have been difficult for McClard to ignore other differences between the two men. While McClard was brusque and at times awkward in social situations, Sweet had a way of getting along with most everybody, even those, like Burns, the brawny football coach, who were as right wing as Sweet was left. Likewise, Sweet was a natural in front of the students, hamming it up. McClard, for all his authoritarian bent and considerable administrative talent, had a habit of becoming a nervous wreck during public speeches. His hands shook, his movements became erratic, and he became so anxious that, when possible, he tried to delegate his duties. Linda Shonkwiler, who graduated in 1971, remembers her shock when, upon being elected class president, McClard told her to stand up and give the assembly addresses in his place. (Little did McClard know that Shonkwiler's greatest fear was also public speaking.)

With each passing year, McClard and Sweet's relationship continued to sour. It seemed inevitable that matters would come to a head.

It sounded like a grand plan. A dozen teachers and administrators would take off on a Saturday morning in the spring and drive down to St. Louis in the VW bus of Phil Sargent, the athletic director. They'd hit some taverns and then head to a St. Louis Cardinals game. Sweet was charged with organizing an itinerary and, as usual when it came to such matters, took great delight in doing so, especially since he was a diehard Cubs fan. The Friday before the trip, he passed out a sheet to all involved.

Scanning the paper, superintendent Britton began chuckling. On it, Sweet had included a roster of "Members of the Excursion" under three headings.

The first read "Cardinals fans and gentlemen of position" and included McClard, identified as "Principal of Macon High School, Macon, Illinois"; Ralph Coate, "Head of the Science Department, Macon High School, Macon, Illinois"; Britton; and three others.

The second heading, however, read "Cubs Fans—people of questionable background including deviates and assorted degenerates." In this group Sweet included himself, identified as "known alcoholic and chaser of females"; a teacher named Guy Carlton ("Wino and part-time street fighter"); a teacher named Ralph Lancaster ("Pepsi addict and known cigar smoker"); and a Champaign buddy named Fred Schooley ("A friend of Sweet's, suspected sex fiend").

Finally, a third header read "Others: This group is made up of people who know *nothing* about baseball." Here Sweet included his friend and former baseball coach, Tim Cook, described as a "Yankees fan, non-drinker, ex-Coach, and suspected psycho," and a teacher named Dale Sloan who, based on his allegiance, was demeaned as a "Giants fan, non-drinker, henpecked dullard."

Then there was the itinerary itself:

Destination	Arrival	Departure	Comments
Macon Motel Dining Room	9:00 A.M.	9:30 A.M.	Breakfast
Midway Tap (Stonington)	9:45 A.M.	10:00 A.M.	Refreshment
Sam & Louie's (Stonington)	10:05 A.M.	10:30 A.M.	Refreshment
Zebra Room (Taylorville)	10:45 A.M.	11:00 A.M.	Refreshment
Morrisonville Tap (Morrisonville)	11:15 A.M.	11:30 A.M.	Refreshment
Harvel Tap (Harvel)	11:45 A.M.	12:00 A.M.	Refreshment
The Gardens (Litchfield)	12:30 P.M.	1:30 P.M.	Liquid Lunch
Mt. Olive Tap (Mt. Olive)	1:45 P.M.	2:00 P.M.	Refreshment
Murso's (Edwardsville)	2:30 P.M.	3:30 P.M.	Refreshment
East St. Louis	4:00 P.M.	4:30 P.M.	Refreshment
St. Louis	4:45 P.M.	6:00 P.M.	Free Time
Enter beautiful Busch Stadium at 6:00 P.M. Contact the nearest Budweiser vendor.			

The crew, and the game, did not disappoint. By the end of the evening Sweet had purchased five Styrofoam Cardinals hats and gleefully smashed them up in front of St. Louis fans; the Cardinals had won; and everyone save Tim, Dale, and Phil Sargent was lit. On the ride home, Britton suggested a game of poker. Cards were produced; hands were dealt.

Half an hour into the game, McClard started needling Sweet about his teaching. Sweet laughed it off.

Ten minutes later, McClard came at him again. Sweet chuckled once more, but he was becoming annoyed. Sweet liked to think of himself as someone who could get along with most anyone, but he didn't like to be pushed around.

"Look, I'm going to teach English how I want," Sweet finally said. "Your authority means nothing to me."

The VW bus went silent. McClard's face turned pink, then blossomed into an unhealthy red. This was most definitely not how a lieutenant spoke to his commanding officer.

"*I'll fire your ass!*" McClard yelled, nearly knocking over his pile of chips.

"Go ahead and try," Sweet responded, now yelling himself.

And, best anyone can remember, that was the precise moment when McClard began endeavoring to do just that.

Britton could only protect Sweet for so long. Baseball would have to do the rest.

4

"Practice Is Optional"

The recruiting began in earnest some months later, on a snowy January night in 1970. Worn out after work, Sweet made the short walk from his apartment on Front Street to Claire's Place. Just down from the bank and across from the railroad tracks, Claire's was the kind of small, smoky bar where people went to do some serious drinking. Canvas hunting coats hung from the stools like drapery, and a few beat-up booths gave way to a cigarette-stained pool table in the back, not far from a card table where locals played a game called pitch, a descendent of euchre. The bar had seen its share of fights, especially on Saturday nights, but it was relatively quiet on this afternoon. The regulars were present, of course, a row of old-timers atop their designated stools, settled in from three to seven P.M. each afternoon. There were the Panchot brothers from the grain elevator across the street, and Big Joanne, as well as Stan Farlow and Roger Goin, whom everyone just called "Get." And, at the end of the bar, Comet Johns, who proudly drank nothing but Michelob. Since the bar stocked only one twelve-pack of such a high-end beer at any given time, Sweet and his buddies loved to tweak Comet by walking into the bar and announcing loudly, "One Michelob down here, please!"

On this afternoon, Sweet ordered his regular, a Pabst. He drank it not because he loved the beer but because, at a quarter, it cost a dime less than premium beers like Budweiser and Schlitz. As he cracked open the can, he heard a voice.

"Hey, Sweet, you always drink alone?"

Sweet looked up and smiled. It was Bob Shartzer. The two men had spent some good nights drinking together, and were friendly. Shartzer pulled up a stool next to Sweet and order a Pabst himself.

"So, you hear the boys still don't have a baseball coach?"

Sweet had and, frankly, it didn't surprise him. There were few less-desirable gigs at Macon High. Baseball may have been the national pastime, fueled by the popularity of players like Bob Gibson, Pete Rose, and Carl Yastrzemski, but central Illinois was football and basketball territory. Even track was more popular at Macon High, and with good reason. There was little to no fan support for the baseball team; games were often rained out; and, despite some promising young players, the Ironmen had a long history of losing. Three years earlier, the Ironmen had gone the entire season and managed only one win—and that came on a forfeit when the opposing team thought it had a home rather than an away game. The Macon boys celebrated anyway.

The job of head coach had become viewed as an enlistment of sorts at Macon High—serve your time and get out. In the previous three years, the boys had gone through three coaches, the latest of whom, Jack Burns, claimed, with little dispute, to know "not a shit" about the game. Even the players were dubious. One of the town's most talented boys, a junior named Mark Miller, had opted not to come out for the team as a freshman and sophomore, saying he was too worn out from football. No one much blamed him. Dale Otta, the team's junior shortstop, sat in bed at night wondering why no one wanted to coach the team.

Now it was two weeks before the season and Macon once again needed a new coach. Britton had canvassed the faculty and come up empty, in part because he could offer little incentive. Though the job required longer hours and plenty of travel, it came with only a

3 percent bump in salary. Eventually, the parents of the players had decided to take matters into their own hands, which explained why Bob Shartzer was at Claire's.

"You know," Shartzer continued, taking a deep swig of his beer. "Me and the Glans were thinking you'd make a pretty good coach."

"That so?" Sweet said, trying to sound casual. He knew what was coming next. While plenty of parents at Macon High didn't approve of his teaching methods, the baseball dads weren't among them. Sweet had played softball with some and watched Cubs games with others. In turn, the men had seen how their sons responded to Sweet's English class, and they respected how he maintained control of his students while still making class enjoyable. Some, like junior pitcher John Heneberry's father, Jack, had heard Sweet was "too out of the ordinary, too much of a hippie longhair." Still, it wasn't like they had many other choices.

For his part, Sweet wasn't against coaching, and had quietly mulled the option ever since Shartzer had first brought it up at a pig roast. In theory, the job appealed to him. It was the reality that worried him. Coaching baseball would require a large time commitment, and he'd have to fight McClard over every budgetary issue.

There was also the small matter of the fact that not only had Sweet never coached baseball, but, as he now reminded Bob Shartzer, he'd never coached *anything*.

"Who cares?" Shartzer replied. "Hell, the boys did fine with Burns." He paused. "Besides, we got some talent out there, L.C., and you know it."

This was true. In 1969, boosted by a group of young players, the Ironmen had built on a mediocre season to go 10–5 and win the school's first conference title since 1962. Sweet had wandered by a few of the games and was impressed by how smooth the team looked on the field.

Despite his claims to the contrary, Sweet actually knew plenty about the game. As a boy, he'd played on military bases, where he developed an easy, compact swing, and a snap throw that he released from his ear, like a catcher. Eventually he became skilled enough that, upon falling in with some baseball players in Champaign, he was invited to try out for a local semipro team during college. To the surprise of everyone, he made it. Though not a power hitter, Sweet had enough pop in his bat to hit the occasional home run, was a fine third baseman, and could take the mound in a pinch. His talent, combined with his fun-loving personality, meant he was always being asked to play for someone, somewhere, whether it was the Eastern Illinois League in Champaign or semipro circuits in southern Illinois. He was never paid for his services—unless you count beers at the tavern afterward—but he played with plenty who were.

He turned back to Bob Shartzer.

"You know I love the boys," Sweet said. "But I'll have to think about it."

And with that, Sweet hoped to slip out of Claire's and avoid further entreaties. Before he could make his exit, though, reinforcements arrived in the form of Ernie Miller. "If there's anyone who can get my boy Mark out there to play ball," Ernie said, "it's you." One beer led to two, which led to four and, pretty soon, arms were around shoulders and lineups were being discussed.

Under a hazy ceiling of cigarette smoke, buoyed by the Pabsts, Sweet began to see the job in a new light. It would require a lot of time, but he was a single guy in Macon—all he had was time. And the more he thought about it, those boys did have potential. It might not be evident to most in the town, but it was to him. They could be good, he thought, *real good*. All they needed was someone to believe in them.

A week later, he walked into Britton's office and made an announcement: He'd take the baseball job.

If Sweet needed reason to doubt his decision, he got it on March 4, 1970, the first day of practice. After two days of rain, the morning dawned cold, dark, and misty. That afternoon, when Sweet made his way out to the field at 3:30, it was through a marshy outfield.

The players were accustomed to playing in brutal conditions. Historically, Macon's weather cycle was uncannily in sync with the baseball season, the rains increasing through the spring and peaking in late May, during the heart of the schedule. Early season games were often held in a light drizzle or, if it happened to be dry, a 45-degree temperature that felt ten degrees colder due to the winds tearing across the Illinois plains. Snowfall had forced many a March practice inside, where the boys made do with tennis balls and Wiffle balls in the cramped gym. Because of all the cancellations, Macon sometimes played as few as eight conference games a year.

By these standards, Sweet's first day was downright temperate, plagued by only an early morning shower. As the boys warmed up on the waterlogged grass under a weak spring sun, Sweet stood near the backstop with his glove under his arm. Scanning the field, he mulled potential lineups.

On the mound, throwing half-speed, was Doug Tomlinson. A senior, Tomlinson was the closest Macon High had to a big man on campus—a star on the basketball team, the quarterback of the football team, and a member of the National Honor Society. He was both Macon's best returning hitter and its ace, armed with an overpowering fastball and an effective curveball. Tall and handsome, with dark hair, droopy eyes, and broad shoulders, Tomlinson was the kind of kid for whom it seemed everything came easily. Even so, as the only remaining starter from the 1968 team that won only one game, he of all the boys most felt the weight of the team's history.

Behind the plate, thick and imperturbable, squatted junior Dean Otta. Sweet had never seen a catcher quite like Dean. A tough country boy, he eschewed signs, instead telling his pitchers to "just throw it up there and I'll catch it." This might have proved disastrous had Otta not possessed an eerie ability to stop most any pitch. He blocked balls with his body, snared them above his head, and, if they sailed too far off the plate, was known to catch them barehanded.

Out at shortstop, his brother, Dale, scooped up grounders. Though twins, the two were easy to tell apart. While Dean was wide and solid with a wedge for a jaw, Dale was tall, thin, and light on his feet. He'd led the team in batting average as a freshman and finished his sophomore year tied with Tomlinson for the best mark, all while displaying one of the best arms on the team. A serious, introverted boy, Dale provided a counterbalance to some of his fun-loving teammates. Sweet expected him to emerge as a team leader, if not a vocal one.

To Dale's right, chin jutting out, Steve Shartzer emitted a steady stream of smack talk. Shark had grown into a strong-armed third baseman, talented hitter, and imposing pitcher. He was also perhaps the cockiest sixteen-year-old Sweet had ever met. Still, the coach had developed a soft spot for the boy.

Next to Shartzer, taking turns at third base and in the outfield, was wispy junior John Heneberry, the last of the team's trio of starting pitchers. So lanky as to appear almost undernourished, Heneberry had missed all his sophomore season with mono. He mystified Sweet. Even though the other boys swore he had great stuff, to Sweet's eye the kid had one of the weaker arms on the team. At one point, Sweet wondered aloud why Heneberry kept practicing his changeup. Finally one of the boys had told him that wasn't Heneberry's changeup. It was his fastball.

Across the diamond, doling out grounders, was first baseman Jeff Glan. In most respects, Glan was the opposite of the prototypical tall, homer-bashing corner infielder. Only five-foot-seven, he was primarily a singles hitter. Not blessed with speed, he had a habit of throwing his chin back when he ran, making it look as if his head might topple off its mooring at any instant. The son of a farmer who worked a second job at the Pittsburgh Plate Glass factory, he was also the best student on the team and a pithy speaker given to occasionally quoting philosophy.

Out in right field, wearing thick black glasses and chewing gum, Brian Snitker shagged fly balls. Though only a freshman, Snitker possessed a smooth, powerful swing. It was a good thing, too, because on a team of speedy players he was even slower than Glan. As Shartzer loved to crack about Snitker, "There's dead people that can outrun him."

In center field was freshman Stu Arnold, the one-time runt of the Elwin team. Now a graceful, dark-haired boy, Arnold had a natural feel for the game, and was renowned for getting ungodly jumps on fly balls. With his high cheekbones and killer smile, he was also the closest thing Macon High had to a matinee idol. Though only a freshman, he'd already been asked to the prom by perhaps the prettiest senior in the high school.

Over in left field, Sweet could make out the diminutive figure of Mike Atteberry, pudgy-cheeked and wearing oval, black-rimmed glasses. A senior and talented hitter, Atteberry was the rare Macon athlete who didn't play multiple sports, though not for lack of trying. Growing up, he'd always loved football and basketball. But while all the other boys hit growth spurts, he remained stuck at a shade under five feet. Baseball was the only sport at which he could succeed. Then, after his junior year, finally and much to his delight, Atteberry sprouted six inches. He now stood a relatively towering five-foot-seven.

Finally, Sweet's eyes turned to the blond boy at second base, the one with the quick feet and sure glove. Ernie Miller had been right: Sweet's hiring *had* convinced his son to play baseball. A natural leader, Mark Miller was funny, charming, and unusually empathetic for a teenager. Sweet had a hunch that if anyone could help him keep Shartzer in line, it would be Miller.

After fifteen minutes, Sweet called the boys over. One by one they jogged in until all fourteen were present. It was not an imposing crew. Those that weren't scrawny were small, and those that weren't small were scrawny. After performing a head count, Sweet cleared his throat. "I've got good news boys," he said, affecting a mock serious tone. "You've all made the team."

The players looked around, unsure whether they were allowed to laugh.

Sweet continued.

"Alright, I've got some rules to go over," he said. "The first one is that I'm not going to have many rules."

Next, he announced that practice was optional. If any of the boys didn't want to play ball, he wasn't going to force them. Also, there would be no wind sprints, punishments, or lengthy pregame speeches. When it came to strategy, if a player felt he could steal a base during a game, he should signal Sweet that he was going, not the other way around. And as far as who played where, Sweet told them to work that out among themselves. After all, they certainly knew better than he did.

The boys stared at him, then at each other. Was he for real? *Optional practice? Pick your own position?* It was quite a contrast from Burns, who'd known little about baseball but plenty about discipline.

Burns had been a Britton special, hired to toughen up the kids. Standing six-foot-two and weighing in the neighborhood of 250, he looked like a tractor with a flattop. Burns grew up in Kennett, Missouri; played tackle at Arkansas State; and was fond of ordering the boys to lie on their backs and close their eyes while he recited speeches from *Patton* at a tremendous volume, yelling, "NO DUMB BASTARD EVER WON A WAR BY DYING FOR HIS COUNTRY!" During football practice, if a running back missed his cut, Burns grabbed the poor boy by the shoulder pads and yanked him onto his ass, whereupon he loomed over him and shouted, "Where are YOU going, you little BIRD-HEADED BASTARD?!"

Under Burns, the kids knew to await orders, just as they had with Tim Cook, their hard-driving junior high coach who believed yelling was the primary component of coaching. But now here was Sweet, who seemed intent on not giving any orders at all. What's more, just as in English class, he told the kids to call him not "Coach" or "Sir," but just "Sweet." Dale Otta looked around at his teammates, then back at his new coach, with his long hair and crazy sideburns. *This*, Otta thought, *is going to be an interesting season.*

During the first week of practice, Sweet was struck by how fluid the boys looked. Dale Otta and Miller turned the double play as well as anyone he'd seen at the high school level; Glan ran infield practice with a coach's precision; and Shartzer and Dean Otta appeared to have an innate understanding of each other when on the mound and behind the plate.

Then again, the boys should have looked smooth, for they had been playing with or against each other their entire lives. Unlike schools fed by a number of communities, Macon High drew from only two towns: Macon and Elwin. Since there were only so many athletic kids of a certain age, this meant the Macon sandlot team looked an awful lot like the Little League team, which looked an awful lot like the junior high and high school teams. The same held true for other sports. If the baseball players didn't play football, or vice versa, there wouldn't have been enough kids for either squad. So Dale Otta was Macon's shortstop . . . and small forward . . . and tight end, while Glan was also a quarterback and point guard. At times, the school's shallow athletic pool led to some comic lineups. The starting center on the basketball team was Shartzer, who stood but five-foot-eleven, while Heneberry made for one of the more improbable defensive ends imaginable at five-foot-nine and 125 pounds.

If the teams were makeshift, the program itself was even more so. When Sweet took the job, there was no scorekeeper, no assistant coach, no bus driver, no trainer, no equipment manager, and little in the way of funding. When Sweet retrieved the uniforms from a dank storage room underneath the junior high, he was surprised to find that they were the consistency of burlap sacks. Gray with faded purple lettering, a sportswriter would later describe them as looking like "World War II rejects." The rest of the gear wasn't much better. The hats were mismatched and the collection of baseballs so sparse that in years past when the boys lost them during warm-ups, they'd occasionally been forced to ask their opponents for replacements. As for bats, Sweet started the season with only five and knew that when one broke, it would be a battle to get McClard to free up the five or six dollars required for a new one.

Despite all the logistical issues, the biggest problem—as Sweet saw it—was all the rainouts. How could the boys get better if they never played? Thus his first act as coach had been to walk into the office of athletic director Phil Sargent.

"How can I double the games on our schedule?" Sweet asked.

"Double?" Sargent looked surprised.

"We've got a good team and these boys need to play. Not just in our conference but some of the bigger teams around."

At Sweet's insistence, Sargent made some calls. Soon enough, Macon had twenty-two games lined up for the season. Sweet figured that would be enough for the boys to get noticed.

5

Lost in the Corn

Of course, to get noticed a team has to play well.

On April first, after nearly a month of practice, Macon opened its 1970 season at home versus Pana High, a school of five hundred students located twenty-five miles south of Macon. Sweet arrived at the field by 2:30. He was not the first one.

"Coach Sweet, I've chalked the field and got the bats out," said a small, freckled boy.

Sweet smiled. Sam Trusner was the first and only member of his baseball staff. An energetic if uncoordinated freshman, Trusner grew up playing sandlot ball with the rest of the Macon boys. The older he got, however, the clearer it became that he would travel a different athletic path. In eighth grade, the junior high track coach approached Trusner and asked if he wanted to be his equipment manager. If he accepted, Trusner would get to go to the state track tournament, all the way up in Peoria. Trusner jumped at the opportunity and did such a fine job that when Jack Burns got word of it, he lumbered over to the junior high one afternoon during lunch and tracked the boy down. When Trusner looked up, cowed by Burns' size and reputation, the coach announced that he'd heard the young man was a damn fine equipment manager and informed him he'd be doing the same job for the football team in the fall. Trusner swelled with pride. *The high school coach came all the way to the junior high just to see me? How cool is that?* Soon enough, word got around that there was a short, industrious kid who could ease a coach's load. Within a month of arriving at Macon High, Trusner was recruited for the basketball team. When Sweet got the baseball job, Trusner signed on for a third sport.

Now, as Sweet jotted down his lineup, Trusner laid out the first aid kit, the team's four scarred batting helmets, and a small bag of baseballs. Next came the bats, five in a row. They were all different models of Louisville Sluggers: two Mickey Mantles, a Nellie Fox, and a couple of old, beat-up ones. These were the team's most precious commodity. Other than one ancient fungo bat, an old "unbreakable" model with a fiberglass grip that drained the pop out of the barrel, all the bats were wood, and the team usually broke at least one per game. When that happened, the boys made do with what they had. If all that was left were longer bats, the boys choked up; if only short ones were left they slid their bottom hand down the knob of the handle. This was still an upgrade from what many had grown up with. For many of the boys, the only way to acquire a bat while young was to loiter outside Fans Field in Decatur, home of the Class-A Commodores, and ask for the broken game bats, which they then took home, nailed back together, and wrapped in electrical tape.

Presently, Sweet walked over and handed Trusner the scorebook. Upon reading down to the number seven hitter in the lineup, Trusner looked up, surprised. After some thought, Sweet had decided to start Stu Arnold in center field over a junior, Gary Mathias, even though Arnold was only a freshman. Since Glan was out with an injury, Sweet had also penciled in the light-hitting Heneberry as the first baseman, batting ninth.

Thus the Macon lineup looked like this:

1. Mark Miller 2B
2. Dale Otta SS
3. Steve Shartzer P

4. Mike Atteberry LF
5. Doug Tomlinson 3B
6. Dean Otta C
7. Stu Arnold CF
8. Brian Snitker RF
9. John Heneberry 1B

As the boys arrived and began warming up, Sweet walked the field, checking its condition. Even on a good day, it was a difficult place to play baseball. Home plate abutted the industrial arts building, and there were no outfield fences, unless you counted the cornfield in deep right, which at roughly four hundred feet was considered in play. This led to the unusual sight of outfielders sprinting into the corn and tramping into a forest of knee-high stalks, while a runner madly circled the bases behind them. Sometimes it took minutes for the right fielder to emerge. Other times, the fielder recovered the ball so quickly that Macon's opponents accused Ironmen players of stashing extra balls amongst the corn.

Next, Sweet made his way over to center field, which presented a different challenge. Through the heart of it arced the school's running track, ready to upend any backpedaling fielder. Since shallow center also doubled as the landing area for the discus, the ground behind second base was a minefield of divots and crevices. Thus any ball that reached the outfield on the ground was liable to change direction unexpectedly or, worse, hit a crater and stop dead.

The infield wasn't much better. The mound was a flat patch of dirt, and the loose soil of the basepaths housed so many rocks that Sweet asked the players to periodically comb it with five-gallon buckets in hand. More often than not, the buckets were full in no time.

On this day, the usual challenges were compounded by a game-time temperature of 39 degrees that felt even colder due to a brutal wind. It roared in off the barren cornfields, tearing off the boys' hats during warm-ups and giving new meaning to the term "wild pitch." Games had been called on account of wind in central Illinois plenty of times before, and this one probably should have been, too. Still, both coaches agreed it was better to at least try to play.

As the game began, Sweet occasionally glanced over at the sideline, waiting for fans to arrive for the home opener. He knew there wouldn't be many, especially early in the season and on such a cold afternoon, but even he was surprised by how lonely it was. In all, maybe a dozen people showed up. Since there were no bleachers, most stood by the fence or sat wrapped in blankets on folding chairs. All of them were parents.

Maybe that was for the best. Macon struggled early, unable to read the conditions. Balls ricocheted off gloves and routine throws sailed wide. Shartzer uncorked a wild pitch and the errors piled up, three in all. On offense, the Ironmen couldn't sustain a rally. In seven innings they managed only two runs on four hits while Pana scored four on six hits. It was little comfort that all four Pana runs were unearned.

Afterward, the Macon players dispersed into the night, stewing about the errors and hoping the loss wasn't the start of another long season. Sweet showered at the gym and drove back to the house in Decatur where he'd recently begun renting a room, replaying the game in his head the whole way.

He wasn't too worried, at least not yet, but he knew if the team lost a couple more games it wouldn't take long for people in Macon to begin branding him a failure. Then again, he'd been called worse.

Some months earlier, a parent walked into a Macon school board meeting, looking agitated. Held at 7:30 P.M. in the high school library, the monthly meetings were usually quiet affairs. The seven members were joined by a treasurer, the principal, and the superintendent. Meetings lasted an hour or so and the board voted on proposals using a simple "yea" or "nay" procedure. Monthly finances were discussed, expenditures recorded, and school matters debated. Most of the time, matters tended toward the mundane. "It was mutually agreed upon that no further consideration be given to the purchase of another lawnmower," read the minutes for June 16, 1969, "and that the superintendent hire a boy in the community to mow the grass with present facilities at the salary of $1.50 an hour."

Occasionally, as on this night, townspeople attended. Most of the time, they came to ask the school for something: money for a graduation float, better concessions, new textbooks. This parent, however, had a grander concern. When called upon, he stood up, looked around the room, and made a proclamation. "You've got to get rid of Lynn Sweet," he said. "That man is a communist."

Roger Britton was taken aback. He'd heard plenty of accusations leveled at Sweet. One time, Sweet and Ernie Miller walked out of Claire's and, seeing pigeons perched on the grain elevator, grabbed a hunting shotgun from a friend's car, took aim, and fired. That led to a fine of $50 for Sweet for "possession of a loaded and uncased gun," and $35 for Miller. Another time, McClard became livid when he found Sweet in the gym, playing basketball with his students after hours, and the two men had engaged in a heated shouting match. In each case, Britton had stepped in, calmed the waters, and defended his friend. But *communist*? That was a new one.

The agitated parent proceeded with a litany of reasons why he believed this to be the case, including Sweet's reading selections, his politics, and the fact that, plain for all to see, the man was a hippie who'd be better off taking his act to California.

It wasn't the first time someone had suggested Sweet leave town. To many Maconites, Sweet seemed more foreign than ever by the spring of 1970. Rather than the town having an effect on him, the opposite appeared to have occurred. Not only did Sweet look like a peacenik, but instead of settling down he'd become even more of a vagabond. For a while he lived in an apartment on Front Street, then in a house with Jack Burns down the road in Radford. Now, of course, he lived in that house in Decatur with a bunch of basketball players, some of whom, the women down at the Country Manor restaurant whispered, were *colored*. At times it seemed Sweet just lived out of his car. To invite him over for dinner was often to find Sweet, a few days later, still camped out on your couch. Not that anyone ever minded, for he was excellent company and a conscientious guest. Steve Shartzer remembers a couple of mornings when he awoke to find Sweet on the family's couch, bleary-eyed after a night of carousing with Burns, Britton, and Bob Shartzer. Unfailingly, though, Sweet was always up by 7 A.M., groggy but dressed and ready. By eight he was at school and teaching, lest he break one of Britton's cardinal rules: Have your fun but always, *always* stand tall the next morning.

Then there was that strange business with the slippers. One morning, Roy Roush, the vice president of the school board, was walking in the post-dawn hours near his house on the eastern edge of Macon when he'd seen the most peculiar thing. There, silhouetted against the morning light, was a man in shorts and canvas slippers, tearing down the street. As the figure got closer, Roush recognized the mop of brown hair and realized it was Sweet, pumping his arms and sprinting around town for what appeared to be no good reason. "Hello there, Roy!" Sweet called out, and then he was gone.

This being 1970, the idea of running for fun hadn't yet entered the national consciousness. *Runner's World* had only recently graduated from being a pamphlet printed out of the Kansas home of a man named Bob Anderson, and it would be a year before a University of Oregon track coach would oversee the release of a shoe called Nike. Sweet was already hooked, though. He loved how running cleared his mind and energized him—"better than a pill," he told people. He began while living in Champaign in 1962, starting each morning by clocking four miles around town. Macon was not Champaign, though, and concerned neighbors sometimes stopped and asked if he needed help—why else would he be tearing off at such a pace? Other times, pickup trucks swerved as if to hit him, the drivers cackling as they zoomed by.

Indeed, little about the man made sense to the people of Macon. Still, while there were plenty of words one could use to describe Sweet, "communist" was not one of them. So when the parent made his accusation, Britton pushed back. Addressing the parents, administrators, and board members, he reminded them how much the students loved Sweet. The man was just a bit progressive, that was all.

Later, however, Britton cornered Sweet to tell him what had happened. "L.C.," he said, "you know that one of these times I really am going to have to fire you, right?"

Sweet nodded, then thanked his friend for having his back. He was aware of how McClard and the school board viewed him, but if anything he found it amusing. Sweet saw himself not as a troublemaker but as a catalyst. In his view Macon clung to antiquated views and part of his job was to introduce new ones. That's why he'd done away with the old English curriculum almost immediately; why he'd taken out the individual desks in his room and hauled in those round tables to encourage a flow of ideas; why he had his students read books that forced them to confront new concepts; and why he kept giving them assignments, like the obituary exercise, that encouraged the kids to think about life outside of Macon.

Getting fired? That didn't worry Sweet too much. After all, he was sure he could find another job if he needed to. Hell, he still got calls from the Chicago schools and from as far away as Alaska. What did he have keeping him in Macon, anyway?

6

He Ain't Got Shit

Five days separated the Ironmen's season opener against Pana and their next game, at home against Assumption. For Steve Shartzer, they were five agonizing, interminable days. Most of the players had shaken off the Pana game after a night. Not Shartzer. After the loss, he'd thrown his glove in the locker room, then gone home to stew in silence. Each afternoon afterward at practice, he reminded his teammates that they just *could not* make those kinds of errors again, that they must *kick the shit* out of Assumption.

Sweet noticed this and it both impressed and concerned him. He loved Shartzer's intensity but it could be almost scary at times. At sixteen, Shartzer was in many respects still that kid chucking tomatoes, racing around the house, and trying to will his way to victory. Stronger and faster than the other kids, he threw as hard as he could during warm-ups, as if trying to impale Dean Otta with each pitch. His mindset, as he put it, was, "Here she comes, boys, right down the middle, the best I got." He turned batting practice into a competition, endeavoring to make his line drives cleaner than the other boys', his home runs more towering.

Despite all his talent, Shartzer remained driven by a sense of inferiority, always trying to prove to somebody, somewhere that he was good enough. Growing up in Elwin, he strived to impress older kids like

Doug Tomlinson. In Little League, it was the boys from Macon, which, though a small town itself, was a metropolis compared to Elwin. In Elwin, the Little League coach arrived at practices on a tractor with the baseball equipment perched on the back, and was often forced to recruit from lower age divisions just to field a team. Surrounded by inferior talent, Shartzer had spent much of his youth losing to Macon. These defeats infuriated him, not just because he detested losing in any context but because no matter how well he pitched, his defense often failed him. So while John Heneberry was backed by Mark Miller at second and Ottas at seemingly every base, Shartzer had a few boys who, as he put it, "couldn't catch a flu during cold season." In all those years, Steve remembers beating Macon only once.

By the time he reached high school, Shartzer had stopped worrying about his immediate peers and shifted his focus outward. Now he burned to prove to kids from larger towns that he was more than just some hick from Elwin; he was a big-time player. As a freshman, he played three varsity sports and, in the spring, had been recruited for track when the coach, Dale Sloan, saw him play football. After watching in awe as Shartzer sprinted away from a gang of would-be tacklers, Sloan decided the cocky freshman might already be the fastest kid at Macon High. In truth, he was underestimating Steve; soon, Shartzer would prove to be the fastest kid in the *county*.

On the diamond, Shartzer hit over .300 as a freshman and drove in the winning run in the game that clinched the conference title. He practiced hard, beat himself up when he made mistakes, and took the game more seriously than the other boys.

In many respects, Shartzer and his new coach couldn't have been more different. Shartzer brimmed with energy, ready to go to war at a moment's notice. Of all the Ironmen, he enjoyed Burns' Patton speeches the most. He also didn't suffer fools kindly. When a new basketball coach took over the junior high team in eighth grade and began his first practice with a happy-talk demonstration about how *Look boys, two balls can fit through this rim*, Shartzer smelled bullshit and stood up to interrupt him. "What's your point?" Shartzer said. "Isn't the object to put the damn ball in this damn rim?"

"Well yes, Steve," the coach said.

"Well when are we going to do that? That's what I came out here for."

If Shartzer treated the game like a military engagement, Sweet seemed to see it more as a great adventure. Already, in only a month, he'd not only changed most of the team rules—who made practice optional, for god's sake?—but had, at various times, joined the boys during scrimmages, held home run derby during practice, and doled out nicknames to players.

Shartzer was wary. If this was coaching, it was unlike any he'd received.

The following Saturday, Tomlinson took the mound for the Ironmen against Assumption. The sun hid behind clouds, and the temperature again fell below forty, but at least there was no wind. The Assumption hitters probably wished there had been. Without it, they stood no chance against Tomlinson, who launched fastball after fastball. Assumption never got a man past second base and Macon won 8–0. The following afternoon, against Argenta, the result was even more lopsided. Shartzer and Atteberry crushed home runs, and the game was called at 13–3 on account of the ten-run mercy rule, which took effect after five innings.

The boys, and Sweet, could rest easy. They'd regained their groove. Granted, neither opponent had been in their conference, but wins were wins. A week later, the Ironmen's first real challenge loomed.

On April 15, Macon readied for its first road trip of the season, a forty-five-minute drive to Maroa High School, north of Decatur. As usual, getting ready was something of an ordeal.

Released from class an hour early, the boys hurried through the basketball gym, past the purple mats bearing IRONMEN in white letters, underneath the American flag, and into the tiny locker room. Narrow and cramped, it contained three rows of gray lockers, two skinny wooden benches, one toilet, and a communal shower. The boys crammed in and dressed as quickly as they could. It was uncomfortable but still better than football season, when the team gave up on the space entirely and erected black curtains on the basketball court, which some boys chose to selectively ignore—the better to show off their torsos for any teenage girls who happened to walk by.

Once dressed, the boys jogged out to the parking lot, where the long, yellow bus was already idling. Behind the wheel, beaming and welcoming them in a mock tour-bus tone, was Sweet. Unable to get funding for a bus driver, he figured he'd just do it himself.

As Sweet steered the creaky bus, bumping over two-lane country roads, the players laughed, joked, and tried not to get carsick. Toward the back of the twenty-odd rows of vinyl seats, one boy sat quietly. Hat pulled down over reedy brown hair, John Heneberry stared out the window, thinking about everything that could go wrong in this, the first pitching start of his high school career.

By far the least imposing kid on the team, Heneberry was neither tall nor strong. To the untrained eye, a good 40 percent of his body mass appeared to be elbows and knees, and his delicate features and thin face only added to the impression. He was the worst-hitting regular on the team, bereft of power or speed, and Sweet regularly batted him ninth. Especially following Tomlinson and Shartzer in the rotation, he looked like a JV pitcher summoned for a spot start. His fastball, if you could call it that, floated in at a leisurely pace, as if taking in the surroundings en route. As Shartzer liked to say, Heneberry had three speeds: "slow, slower, and slowest."

The Maroa field, like most in the Meridian conference, presented unique challenges. The infield consisted entirely of grass and home plate sat at the intersection of a cow pasture and a cornfield. The left side of the diamond was also the football field, so batters hit from one end zone toward the other. In lieu of a left field fence, a tall row of apple trees buttressed the four-story brick edifice of the high school four hundred feet out. Pursuing balls in deep left required navigating a runoff depression that became so soggy during the rainy season that one football player is said to have almost drowned when opponents piled on top of him for too long. Right field, on the other hand, was a lefty hitter's dream, flat and exceptionally short, ending about 250 feet out where South Cedar Street provided an asphalt barrier.

As Heneberry walked to the mound for warm-ups, the Maroa hitters took casual swings and talked among themselves. Until, that is, they got a load of Heneberry lofting pitches toward the plate, each as soft and fluttery as the last, as if made of papier-mâché. One by one the Maroa boys turned and began to watch. *That's his fastball?* Within minutes, they were visualizing monster home runs, 4–4 stat lines, and the cute girls who'd be impressed by them. One even said it out loud: "We're going to rock this guy."

On the mound, Heneberry could hear the Maroa players and it brought back bad memories. More than any of the Macon boys, he was a self-made player. From the time he was five years old, throwing dirt clods and walnuts on his grandfather's farm in Decatur, Heneberry had dreamed of being a pitcher. By the time he was seven, his father had fashioned a backstop out of a couple of steel posts and chicken wire, and the two played catch in the yard every afternoon, until the light got so dim that bats swooped around John's pitches. All that practice couldn't overcome a core problem, though: John just couldn't throw the ball very hard. During his first couple seasons of Little League, opponents teed off on his fastball, and one game after another ended with Heneberry walking off the field with his head down.

And now, for the third time in three seasons, John had to try to make a good impression on a new coach. And this time it mattered.

He'd barely played during his freshman year and had lost his sophomore year to mono—not that he would have pitched anyway, since the Ironmen had Tomlinson, Shartzer, and a senior named Ray Martin.

The first Maroa batter stepped in, eager to get a crack at Macon's goofy-looking pitcher. On the mound, Heneberry knew how important this first pitch was; as someone who relied on finesse, he needed to have his good stuff right away or the game could spiral out of control. Beginning his slow windup, he kicked his leg high and twisted at the hip, as if all that motion might somehow generate more velocity, then released the ball. It sailed in, headed toward the hitter's chest then—bam!—fell right out of the air. The boy swung as hard as he could. He missed by a foot.

The next pitch never even entered the strike zone, but it looked so tantalizing that the Maroa hitter took another cut. When the third offering started nearly head high yet somehow looped in for strike three, the boy was pissed. He headed back to the dugout grumbling.

The next batter fared no better, nor did the next. All went up looking for fastballs; none saw one in the strike zone. Instead, Heneberry delivered a steady stream of junk. The breakthrough had come one night years earlier while watching the *Game of the Week* on TV. John heard Dizzy Dean refer to a curveball as "the great equalizer" and immediately asked his father about it. Knowing little about the pitch, Jack Heneberry canvassed his coworkers at the post office until he found one who'd played ball in college and could teach him a proper curve. That night, Jack returned home and took his son out to the backyard, where they practiced throwing hooks for hours.

It wasn't pretty at first. John had trouble gripping the ball and, even once he could, had no luck controlling the pitch. Errant breaking balls sprayed the Heneberry lot, some so far off-target that Jack considered building a bigger backstop. Slowly, though, John began to get the hang of it. Within a year his pitches were dipping and darting, sometimes even by design. By the fifth grade, after his family moved to

Macon from Decatur, John felt confident enough with his new weapon to use it in a Little League game. At the age of ten, he threw his first no-hitter.

Now he relied on the curveball the way most kids did their heater. Packing the ball back in his hand, he delivered it from a seventy-degree angle, holding the pitch out from his body to get more torque. He could throw curves early in the count, late in the count, or when he needed a strikeout. When he was going good, he could even aim for specific spots in Dean Otta's glove. Most of the time, the pitch did what he wanted. When it didn't—well, hence his reputation as a notoriously poor batting practice pitcher. If he spun one up there and it didn't break, it usually ended up popping the batter. Already, Mike Atteberry had dislocated the middle finger on his left hand during batting practice while smacking down a Heneberry breaking ball that never broke.

They were all snapping today, though. On the sideline, Sweet watched, rapt. By the time Heneberry racked up his twelfth strikeout of the game in the seventh inning, Sweet was a believer. Not only had Heneberry allowed only two hits in shutting out Maroa 5–0, he'd done so in what Sweet considered an exquisitely entertaining manner. As the game went on, the Maroa boys had become increasingly agitated, cursing after each strikeout. "He ain't got shit!" one muttered on his return to the dugout. Sweet thought this so wonderful that, some time later, he bestowed upon Heneberry an unofficial nickname: *Ain't Got Shit*. To Sweet, it not only summed up the boy but, in some respects, the whole team.

By mid-April, Macon boasted an impressive 5–1 record but that wasn't what caught the attention of Joe Cook. Rather, he was more interested in how the Ironmen had won those games.

As preps writer for the Decatur *Herald & Review*, Cook covered roughly one hundred schools, from Lincoln in the north all the way down to Alney and Greenville in the south. He knew most every highway and back road in central Illinois and was always on the lookout for potential feature stories. Upon glancing at Macon's schedule, he suspected he'd found one. He checked the box scores, then checked them again and came to the same stunning conclusion: Not only were the Ironmen undefeated through four conference games, but they had yet to give up a run. What's more, in six games total, Macon had yet to allow an earned run, period. *Forty-two innings and a 0.00 team ERA*. Even in an area where it seemed every team had an ace, this was a remarkable feat, especially coming from a school with little to no baseball history.

Cook picked up the phone and called Macon High, whereupon he asked to speak to the baseball coach, a man by the name of L. C. Sweet. This was a story he needed to hear.

The next morning, the residents of Macon opened up their papers to see a headline in the sports section that read "How Sweet It Is." The article, which filled a good quarter of the page, mentioned Tomlinson, Heneberry, and the Ottas, as well as a boy identified as "sophomore John Shartzer," a mistake Steve Shartzer proceeded to take as a personal affront.

A full half of the piece, however, was devoted to Macon's first-year coach, whom Cook depicted as a quirky, candid, fun-loving "bachelor in his mid-twenties" who "got the baseball job by forfeit." Sweet was quoted as saying, "I wasn't too excited about doing [the job] at first, but it's been a very enjoyable season." When asked about his coaching acumen, Sweet deferred to the boys' talent. As for his own priorities, said Sweet, "I'm still an English teacher first."

This may have been true, but baseball coach was becoming an awfully close second.

In one game after another, Macon prevailed. The boys crushed

Niantic 10–0, Moweaqua 9–2, and prevailed 4–2 over archrival Mt. Zion, a team the Ironmen hadn't beaten in years. Sweet's boys were bordering on dominant.

By now, the team had fallen into a loose rhythm, egged on by Sweet, who not only spent a good chunk of practice joking with the boys but nearly all of it on the field. At first, the players weren't quite sure what to make of it; coaches were supposed to stand on the side, with a whistle, chewing them out. But here was Sweet, taking his cuts, running in the outfield, and throwing batting practice most every day. And what a BP pitcher he was. Heneberry remembers it as, "like having a pitching machine." Even though some of the balls were torn up, with the stitching loose and the cover flapping, Sweet had tremendous control. If you needed confidence, he could groove one. If you had trouble with outside pitches, he put one fastball after another on the outside corner. And if you got too cocky, as Heneberry says, "He could gun you down."

Sweet pitched because he enjoyed it but also for strategic reasons. Whereas most teams in the area employed their starting pitchers to throw batting practice, Sweet tried to dissuade his from doing so. "What's the point of that," he said to Heneberry and Shartzer. "Why would I want you to learn to throw the ball so guys can hit it?"

So instead it was Sweet up on the mound, throwing sometimes an hour a day, possessed of a seemingly rubber arm. The fielders got practice in live game situations; the hitters got to face pitching from someone who'd competed at the semipro level; and Sweet got to play ball. "It was amazing," says Heneberry, "how much better we got."

There was only one cardinal sin during practice: getting too serious. "Gentlemen," Sweet said whenever this occurred, "we are here after school because we are no longer in school. This is the fun part." If that didn't work, he had other means. Once, when he sensed the kids getting too testy, he went into his windup and, upon swiveling, turned and mooned the boys.

Day by day, the players became more accustomed to both Sweet's unconventional approach and his seemingly limitless confidence in them. During games, they took off running whenever they wanted, often with great success. They bunted when they saw an opportunity and pitched out when it seemed prudent. Instead of deputizing a parent to be the first base coach, or bringing in an assistant, Sweet named Heneberry to the job. He did this in part because Heneberry was a part-time player but also because he knew the responsibility would boost the boy's confidence, which Sweet saw as the ultimate goal of much that he did. During games, no matter how bad Tomlinson, Shartzer, or Heneberry looked on the mound, Sweet left them in. "You'll work through it," he said. Or, if they appeared tight, he pulled them aside between innings and asked them why they played baseball. If the boys looked back at him blankly, he smiled and said, "Because it's fun!" And then, without discussing strategy, he walked away.

Shartzer in particular was warming to Sweet's methods. If the new coach had come in and said, "Drop down and give me twenty," Shartzer's response would have been, "You pitch this ball. I do more pushups and sit-ups at home when I'm done than you do all week. Don't give me that."

But Sweet felt like more a mentor than an authority figure. Despite his laissez-faire attitude, he also struck Shartzer as a man who knew baseball, respected the game, and understood that coaching was about discovery, not dictates. "Try holding the bat in your fingertips so you're quicker and stronger and they can't throw it by you on the inner half of the plate," Sweet told him. Or, "When you're hitting, pretend you're on the mound. What would you be throwing here? Why? Then be ready for it."

The proof, as Shartzer liked to say, was in the goddamn pudding: The team was piling up victories. Winning games was one thing, though. Gaining respect was another.

By May 9, when the Ironmen hosted Argenta, they were 10–2 and on the verge of the postseason. It was a gusty afternoon and the wind blew northeast, out toward left field, giving wings to any ball pulled down the line. It was Heneberry's turn on the mound, and after three innings he was already in a 4–1 hole. Then, in the top of the fourth, a tall, muscular Argenta player named Mike Ferrill stepped to the plate with two men on. It was one of those days when Heneberry's off-speed pitches were wandering, held up even further by the wind. After sending a couple breaking balls into the dirt, Heneberry had no choice but to pitch to Ferrill. He left one up in the zone and Ferrill sized it up and reared back. The impact of bat on ball made the kind of booming, resonant crash little boys dream about when hitting imaginary home runs in their backyards. Said Heneberry: "Oh shit."

The ball gained elevation as it went, soaring above the infield, over the discus pockmarks, and past the running track before finally touching down on the football field, which doubled as deep, deep center. It traveled so far that the Argenta base runners slowed to a leisurely trot as they rounded third base. And so it was that Denny Hill, an Argenta outfielder, sauntered in to touch home plate and, as he did, turned toward the Macon bench and, loud enough for all to hear, posed a question.

"They found that ball yet?"

At third base, Shartzer's face reddened; as he saw it, he was the only one allowed to make fun of his teammates. He took three quick steps toward Hill and pointed his finger. "Don't you ever do that again, fat boy," he yelled. "Because the next time you're going to face me." Then, for the rest of the inning, Shartzer muttered under his breath, stockpiling anger. By the time he came to the plate the following inning, he was practically twitching. He crushed one to center and stretched it to a double. From his perch on second base, Shartzer turned and cupped his hands around his mouth. "Hey, you find that ball yet?" he yelled, a refrain he would continue to utter after every Macon hit and, as it turned out, every time he saw Ferrill or Hill for years afterward.

Energized, the Ironmen bats came alive. They cut the score to

8–6 and then, with the bases loaded and two outs, Heneberry came to the plate, hitting ninth as usual. The Argenta pitcher threw the first two balls off the plate to start out 2–0. This did not sit well with his coach.

Slamming the scorebook into the fence, the coach marched out to the mound.

"This guy couldn't hit it if you put it on a tee. Just throw it over the damn plate!"

And so the Argenta pitcher did. Remembering what Denny Hill had said earlier, Heneberry reached back and swung with everything his bony arms could manage. He met the pitch head-on and yanked it down the left field line. The ball sailed over the infield, then instead of alighting, as most of Heneberry's hits did, it kept soaring. In three years of games and batting practice, Heneberry had never come within twenty feet of hitting one to the running track. Now he watched as the ball flew over it and rolled onto the football field. Only his slow feet kept him from a home run, and he coasted into third with a stand-up, three-run triple. It was the farthest he had ever, or would ever, hit a baseball.

If Sweet had harbored any concerns about his team's confidence or resilience, they were put to rest. By the end of the game, Macon had erased a six-run deficit to win 13–9.

Wins like this didn't exactly lead to baseball fever, but people in Macon were becoming increasingly curious about the Ironmen. With each victory a new headline appeared in the *Herald & Review*: "Macon Scores Fifth Shutout in Meridian"; "Another Shutout for Macon"; "Macon Clips Moweaqua." New faces began to appear at games. There were uncles and brothers and curious townsfolk but also, on occasion and much to the boys' delight, the occasional teenage girl. Sometimes there were up to thirty or forty fans, though the core still consisted of the baseball parents: Bob Shartzer, along with Dwight and Maxine Glan; the Arnolds; the Snitkers; Ernie Miller; and Jack

Heneberry, always alone because his wife, Betty, became too nervous at games to watch her son.

On occasion, even school board members stopped by. And the more the Ironmen won, the more ambivalence some felt about Sweet. Maconites may not have agreed with his political or religious beliefs, or liked his teaching curriculum, but baseball was a common language. He couldn't be all bad if he had the boys playing so well.

By mid-May, the Ironmen were 13–2 and Meridian Conference champions. Heading into the district title game they were also, amazingly, the favorites.

Winning the conference was impressive for a school like Macon, but the feat was tempered by the level of competition. Most of the other schools in the area were also rural outposts, with enrollments between 200 and 450. Few had large budgets or extensive rosters, and most played on fields that, like Macon's, bore only a passing resemblance to a proper baseball diamond. There was one exception though: Mt. Zion.

Ten miles northeast of Macon, Mt. Zion was a thriving suburb of Decatur with a population of roughly twenty-five hundred. As commuters moved in, the town had continued to grow. As a result, over the years the rivalry between Macon and Mt. Zion had become increasingly lopsided. Mt. Zion's team was deeper, its uniforms nicer, and its town more affluent. The team played on a handsome field with fences and combed dirt base paths. All this filtered down to the players, who acted, as Dale Otta remembers it, "Like they were higher class than us."

So on Friday, May 15, when Doug Tomlinson pitched seven innings and Shartzer knocked in two runs with a fifth inning double to power Macon past Mt. Zion 5–3 for the district title, it was a cathartic victory for the Ironmen. More important, it was also a sign that

Macon wasn't merely a good team in a weak conference but perhaps a good team, period. That the Mt. Zion players left the field cursing, unable to believe they'd lost to Macon again—twice in one season!—made the win all the sweeter.

Within hours, the news spread around town, from Claire's to the Country Manor and then, by telephone, up to Elwin and down to neighboring Moweaqua: The Ironmen were headed to the regionals.

Shartzer was the first to say it, the following week during practice: "Why can't we go all the way to state?"

After all, as Shartzer pointed out, "It ain't like there's a rule against it." And indeed, this was true. There were, however, years and years of precedent. Schools like Macon didn't make it to state, and with good reason.

In 1970, the Illinois high school baseball playoffs were one big free-for-all, bereft of divisions or the classifications that were later created to ensure that small schools need only compete against other small schools. As a result, the competition was staggering. There were roughly seven hundred high schools in Illinois that fielded baseball teams, encompassing nearly seven hundred thousand students, and all were fighting for the same prize. To advance all the way to the state tournament required an incredible run. A team needed to win its conference, then prevail in two games at the district playoffs, two at the regionals, and two at the sectionals. And that was just to *qualify* for the state tourney, an eight-team affair held at Meinen Field on the campus of Bradley University in Peoria. To capture the title a school had to win ten consecutive playoff games, or four more than the champion of the modern-day NCAA basketball tournament.

The teams that prevailed usually hailed from the largest schools, sports powerhouses like Waukegan High in Waukegan; Griffin High in Springfield; Adlai Stevenson just outside Chicago; and, most feared of all, Lane Tech on the North Side of Chicago. The largest school in

Illinois by both enrollment and physical size, Tech boasted fifty-two hundred students, all of whom were boys. It splayed out on a thirty-three-acre campus, its five-story, fortress-like structure so large that students sometimes went an entire school year without running into each other in the halls. Both an academic and sports juggernaut, Tech drew talent from across the Chicago metro area and spit out a steady succession of Division I and professional players, including Giants outfielder Phil Weintraub; Cubs slugger and 1945 National League MVP Phil Cavarretta; Cubs pitcher Len Church; and, most recently, Mets draftee Buzz Capra, who would go on to be an All-Star and lead the National League in ERA in 1974. Upward of five hundred freshmen tried out for the Lane Tech team every spring, each one assigned a number and sent through a series of sprinting, fielding, and hitting drills on which they were judged on a scale of 1–8. To even have a shot at making the squad a player needed to grade out at five or better in every category. For many an Illinois schoolboy, just making varsity at Lane Tech was enough athletic accomplishment to last a lifetime.

If Tech represented the top of the system, then metro schools like Stephen Decatur (2,500 enrollment) and Eisenhower (2,000) represented the next rung, followed by suburban powers and large schools in small towns. Finally, there were the rural outposts like Nashville (enrollment 450) and, below them, the Macons of the world. These schools were usually fed by a lone junior high and populated with the offspring of farmers. Their teams played sporadic schedules and logged long hours on buses, rolling down rocky back roads. For such schools, just advancing to the regionals was akin to winning a title.

All of which made Sweet's next decision even more unusual. All year, Tomlinson had been the team's ace, finishing the season with a 5–0 record and a staggering fifty-one strikeouts in 32⅓ innings. But now Sweet pulled Tomlinson aside on the eve of the regional opener against Stewardson-Strasburg and the two spoke in low voices. Tomlinson nodded, if reluctantly. Then Sweet walked over to Shartzer.

"Steve, I want you to pitch against Stew-Stras."

"Me?"

Shartzer was genuinely surprised. He'd had a great season, finishing with a 6–1 record and 44 strikeouts in 41$\frac{1}{3}$ innings, but he didn't expect this. Not only because he was a sophomore, and because Tomlinson had been so dominant, but because Shartzer had long idolized the older boy. The Tomlinsons lived between Macon and Elwin and, for years, Steve yearned to be accepted as an athletic equal to Doug. He hadn't prepared to actually get the chance, though. At least not so soon. But Sweet had a plan.

7

It Only Takes One

There are moments in a boy's life that are seared into his memory. For the Ironmen, one was the first time they walked onto Fans Field in Decatur, Illinois, site of the regionals.

The home of the Commodores, a Class-A team in the Midwest League affiliated with the San Francisco Giants, Fans Field was located at the corner of East Garfield and North Woodford Streets in a residential neighborhood just north of downtown Decatur. Built in 1924, it was one of the last wooden stadiums, an elegant throwback to the ballparks of the early part of the century. By 1970 it had seen better days, but to the Macon boys, for whom even a chain-link outfield fence was a rarity, it looked like Yankee Stadium.

Entering through the back of the dugout, Heneberry stepped onto the cropped grass and paused for a moment, taking it all in. Having spent the first eight years of his life in Decatur, he considered Fans Field to be hallowed ground. This was where Tito Fuentes played, where a nineteen-year-old super-prospect named Gary Matthews now starred. And on this afternoon, Heneberry was going to be the one playing, not watching.

The outfield stretched before him, flat and green as a golf course. The infield dirt was fine and loose and the pitching rubber sat atop a small hillock, one of the first raised mounds he'd ever encountered. Above him, great banks of lights looked down from the top of the stadium walls. The fence, adorned with ads for auto care and Hostess bakeries, seemed miles away at 340 feet in right, 370 in center, and 340 in left. Wooden roofs extended over the bleachers, which rose above roped-off box seats. In all, the park seated over 5,000, a staggering figure to boys accustomed to a turnout in the teens.

One by one, the players walked onto the field as if in a daze. Finally, lugging a sack of bats and wearing a uniform he'd washed the night before, came Sam Trusner. Of all the Macon boys, he might have been the most elated. For once, he had a real dugout to stock. Ever so carefully, he lined up the bats in the wooden rack, then made his way down to the bullpen—an actual bullpen! He pretended to inspect its readiness for warm-ups but really was just thrilled to stand atop the rubber. Perched there, he looked up at the press box and saw, peering down as he peered up, a pair of reporters. It was the first time he'd ever seen anyone from the media at a Macon game.

Across the infield, the Stew-Stras players warmed up, decidedly less starry-eyed. Stewardson-Strasburg was a rural school based in a southern Illinois hamlet where the population of German immigrants took two things very seriously: baseball and drinking. Stocked with talent, the team had advanced to the regional final only a year earlier, when it lost to MacArthur, one of the big Decatur schools. Now, after blowing out Shelbyville 8–2 in the semis, the Stew-Stras Comets entered the game at 11–3 and brimming with confidence. And who could blame them? Instead of a power like MacArthur, they'd drawn a tiny school full of farmers' kids. What's more, for reasons the players couldn't fathom, Macon wasn't even starting its ace pitcher.

By 4 P.M., it was pleasantly warm, if a bit humid. In the stands, nearly 150 fans clustered above the dugouts, roughly half of whom were from Macon. Looking up, Sweet not only recognized parents, teachers, and administrators, but also townspeople like Bob Taylor, an imposing bank manager and Macon booster whose flattop towered above the crowd. Behind home plate, Sweet spotted a small cluster of raucous Macon students.

On the mound, Shartzer warmed up, rocking, firing, and grunting. As Sweet watched, he felt good about his decision to start the boy. He'd done so for two reasons. First, if the Ironmen were as good as he suspected, he would need Shartzer to pitch down the line, when tournament games are held on back-to-back days. To do so, the young man needed confidence. Second, Sweet knew that, as good as Tomlinson was, Shartzer was the key to Macon, both that season and for two years to come. No one's fire burned hotter.

Maybe it was the enormity of the moment. Maybe it was playing on that fancy field. Or maybe it was all those eyes watching. Then again, maybe it was just that the Ironmen had finally met their match.

Whatever the case, Shartzer trudged off the mound after the top of the seventh, looking despondent. Sweet would have none of it. "C'mon, this game's still going," he said. "Let's get some runs here." But all Shartzer could think about was how he'd let the team down.

Really, though, it was the other way around. In seven innings, Shartzer had pitched well, allowing only two earned runs on five hits. The problem was that John Geisler, the pitcher for Stew-Stras, had been better, stymieing Macon with exceptional control and an impressive repertoire that included a knuckleball, a pitch most of the Ironmen had only heard about on TV. All season, the Ironmen had scored in bursts, averaging over six runs a game. Now their offense had gone cold at the worst time. Heading into the final half-inning, Macon trailed 3–0.

Now, of all the kids to lead off, the team's hopes were pinned on

Brad Roush. Roush was a senior who'd joined the team a month earlier, when track season ended. Handsome and well-liked, he was a natural athlete who set the school record in the 880. He was renowned for his resolve late in races, often relying upon pure determination to fend off an opponent's finishing kick. That was track, though. On the baseball field he was fluid and quick but ungainly at the plate. To date, Roush had only one hit for the season. What's more, this would be his first time against Geisler. Sweet had inserted Roush in the top of the sixth for Brian Snitker, the freshman right fielder who was the opposite of Roush—"Good hit, bad wheels," as Sweet said. But hit Snitker could; he finished the season with a .379 batting average, the third-best mark on the team.

Taking Snitker's bat out of the lineup was a risky move, but Sweet was playing a hunch. Roush was not only older, stronger, and more experienced, but also much faster and a better fielder. If he did get on base, his speed gave him the chance to create a run.

Or at least that's how Sweet figured it in his head. Now, as Roush walked casually to the plate, devoid of the typical slugger's swagger, Sweet rose and clapped along with his players, trying to generate momentum. Inside, he began to have second thoughts.

The first pitch from Geisler was a fastball down the middle. Roush sized it up and, as if admiring a particularly impressive rainbow, watched it pass by before finally swinging. STRIKE!

The next pitch was the same thing: pure heat. Determined to at least give himself a chance, Roush threw back his shoulders and took a mighty cut. There was only one problem: Geisler had thrown the ball roughly three feet above the strike zone. "STRIKE TWO!"

On the bench, Sweet felt his heart sink. "Oh, shit," he murmured. "This is bad."

Then, for whatever reason, Geisler went for the kill. Even though he had Roush 0–2, he didn't force him to chase a ball away, nor did he test one of his breaking pitches. Instead he threw another high heater. Now, Roush may not have been a great baseball player, but he was a good athlete, and, given three chances to hit the same pitch, he could time it. With a high, forceful tomahawk swing he met the ball square on and sent it soaring toward the gap in right center.

The Macon bench rose. Sweet let out a little whoop. All had the same thought: *That thing has a chance.*

For a moment, it looked as though the right fielder had a bead on it. But the ball kept rising, soared over his head, and struck the old wooden wall on one hop, some 350 feet out. Meanwhile, Roush took off like he was running the 100 meters. If he saw Heneberry signaling at first base, he didn't acknowledge him. Roush was a runner; this is what he did. He sprinted to second and then, without hesitating, made a wide turn and bore down on third. The throw bounced in at the same time as Roush began his slide, but the boy was too quick. He had a lead-off triple. It was one of the only extra-base hits of his high school career.

In the stands, the Macon contingent roared and Bob Taylor leapt up, hands in the air. Down in the dugout, there was a corresponding surge of energy on the Macon bench. If Roush could hit Geisler, maybe others could, too.

To the plate strode Jeff Glan, whom Sweet often called the "king of the dribbler." True to form, he sent a seeing-eye single back up the middle, just out of the second baseman's reach, bringing in Roush. Macon was on the board, down 3–1 with no outs.

Bearing down, Geisler retired Mark Miller on a fly ball and induced Otta to hit a routine grounder, but the third baseman threw it away, allowing Otta to reach. Now it was Stew-Stras' turn to feel nerves. Catcher Brad Friese walked to the mound for a conference with Geisler. Moments later, Geisler pitched out with the goal of nabbing Otta on the run. Only, behind the plate, Friese was expecting a fastball. The ball bounced to the backstop. Glan didn't hesitate. Throwing his chin back, he broke for home and scored easily. Behind him, Otta advanced to third. Another roar went up from the bleachers. Macon was down only a run, 3–2.

Still, other than Roush, no one had hit Geisler hard all day. Between the dribbler, the error, and the wild pitch, the Ironmen were lucky to have scored at all. Sweet knew this, but he sensed perhaps that the boys did not. He certainly wasn't about to tell them. As Shartzer walked to the plate, Sweet began clapping. "C'mon Steve, let's win this thing!" he bellowed.

All season Shartzer had been Macon's run producer, leading the team in hits and home runs. Now he had a chance to avoid taking the loss, to make up for his failure on the mound. He was damned if he would go down swinging. On the third pitch he smashed the ball toward second base, just hard enough that Otta could beat the throw home. Tie game.

The boys leapt out of the dugout. In the stands, the Macon students whistled and howled. The Ironmen were not only still alive but, against the odds, had a chance to finish off Stew-Stras right here, in the bottom of the seventh inning. With two outs and a runner on first, the game lay in the hands of Mike Atteberry, the diminutive senior.

Of all the boys, Atteberry perhaps needed this opportunity the most. Two-and-a-half years earlier, when he was fifteen, his father starting having blind spots while driving. When it persisted, Mike's mother took him to the doctor. The diagnosis came back as brain cancer. Charles Atteberry lasted less than a year before succumbing at the age of forty-eight. Ever since, Mike's mother had been distant. He often walked into the kitchen to find her standing silently, staring off into space. As a senior and a one-sport athlete, Mike dealt with the loss in his own way, pouring his energy into baseball. It was something he understood, something he could control.

He adjusted his black-rimmed glasses, took a practice cut, and stepped in. *Just make hard contact*, he thought. Geisler started in, then drew back. His first pitch was off the plate, his second a strike on the corner. Then came his third: a fastball, high and hard. Atteberry cocked his elbow, took a small step forward, and tried to murder it.

Instead of a mighty *boom*, though, there was only a weak *crack*. Atteberry watched, aghast, as the ball rolled harmlessly toward third base. His only hope now was to beat the throw. He tore off toward first, and as he sprinted he thought about making the last out of his high school career, of being the one who killed what could be the final Macon rally. He heard the defense yelling. He heard Heneberry yelling. And then he saw the first baseman's eyes widen and his glove rise as the ball approached. Desperately, Atteberry launched himself at the bag, flying through the air and sliding into first in a bloom of dust. The dirt cleared. He looked up at the first base ump.

"SAFE!"

The bench went nuts. Atteberry exhaled. Macon's rally lived.

On the mound, Geisler looked exasperated. It had been a long inning, and his defense had now failed him twice. If he was getting out of this, he needed to bear down and strike out the next batter, Macon's star, Tomlinson. This was no time to mess around with the knuckler. So, just as he'd done with Roush, Geisler fired one toward the outside half of the plate, as hard as his arm allowed. It was the same pitch he'd used to strike out Tomlinson earlier in the game.

It's possible Geisler had lost some velocity after seven innings. Or perhaps Tomlinson finally got a read on the pitch. Either way, he connected on the fat part of the bat. To the Macon parents in the stands, it sounded like a gunshot, the noise echoing off the wooden bleachers.

On contact, Shartzer broke from second, head down. At no point did he turn to watch the ball or look up as he approached third. The fastest kid in Macon County had one goal, and it lay 180 feet away.

Behind him, the ball rocketed into left-center and bounded off the grass. By the time Stew-Stras' center fielder picked it up, Shartzer was already around third, legs a blur. Had it been Glan, Heneberry, or Snitker, the center fielder might have had a shot at him, but it would take an unreal throw to catch Shartzer.

Shartzer didn't know this. All he knew was that he had to score the winning run at any cost. He couldn't hear the Macon fans in the stands, standing and yelling. He couldn't hear his dad, down by the sideline, demanding that he "BRING IT HOME, STEVE!" And he couldn't hear his teammates, now on their feet and out of the dugout, yelling and pinwheeling their arms, a dozen third base coaches directing him toward the plate. All he could hear was the thudding of the blood in his temples and the *scritch* of his cleats on dirt.

The throw skipped onto the infield grass, bound for the catcher. Shartzer was way too fast. With room to spare, he beat the ball home, scoring standing up. Within moments of touching the plate he was mobbed by his teammates. In the stands, parents raised their hands into the sticky sky, exulting. Bob Shartzer looked so proud he might burst. Macon students hurdled the fence and tore onto the field, joining the players in one happy mass. The boys slapped hands and cheered.

For the first time in school history, the Ironmen were headed to the regional finals.

That night felt different from any that had come before. The boys headed out to the Country Manor and sat on the hoods of their Fords in the parking lot, smoking cigarettes and listening to Johnny Cash's "At Folsom Prison." Again and again, they relived the moments: the way Roush looked as surprised as anybody when he hit that ball, the way Glan chugged around third, pumping so hard that his chin was pointed to the sky. There was something else, too, something beyond elation. The boys felt *important*. Heneberry was the one who voiced it, how it felt like "Now we're playing for all the small schools, the Blue Mounds and the Moweaquas and places like that."

As for Sweet, he was still beaming the next morning when he walked into the teacher's lounge at Macon High. There, he sat down to write up his customary postgame sheet. In addition to updated statistics, he included a quick note next to each player's name. Beside Shartzer's he wrote, "Clutch hitter, gutsy performance." For Atteberry he wrote, "Socking the old apple." And next to Brad Roush's name, thinking back on that timely third swing, Sweet wrote, "It only takes one."

Throughout the day, congratulations poured in. Britton stopped by. So did Carl Poelker and Burns, coaches who understood just how hard it was to advance to the regional finals in this part of Illinois. Left unspoken was what one more win would mean: sectionals. No Macon team in any sport had advanced that far in nearly a decade.

First there was the matter of the regional finals, though, and when Heneberry heard who the Ironmen would face, he didn't know whether to be thrilled or scared. "We get the Reds?"

As the only Decatur native, he knew it was one thing to play schools like Mt. Zion and Stew-Stras and another to play the Running Reds of Stephen Decatur High. With two thousand students, Stephen Decatur dwarfed Macon. Not only were the Reds a traditional big-city power, but they'd also been dominant in the tournament so far, needing only five innings to trigger the mercy rule against Clinton High in the semifinal. It was the kind of team Macon never got to play, the kind of opponent they dreamed about getting a shot at. It would be an outsized test.

If the boys were nervous that afternoon at practice, they had a strange way of showing it. They took turns trying to hit the longest home run, cracked jokes, and talked about girls. Sweet was equally loose. As he saw it, there was no point in making an inspirational speech and, besides, he didn't believe in those anyway. So instead he joked about Glan's dribbler during the Stew-Stras game, and the look on Atteberry's face when he was called safe. Then he affected a mock serious tone. "OK, we got a big game tomorrow, boys," he said, staring them down. "So don't go spending the *whole* night with some girl."

The irony was that Sweet went out and did exactly that himself. Her name was Jeanne and, against his better nature, Sweet was falling in love.

Jeanne Jesse never thought she'd date a guy like Lynn Sweet. Not with those sideburns and the long hair and the radical politics. Four years earlier she'd been a senior at Macon High and, like most, had taken Sweet's English class. Plenty of girls had crushes on Sweet, but she wasn't one of them. A cheerleader, she preferred clean-cut types, the kind who played basketball and said "Yes sir" and "No sir."

She wasn't in a rush, anyway. The seventh of fifteen kids in the Jesse family, Jeanne knew plenty about patience. Growing up, she'd shared dinners with up to twelve siblings, each one assigned one piece of the two fried chickens their mom cooked (Jeanne's was the thigh). Her father was a proud, decent man who worked at Caterpillar and, later, as an insurance salesman and a millwright. When he came home, he saved the disciplining for dinner. Thus any Jesse who'd transgressed knew that, at 7 P.M., he or she—but usually he—would receive a scolding. Jeanne rarely got into trouble, though. Quiet, thoughtful, and meticulous, she decided at a young age that to survive in a family as large as hers she needed to be organized and efficient. So she stayed after school each day until she finished all her homework, lest she bring home her books and papers and lose them amid so many others.

College had changed her, though. At Eastern Illinois University she majored in business education and became more curious about the world. She'd been out to bars, been courted by older men. When she returned as a junior for spring break in March of 1970, she looked different, too. Always considered a prize in Macon, Jeanne had only grown more stunning. Her shoulder-length dark hair fell on either side of small, delicate eyes. Her athletic figure had filled out in all the right places. It was impossible not to notice her.

Sweet certainly did when she first pulled up on a motorcycle outside his classroom one March afternoon. *That* was Jeanne Jesse? Just seeing her, he forgot all about the yearbook she held, even if it was the reason for her visit. Technically, the yearbook was for research purposes. Carl Poelker, the affable math teacher, was again trying to set up Sweet with some girl or another, and this one—whose name Sweet now couldn't even remember—was a senior at Eastern. So Sweet had asked one of his students, Jeanne's younger sister Lou Ann, to procure a yearbook. Lou Ann had in turn written a postcard to Jeanne. And now here she stood, passing the yearbook to Sweet through the window in his classroom.

He took it and promptly tossed it on his desk. Then he suggested she come back at noon to grab lunch.

Jeanne agreed. That she brought along her older brother didn't bother Sweet in the least. The more the merrier, he thought.

Besides, Sweet wasn't exactly lacking for companionship. Already casually dating a few girls, he found the prospect of adding another to the mix exhausting. But the more he talked to Jeanne, the more interested he became. In many respects, the two were opposites. Her family was Catholic; he was agnostic. She was a small-town girl; he was a product of larger cities. She was reserved and patient; he was gregarious and spontaneous. Almost instantly, they clicked.

They saw each other again that night, talking for a couple hours at Jack Stringer's house over beers, and then went their separate ways. Each had dates that Saturday night, but as they went through the motions, he in Champaign and she in Chicago, neither could shake the thought of the other.

This sense of longing was new for Sweet, and he didn't like it. For a man who'd led an itinerant life, who'd dated dozens of women, who'd been, in the words of Champaign friend Fred Schooley, "a real cocksman," Sweet's fall was remarkably fast. He saw Jeanne again on Sunday for a motorcycle ride, which led to a night at Claire's Place, which led to Jeanne skipping two days of school to stick around in Macon. That week, they saw each other every night. By the end of the month, Sweet was smitten.

Now, on the eve of the regional finals, Sweet headed off to see her again. It was probably better that he didn't know what awaited in the morning.

8

The Announcement

The call came over Macon High's loudspeaker on Wednesday, May 20, the morning of the regional finals.

"All Macon baseball players and Coach Sweet, please report to the library to see Principal McClard."

John Heneberry was in class at the time, and he felt a tingle of excitement. Breezing down the hall, he entered the library expecting a good old-fashioned pep talk—perhaps a blustery pronouncement of how proud McClard was of the boys for "representing the school, God, and country," followed by a send-off.

After all, what else was there to talk about? Though the nation was in turmoil—the front page of that morning's Decatur *Herald & Review* featured a South Vietnamese army tank churning through a mud-choked stream in eastern Cambodia—in Macon, the world had narrowed down to one game: the Ironmen versus the Running Reds. The boys would load onto buses in the early afternoon to make the trip to Johns Hill School in Decatur. A group of parents and students planned to caravan behind them. Even board president Merv Jacobs was considering making the trip. In less than two weeks, the Ironmen had gone from local curiosity to a genuine source of civic pride.

And now McClard was going to rally the troops, or so the boys assumed. Only, instead of doing so, McClard began talking about

Macon High in general, or maybe it was athletics in general, no one much remembers. He continued on like this for about fifteen minutes. Finally, he came to his point. "I want all of you whose names I'm about to call to raise your hands." And then McClard began to read from a roster: "Mike Atteberry, Jeff Glan, John Heneberry, Dale Otta, Dean Otta . . ."

When McClard finished, he'd read fourteen names. He looked up at the boys. "Is there anyone whose name I didn't call?"

In the back, against the wall, Brad Roush raised his hand.

McClard frowned, then looked down at the paper in his hands. He walked over to Sweet and they had a brief discussion in the hallway. After a moment, the two men returned, McClard looking serious and Sweet angry. Then McClard announced that he had bad news: Mr. Roush was not on the official postseason roster that Macon had sent in to the Illinois High School Association prior to the playoffs. He had to report this.

Heneberry waited for McClard to smile. It had to be a joke, right? Instead, the principal dismissed the boys. Then McClard called Hal Prichard, the Athletic Director at Stephen Decatur, who in turn called the Illinois High School Association (IHSA). Two hours later, the IHSA called back with its decision: Since Roush's name hadn't been submitted prior to the playoffs, Macon had won with an ineligible player. The school had to forfeit its victories and exit the tournament. Stewardson-Strasburg, the team the Ironmen had just beat, would face Stephen Decatur in the regional finals that afternoon.

Sweet gathered the boys and broke the news. He knew it was his role to be diplomatic, to take the school line, but he couldn't help himself. "This," he said, "is absolute horseshit."

Doug Tomlinson felt like he got hit by a truck. Heneberry was stunned into silence. Shartzer flew into a rage, demanding answers. It was one thing to lose a game, but disqualified? It wasn't like Brad Roush was some ringer who had just moved to the district. He was a senior honors student who had played baseball his first three years at Macon High. How the hell could a kid like that be ineligible?

Sweet felt disgusted and betrayed. He knew he'd updated the roster and filed it. What he didn't know was where along the bureaucratic ladder the roster had stalled, whether it was with Phil Sargent—the school's well-meaning athletic director—or perhaps at another administrator's office. He also couldn't help but wonder about the timing. Why would McClard decide to recheck a logistical item on this, the morning of the team's biggest game, then report it himself? Sweet was pretty sure he knew why.

Sweet felt the worst for the seniors. That evening, he drove to Doug Tomlinson's house, near Elwin. For two hours, he, Doug, and Doug's parents sat in the kitchen, commiserating. Sweet told them how sorry he was. How he felt like it was his fault. How he felt powerless. All of them were angry, but none knew how to channel that anger. When they'd said all they could, Sweet took his leave.

Meanwhile, across town at the Jesse house, Jeanne was standing in the kitchen with her mother when one of her sisters came running into the house, crying. It was Lou Ann, who was dating Shartzer at the time. "The team's been disqualified," she sobbed, then sprinted upstairs to her bedroom. Jeanne's heart sank. A couple hours later, she heard the throbbing of a motorcycle engine outside the house.

Jeanne walked out into the night to see Sweet on his Triumph Bonneville, looking strangely vacant-eyed.

"Wanna go to Decatur?" he asked. "I need to get out of here."

It was the first time Sweet had invited Jeanne to his place in Decatur. She knew he must be taking it hard.

They roared through the darkness, past the silhouettes of cornfields, until they reached Decatur and the small, run-down house where Sweet was renting a room. He dropped his stuff and then slumped into a chair. There, he told her what had happened: how McClard had delivered the news, how crushed the boys had looked. Jeanne remembers Sweet as "reeling" and "inconsolable."

She suggested they go see the Shartzers or the Glans—maybe getting the team together would make him feel better. He said he couldn't bear to. She suggested going to a bar but that held no allure, either. So there they sat. No music, no drinks. Sweet was the most joyful, lively person she knew. Now it was like the light had been drained right out of him.

What was there to do? In the days that followed, the parents held an emergency meeting in the cafeteria at school, then urged Sweet to help them find a culprit. They wanted to take their case to the board. They wanted to bring down McClard or Sargent. Sweet declined the parents' entreaties. It wouldn't change things, he said. They still wouldn't get a chance to play Decatur.

Still, the disqualification gnawed at him. The following week he descended to the equipment room in the basement to organize all the gear and file an end-of-the-year inventory. Only, instead of doing so, he dumped everything in a pile and left it there. Then, when he saw the players that afternoon, he told them to keep their uniforms. The school didn't deserve them back anyway. Besides, if McClard was suddenly so interested in the team, let him buy new ones.

Sweet knew this wouldn't go over well, but he didn't care. He was too angry. Not just for himself but for the boys. He'd watched them come together and seen their pride in the team and the confidence they'd gained. Usually, he felt there were important lessons that came from losing. He didn't see much of a lesson here.

9

Long Summer Nights

Sweet needed to get out of Macon. After graduation, he headed to Champaign and got a job painting houses with two buddies, a world away from small-town politics. Some nights, he jumped on his Triumph and cruised the fifty-some miles to Eastern Illinois University, in Charleston, where Jeanne was living in the Delta Zeta sorority house. In the hope of graduating early, she'd petitioned the school to take twenty hours of summer classes. When Sweet visited, the couple spent evenings driving around the country, he cracking jokes and she giggling. At the end of each night, she walked into the sorority house and he climbed to the top of it, ascending the fire escape to the flat tar roof. There, on a wool blanket, he lay down under a canopy of stars, marveling at the new turn his life had taken.

As Sweet was busy clearing his head and falling in love, the Ironmen players were spending their summer trying not to dwell on the disqualification. For those who remained, an unspoken pact was formed. To get better. To play tighter. To return to the postseason and advance to sectionals the following season. In the thick Illinois heat, the returning players gathered for impromptu games at the old elementary school just north of the Macon Library. Brian Snitker rolled up on his bike, and Heneberry walked from his parents' place on Front Street. The Ottas arrived in Dale's midnight blue 1964 Chevy Impala, the one with the bucket seats Dale was so proud of. Some days they played over-the-line, other times it was home run derby or a full-fledged scrimmage. If only two boys showed up, the pair took turns hitting balls against the brick façade of the high school, the crack of the bat followed by the thud of ball on mortar.

At night, the boys cruised out to Mile Corner listening to Led Zeppelin. Gas was thirty cents a gallon, and nobody ever put in more than a dollar's worth at a time—for a dollar was a lot to the boys back then, and few had more than two or three in his pocket at any given time—so a trip to Decatur was only for special occasions. Other times, they'd sit at the Country Manor and tell lies. Each night, it seemed, a different parent hosted dinner. One evening you could have shown up at the Shartzers' house and found three sweaty kids scarfing down chili and dumplings; the next the house was empty because they'd all be over at the Snitker place, eating chicken.

Of all the boys, though, Shartzer and Heneberry bonded the most that summer. As the two returning pitchers, they knew they would form the team's backbone in 1971, but it went beyond that. John was an only child and Shartzer had only an older sister. In each other, they found something of the brother they'd never had.

Sports formed the foundation of their friendship, but they rarely discussed them. Instead, once a week or so during the summer, the duo borrowed either Bob Shartzer's cream-colored Ford Fairlane 500 or Jack Heneberry's white Ford Fairlane and drove to the southeast leg of Lake Decatur, a sprawling man-made lake twenty minutes from Macon. There, on grassy banks thick with shrubs and shadowed by sycamore trees, they set their fishing lines with crawdads, minnows, or, if those proved too expensive, pieces of dough. Where they could along the banks, the boys tied extra lines to trees that overhung the dark green water, using the branches as makeshift poles to troll for "grays," the long-whiskered, spotted channel catfish that lurked near the banks. If one of your tree branches came to life and started thrashing, you knew you had a cat on the line.

Since channel cats prefer to eat in the dark, the boys usually settled in for the long haul. Some nights they brought blankets and pillows and slept under the stars, just as Sweet was doing sixty miles away on a sorority roof. Other times they stayed up till dawn, reveling in feeling young and invincible as the sun's first rays colored the water. Always, they communicated through the language of boasts and jabs, Shartzer bragging about how many fish he intended to catch while Heneberry, whose slow drawl sounded to many like a Southern accent, announced each of his bites with great drama. "Shaaarrk, I got one and I'm playing with it over here. . . . You know, he's going to take it here, gonna go *dowwwwwn* with it."

The fishing trips weren't a competition, at least not explicitly, but of course on some level they were, as everything was with Shartzer. So each boy kept an unspoken tally of the number and size of catfish caught, then stored the information for future reference.

Once in a while, when the conversation did turn to baseball, it usually ended up on Sweet, for the boys shared a deep admiration for their coach. For Shartzer, Sweet provided a counterbalance to his own demanding father. For Heneberry, Sweet embodied the promise of a larger, wilder world. Neither boy could imagine playing baseball at Macon without him.

Usually, special meetings of the Macon school board weren't called until during the school year, when unexpected issues arose. Thus it came as a surprise to the board members when word came that one was scheduled for September 3, 1970, the start of the semester.

That evening, all the usual cars pulled into the Macon High parking lot. Presently, they were joined by one rarely seen at the school that late at night.

At 7:30 P.M. in the small school library, new board president Bob Glass took roll call. Former president Merv Jacobs was there, as were Dick Snitker and Don Craft, along with Neal Lentz, Scott Towson, and Roy Roush. Joining the board, as always, were Bill McClard and Roger Britton. Also present, for the first time since being hired by Macon High, was, as the minutes recorded, "Mr. Lynn Sweet, a teacher in the Macon Schools."

Glass stood up and announced that the purpose of the meeting was disciplinary and the employee in question was Mr. Sweet. Then, for what felt like fifteen or twenty minutes, various board members described what they believed to be Sweet's unbecoming conduct. First to speak was Roush, a conservative man who, while a cousin of Brad Roush's father, was not much of a baseball fan. He spoke of how Sweet drove around town in his red Scout, a four-wheel drive jeep that most considered outlandish. Roush said it reflected poorly upon Macon High when the Scout was parked outside bars at all hours. Sweet's mop of hair was also a topic of conversation, as was his laissez-faire attitude with the students. Most troubling, however, was the way he'd handled the end of the baseball season the previous spring. Not collecting the uniforms was bad enough, but criticizing the administration could only be construed as willfully disrespectful.

Throughout the proceedings, McClard likely didn't say much but he didn't need to. Sweet knew who was behind the meeting. All summer, the baseball parents had continued to look for someone to blame for the disqualification, and Sweet suspected that McClard viewed him as the instigator. This no doubt only added to McClard's lingering anger over countless slights, perceived and real, as well as his clear disapproval of the company Sweet kept.

In particular, McClard wasn't fond of Ernie Miller, Mark's dad. Ernie worked at the state employment office and could be a funny, charming man, but he turned dark when he drank. He wore a leather brace where his left hand had been, the result of a shotgun accident when he was young, but his right hand could inflict some serious damage. A hulking man at six-foot-two and 240 pounds, he gained a reputation as the best fighter in Macon, and tough guys from neighboring towns sometimes showed up in the taverns hoping to take a crack at

Ernie. Most left nursing a busted nose, wounded pride, or both. As much as McClard disliked Miller, the feeling was mutual, and Sweet was pretty sure that if Ernie believed he could get away with it, he would have kicked McClard's ass.

Now Sweet sat in his chair, incredulous. Finally given a chance to answer for himself, he stood up. "What's the charge here?" Sweet asked. "What have I done wrong?"

And on it went, for half an hour, Sweet alternately defending himself, listening to new charges, and cracking jokes at what he saw as the absurdity of the situation. If enjoying life was a crime, he was guilty, but how did that make him a bad teacher or coach? When the meeting was over, the minutes read as follows: "Mr. Sweet talked with the Board at length about the past and future status of his association with the Macon Schools. The Board in turn discussed with Mr. Sweet their reaction to his conduct and association with the school during past years. Upon conclusion of the discussion Mr. Sweet retired from the meeting."

With Sweet gone, the board went into its executive session, the off-the-record portion of the meeting where the real dirt went down. The topic: whether or not to relieve the young English teacher of his duties.

Meanwhile, Sweet jumped into the red Scout that irritated Roy Roush so much and drove to Jack Stringer's. He needed some whiskey, and fast. After all, tomorrow was his wedding day.

At noon the following day, the Friday of Labor Day weekend, Sweet left work early, still not sure if he'd have a job or not come Monday but determined not to let it ruin his weekend. He picked up Jeanne in Decatur, where she was student teaching at Lakeview High School, and two hours later the pair appeared in front of a judge in Charleston, Illinois. The bride wore a short, red, white, and blue sailor print dress, the groom a white shirt and black tie. At the end of the ceremony, Sweet kissed Jeanne, after which the two newlyweds began to walk away. They didn't get fifteen feet before they heard a voice behind them.

"Excuse me," the judge said. "That'll be ten dollars."

The couple spent their wedding night at the US Grant Motel in Mattoon, the only honeymoon they could afford. The next morning they arrived at Lynn's parents' house in Champaign. When Sweet's mother appeared at the door, her son held up his ring finger. "Hey, Mom, I'm married!" Sweet announced. "Can we spend the weekend?"

Lillian Sweet was elated, as she tended to be whenever her son was happy. In some ways she was the opposite of Lynn's father: emotional, outgoing, available. A lover of music and literature, she was smart and tough and regretted to her last day that she didn't have the opportunity to further her education. Her father had three children but only the money to send two to college. Lillian had the misfortune of being the only girl.

She'd met Lynn's father one night in 1936 when he was hitchhiking through town on his way to an air base. He moved on but regularly wrote her long, eloquent letters. Later, he sent her books from overseas, including a thick copy of *War and Peace* with gilded edges. To the distress of Lillian's parents, who'd never approved of Lynn Senior, the couple married in 1938. Lynn was born two years later, his sister, Libbie, six years after that.

The family's life had been dictated by Lynn Senior's career. Since he was away for months and sometimes years at a time, it fell to Lillian to raise Lynn and his younger sister. The Sweets had little money, and each subsequent move promised a new life that never materialized as they hoped. The family bounced from Crew, Virginia, to Newport News, from Hopewell, Arizona, to Yuma. For a while, they lived in a state park in Illinois. By the time they moved to Champaign, Lynn Junior had experienced far more than most Midwest children his age. He remembers showering with black kids on military bases, and watching as his father coached a black semipro football team. He remembers money being tight enough that his mom saved the tin foil from a pack of cigarettes.

He also remembers the day his mother found that letter, the one addressed to his father and written by a girl in Germany, and the way his mom looked at his father after that.

Now she welcomed her son, ecstatic at the development. When Lynn Senior returned home later that night and learned the news, he was also pleased, for he considered anything resembling stability to be a positive for his son. Then again, he had no idea that his son was on the brink of getting fired from the only real job he'd ever had.

The following Monday, Sweet got the news when he returned to school. The school board's official decision, after some debate, was to take no action. He still had a job at Macon High.

The question, as he soon learned, was what that job entailed.

Jeanne was the one who first noticed the omission, early that fall.

If it took a while to notice, it was with good reason. After all, it had been a crazy few weeks. After the wedding, she and Lynn moved in with her parents, two more grown kids among all the rest tearing up and down the stairs in the Jesse house. Finally, in late September, their new home arrived.

Granted, it wasn't actually a house, but the seventy-foot trailer felt like one. Situated in Macon's brand-new trailer park, not far from the junior high and the Macon Speedway, it was the perfect size for a young couple. Eventually, the Sweets filled the trailer with a TV, a yellow bean-bag chair, and a coffee table made from a large, upended wooden spool, the kind wire is wrapped around. Beyond that, framing the doorway to the bedroom, hung what was undoubtedly the only bead curtain in Macon.

Since Jeanne was student teaching, and Sweet made only $533 a month, money was tight. They'd only been able to purchase the trailer after a friend cosigned the loan, and even then it was an economy model, built by Amish workers in Indiana. Buying anything else was a significant ordeal. Sears turned them down for credit on their first color TV and it wasn't until their third month together, when Jeanne picked up the beanbag chair for $35 on layaway at a Decatur furniture store, that the couple was first extended credit. Jeanne teared up when it happened.

In Macon, the news of the wedding had come as a surprise to most, as Sweet wasn't one to divulge personal details. However, far from raising eyebrows about a teacher marrying his former student, the union had actually boosted Sweet's reputation around town. At twenty-nine he'd been considered old to still be single in an era when most young men and women married by the time they were twenty-one. And by choosing to settle down with a local girl from a well-respected, cornerstone family, Sweet had given locals the first indication that perhaps he finally intended to put down roots and assimilate into Macon

Befitting his cult hero status at the school, a proper announcement was required. So in the fall issue of *The Ironmen Scene,* the Macon High newspaper, the following ran, under the heading of "Wedding Woes." It was not difficult to divine who wrote it:

> *In a single-ringed, double barreled ceremony before thousands at Charleston, Illinois, the former Jeanne E. Jesse eagerly became the new Mrs. L. C. Sweet last Sept. 4. Featured as Soloists at the wedding were Bob Shartzer singing the Mass in E-flat and Ernie Miller and his Jug band. Attendants to the bride, as of yet unidentified, were resplendently bedecked in a purple chiffon overlacing a delightful sheath of sheer orange burlap and satin that effectively accentuated the lovely pink tennis shoes. The bride looked real good also.*
>
> *Groomsmen in the wedding, reportedly friends of the groom, failed to appear in the ceremony, and are being sought by the Acme Tuxedo rental company, Champaign, Illinois, 61820. A reception was held for the love-struck newlyweds at the Holiday Inn in Mattoon from 4:00 to 4:15. After the reception the couple whisked off to Sigel,*

Illinois for their honeymoon, and now make their home at the Arrowhead Trailer Courts, Macon, Illinois, 62544.

The former Miss Jesse is practicing teaching at Lakeview High School in Decatur, with plans to graduate in November and begin employment at Wagner Castings. A liberal democrat, Mr. Sweet is currently anticipating the forthcoming hunting season, and has no time for the myriad of coaching and educational honors constantly being heaped upon him.

Within weeks of moving into the trailer, Lynn and Jeanne had settled into an easy routine. Sweet handled the social engagements while Jeanne took care of the business and organizational matters. Naturally, then, it fell to her to file away his teaching contract for the 1970–71 school year. As she did, she read it over again. There was his salary, listed at $6,000, and a list of his duties: English II and English IV, junior class advisor, and coordinator of the senior play.

There was one missing, however: baseball coach.

McClard may not have succeeded in firing Sweet, but he had done the next best thing.

10

Un-American, or Unpatriotic

Fall inched toward winter. Nixon announced he intended to pull forty thousand troops out of Vietnam by Christmas, four times his original estimate. In October, the Orioles beat the Cincinnati Reds in the first World Series played on artificial turf while the nation mourned Janis Joplin's death from a heroin overdose. Meanwhile, hopeful Americans signed up by the tens of thousands to join Pan American Airways' waiting list for the first commercial trips to the moon.

In Macon, the Ironmen football team finished 6–2, one of the best seasons in school history. In October, Mark Miller and Jane Metzger were named Homecoming King and Queen. To the cheering of onlookers, the pair rode down Front Street in an open convertible, preceded by cheerleaders, the Macon High Marching Band, and tractors pulling hay racks that students had transformed into floats by painstakingly twisting paper napkins into their chicken wire undercarriages.

As the holidays approached, Bill McClard could be seen in his office after school, working feverishly on something, though no one was quite sure what. Basketball season began and the cold weather moved in. All the while, Sweet remained unconcerned about his contract. No one at Macon High thought much about baseball until after football and basketball anyway. Sweet assumed, perhaps optimistically, that the contract was the result of a clerical error, or perhaps an oversight. At worst, it had to be a bluff by McClard. After all, who in their right mind fired a coach who went 16–2?

Then, in early February of 1971, Sweet heard the news: A new history and driver's ed teacher named Dennis Schley was slated to coach baseball that spring. The twenty-two-year-old Schley had been hired the previous summer with the expectation that he would coach junior high basketball and serve as an assistant to Burns on the football team. Though competent and energetic, Schley had never so much as run a baseball practice, let alone presided over an entire season. Now he would be the Ironmen's fourth head coach in four years.

Sweet couldn't believe it. *They'd actually done it.* He went to Sargent, then McClard, then Britton. From all, he heard the same thing: The board decided it would be best if someone else coached the team. What they really meant, though, was *someone who better represented the school.* This, Sweet thought, was ridiculous. After the disciplinary meeting, though, it was clear he didn't have much say in the matter.

When word reached the players and parents, they were incensed. Shartzer, being Shartzer, argued they should go straight to the top. *How about I just march into McClard's office*, he said. Or Britton's, or Sargent's, or whoever needed to be marched in on. Then Steve would lay it out for them: "If Sweet ain't coming back as coach, you'll need to find a new star pitcher."

His dad had half a mind to do some marching in of his own, as did Dwight Glan. Ernie Miller was ready to bypass the diplomacy and move straight to the ass-kicking. It was Dick Snitker, Brian's father, who prevailed upon them to take a more measured approach. Unlike some of the others, he had a cordial relationship with McClard. Tall and solid, with a wide chin and thinning brown hair, Dick was well liked and universally respected in Macon. He'd worked for twenty years as Illinois state manager for Pabst before becoming a distributor for Jim Beam, a position that made him quite popular around town and earned Sweet's "everlasting respect."

A personable, welcoming man, Snitker was also close with Britton, who was the one who had persuaded Snitker to run for the school board the previous fall. Now, in his first term as a board member and secretary, Snitker took his responsibility to the community seriously. And in this case, he felt it important to go through the proper channels. He suggested to the parents that he take down their feelings, and those of the boys, and present them to the board.

Replacing a coach as beloved as Lynn Sweet was no easy feat, and the closer it got to the season, the more second thoughts Schley had. Schley came from a conservative background, and when he looked at Sweet, with the hair and the peace signs, he at first saw someone who "looked like he was un-American or unpatriotic." That Sweet had been fired as baseball coach didn't exactly surprise Schley.

As an assistant during the football season, however, Schley had gotten to know many of the baseball players, and the more he talked to them, the more he wondered about Sweet. The kids spoke of the man so highly, and trusted him so completely, that Schley figured the strange-looking coach must be doing something right. For his part, Schley's instincts ran closer to Burns—drop the hammer, instill discipline—and he feared that approach would backfire on a team built by Sweet.

Then there were the baseball parents. They were nice enough to Schley, and many knew him from football, but it was obvious they wanted Sweet as their coach. This put Schley in a tough spot.

Besides, he was worn out. Between teaching and coaching junior high basketball, he was never home. He wanted to spend more time with his new wife, to be home on time for dinner once in a while. Two weeks before the season, he approached Britton in private and told him he'd be fine not coaching baseball.

A few nights later, the Sweets heard a knock on the door of their trailer. Unaccustomed to visitors so late, they ignored it at first. But the knocking persisted.

Finally, Lynn turned down the stereo, the one they'd bought on Jack Stringer's credit at Goldblatt's, and walked over to the door of the trailer and peeked out. There on his steps, breath visible in the February night air, stood Bob Glass, the board president.

"Hi, Lynn, I'd like to talk to you about something," Glass said.

Sweet invited him in. With his square head, bristly flattop, and wide jaw, Glass gave the impression of a man who should have a whistle in his mouth at all times, and indeed he'd once led the Macon High basketball team to the regionals. Wearing a suit and tie and carrying a clipboard, he looked comically out of place in a trailer that was only a lava lamp away from a college dorm room.

Jeanne offered Glass a cup of coffee and the three of them sat around the small kitchen table. Sweet figured Glass could only be there for one of two reasons: to offer him back the baseball job or fire him once and for all.

Glass wasn't in any hurry to tip his hand, though. Slowly, methodically, he began to interview Sweet. He asked about not returning the uniforms, about team protocol, about meeting school standards, and about Sweet's idea of a proper educational culture.

Sweet considered being contrarian and challenging Glass. Had it been McClard in his living room, he might have. Instead, he was cordial and diplomatic. Sweet said that he felt bad about the uniforms, and that he understood that the boys looked up to him and it probably wasn't the best thing in the world for the players to see their baseball coach rebelling against the school. After forty-five minutes, Glass rose, shook Sweet's hand, and left.

Watching Glass walk out into the night, Sweet tried to read the man but failed. For the life of him, he couldn't figure out if this meant he would be coaching again.

A week passed and still nothing. The first baseball practice was two days away. Dennis Schley started drawing up a roster. Some of the seniors resigned themselves to yet another new coach.

And then, at 7:30 P.M. on the evening of Monday, March 1, a day before the first practice, the school board convened for another special meeting. After roll call, Dick Snitker stood up. He looked around the table. As usual, all the board members were there, but one man was curiously absent. For reasons Sweet would learn in time, Bill McClard was not in attendance.

Not given to digressions, Snitker likely got right to the point. They'd all heard Bob Glass' report. They knew what the parents thought and they knew what the kids wanted. They knew that while the Ironmen had a chance to be good, there was plenty of work to be done, work Dennis Schley wasn't qualified for, no matter how nice a guy he was. In the end, it came down to this: Who were they really punishing by firing Sweet—the coach or the players?

Then Snitker moved that Lynn Sweet be reinstated as the Macon High baseball coach.

For the motion to go to vote, it required a second. Snitker looked around the room. Finally, a hand went up. It was Neal Lentz, whose daughter Terri had taken Sweet's English class when she was Macon High valedictorian in 1969.

As the board readied to vote, the men had to weigh a number of factors. There were the words of Snitker and the feelings of the parents and players, but there was also Sweet's track record and reputation, as well as the lingering bad feelings from the previous fall. In essence, what the board needed to decide was whether Sweet had changed. For years, he had been viewed as a renegade, someone who lived *in* Macon but was not *of* Macon. Now, whether the men liked his methods or not, it was clear Sweet was having a positive effect on their children in both the classroom and on the field.

Perhaps the vote would have gone differently had McClard been there. Perhaps not. As it was, based on the evidence and the presentation of Snitker, the men were united. As was recorded in the official school board minutes: "Upon roll call it was found that all members voted 'Yea' and no member voted 'nay.' The motion carried."

Sweet doesn't remember how he found out. Maybe it was Bob Shartzer who called, or Dwight Glan who stopped by, ready to start discussing lineups, or perhaps Dick Snitker with a bottle of Jim Beam. He does remember the feeling, though. Ever since he'd lost the coaching job, Sweet had been perplexed as to why he was so damn attached to a team no one else wanted to coach. Now he understood that his bond with the Ironmen went far beyond baseball.

Given another shot, he intended to further push the boundaries of what was acceptable in coaching. No doubt he'd piss off plenty of people but, as Sweet saw it, that merely meant what he was doing was working. Yes, he had big plans for this team.

Even so, not even Sweet could have imagined what the next season would hold.

Part Two

The Forever Season

Courtesy of Dale Otta

(From left to right) *John Heneberry, David Wells, Dale Otta, and Sam Trusner cheer on their teammates during Macon's 1971 playoff run.*

Prelude

The spring of 1971 dawned as a dark, messy time in America. The economy faltered as unemployment rose and inflation kept pace. Abroad, U.S. troops continued to die in Vietnam while at home protests intensified. In March, behind the rallying cry of "Old enough to fight, old enough to vote," the Twenty-sixth Amendment was introduced, allowing anyone over the age of eighteen to vote.

Around the country, alternative voices arose: A new radio venture going by the acronym NPR took to the air, and an environmental group called Greenpeace was founded. In June, the *New York Times* published a story called "Vietnam Archive: Pentagon Study Traces Three Decades of Growing U.S. Involvement," the first in a series that would change the course of American history.

In central Illinois, the national pessimism was compounded by local anxieties. Here in farming country, where thirteen-year-olds routinely drove tractor loads of grain to be processed, the entire community was in some way dependent upon any given year's crop. Weather was not a matter of small talk but rather of grave importance. Most everyone worried about it, and with good reason. If local farmers suffered a down season they spent less money, which meant local businesses suffered, which in turn meant tax collection faltered.

In the spring of 1971, what kept farmers up at night was a sweet corn disease called southern corn leaf blight. It arrived on the air, blown all the way from Florida and Georgia, and transformed corn stalks into ghostly apparitions, the leaves turning white, then curling up as the plant died. A year earlier, southern blight had reduced corn production in Illinois by an estimated 25 percent, and there was worry that the damage would only intensify. Adding to concerns, the spring of 1970 had been a relatively dry one. Those same clear March days that allowed Sweet and the boys to practice in 1970 had also set back the farming schedule. No one wanted to imagine what another down year of crops would mean.

So instead, in towns like Macon people searched for reasons for optimism. Or, better yet, to celebrate.

11

Another Shot

John Heneberry fidgeted on the dark yellow couch of his living room, a familiar sense of unease washing over him. For years, this had been the family routine: John, his father, his mother, and his grandfather arrayed around the small color TV after dinner, watching the news. Once upon a time, the men on the television had talked about moonshots and John F. Kennedy. Now it seemed like all Heneberry saw were images of tanks and explosions in the jungle.

Like his teammates, Heneberry sometimes had a hard time remembering life before Vietnam. When he was in eighth grade, his history teacher had stood at the front of the class, full of confidence, and said, "Saturation bombing. It will be over in six months." But here it was, four years later, and troops were still shipping over. As insulated as Macon was, the town still felt the toll. Two of the Ottas' older brothers had served a tour, as had one of Stuart Arnold's brothers. People still talked about Joe Whittington, a member of the 1965–66 Macon High baseball team. In September of 1968, Whittington was assigned to the first infantry, near Quan Loi, Vietnam. The students at Macon High remember hearing about Whittington's deployment, and reading the updates in the *Macon News*. They also remember hearing the story about how, three months later at the age of twenty, Joe lit a cigarette on a dark night in the jungle and was shot in the head by a sniper, becoming the first casualty from Macon.

Now Heneberry had just turned eighteen years old. The war that had always seemed so distant, fought by others, no longer did. Neither did a lot of things. As a senior, this was the final athletic season of his final year of high school, just as it was for the Ottas and Mark Miller. In three months they would all graduate and either head off to college—as Sweet always pushed them to do, with the pie-in-the-sky dream being to secure a baseball scholarship—or get a job. The future was rushing at them, and awful fast.

As the TV filled with another shot of Nixon, face dour and pinched, Heneberry looked around him—at his parents and the small, one-story house where he'd spent much of his life. More than any of the boys on the team, he understood the illusory nature of this moment in his life. He longed to hold on to the feeling, to treasure the final months of high school and the upcoming baseball season. The world that awaited—the one Sweet spent so much time preparing them for—was exciting and scary and suddenly very real. But it was not yet upon him. As he saw it, he still had one last chance to be a boy.

Maybe this sentiment—the last chance to be a boy—is what drove Mark Miller on that cool Friday night. Then again, maybe it was the six-pack he'd consumed. Either way, the idea seemed genius at the time. *Let's climb the grain elevator.*

Granted, Miller had already outboozed Heneberry, who was saddled with a lower tolerance and had stumbled home for the night. Still, Miller was always up for a good time, especially if it involved friends. A born storyteller and expert practical joker, he was able to stretch a mundane anecdote into fifteen minutes of drawling comedy. Though a natural athlete, he lacked Shartzer's need for validation; if a teammate asked Miller his batting line for the day, he might not remember, even on days he went 3–4. He could, however, recount every detail of a key play someone else made. The year before, as a junior, he'd been deemed the glue of the team by no less than Tomlinson.

If Miller treasured his friends and teammates more than some, it may have been on account of his own family situation. Ernie Miller was a distant father at times, and when he did show up at his son's games there was always a chance it would be reeking of beer, a spectacle that embarrassed Mark (hating how hard liquor made him behave, Ernie had forgone it years earlier but could still put back a case of Pabst in one night). When Mark was young, he had begged his father not to go out in the late afternoon, at times clinging to his legs when he tried to walk out the door. "If he left," Mark later told his wife, "I knew he was going to the tavern."

On this night, though, as on so many others, Mark aimed only to embrace life. Standing on a friend's shoulders, he peered up at the easternmost storage unit of the elevator, a towering vertical column some one hundred feet in height. Gathering himself, Miller leapt up and grabbed the bottom rung of a thin wire ladder that ran up the side of the storage unit, then pulled himself up. The iron dome loomed above him.

The rungs were a foot or so apart, and Miller climbed quickly, gaining elevation. Soon he was thirty, forty, then fifty feet above the ground. Reaching a small grated platform, he stepped up and kept climbing. Moments later, he emerged onto the roof, ten stories above Macon. Steadying himself, he stood up and surveyed the moonlit landscape. Turning in a circle, he could see for miles in every direction, from the oval racetrack of the Macon Speedway in the west to the water tower of Moweaqua in the south to Elwin in the north. For a boy from Macon, this was as close as it got to standing on top of the world.

Somewhere underneath the warm haze of the beers, Miller surely knew what he was doing was foolish. But then the boys had a long history of foolish endeavors. Shartzer and Miller were notorious for sneaking out of school and making donut runs to the general store during class, always returning with "two jellies" for Jack Burns. When someone stuck a snake in the desk of Carl Poelker, who everyone knew was deathly afraid of reptiles, many suspected one of the baseball players was responsible. And of course there was that business with the hogs.

The previous summer, a local farmer had refused hunting access to his land, a position Shartzer deemed less than neighborly. So Shartzer and Miller snuck onto the man's land one afternoon and flipped the latches on his hog pens. The boys then proceeded to herd a parade of squealing, grunting pigs straight into the heart of Macon, a chaotic sight locals remember to this day. Fearing they'd get caught, Shartzer and Miller then abandoned their herd and made for the Country Manor, where they vaulted into a vinyl booth and tried to look innocuous. A short time later, after rounding up his bewildered hogs, the irate farmer came busting into the restaurant, demanding to know who was responsible. As the boys cowered in the corner, boots covered in a patina of hog shit, the farmer made straight for Letha Tomlinson, the town's queen of gossip (and no relation to Doug Tomlinson). As usual, Letha was ensconced in one of the booths, from which she spent most afternoons monitoring the town's comings, goings, infidelities, and embarrassments. The farmer approached and, aiming a finger across the room at Shartzer and Miller, asked, "Was it them?" Slowly, Letha turned toward the boys, weighing her options. Finally, she turned back. "No sir," she said. "These boys have been here all afternoon." Then she winked at Shartzer.

That scheme, like so many others, had been ill-advised. Climbing the grain elevator was different, though. This was also dangerous.

In the end, it was the descent that got Miller. Perhaps he attempted to climb too fast, or maybe he just lost focus, or the beer finally got to him. Whatever the reason, with sixty feet to go his foot slipped. His hands, so sure on the field, weren't quick enough to save him. There was a thud followed by a clank, and a body fell out of the night.

The next morning the phone rang at the Heneberry house. It was Diane Tomlinson, who was over visiting Mark Miller's sister. She sounded distraught. "John, Mark fell off the grain elevator last night. You gotta get over here!"

Heneberry threw on some clothes and hurried to the Miller house. Upon arriving, he found Mark lying on his bed, looking as though he'd lost a fight with a backhoe. A triangular gash ran down Miller's right leg, his back was skinned raw, and his swollen right wrist was the color of rotten fruit. Adding to the sorry scene, his eye was purple.

Truth be told, Miller had been incredibly lucky. As his teammates would say for years afterward, shaking their heads: "If it hadn't been for that cage . . ."

It was nothing more than a thin strip of iron that ran the vertical length of the ladder, secured by circular piping every five feet or so. But as Miller fell, he had caromed from one side of the enclosure to the other, slowing his descent. Those bounces likely saved his life.

Now Miller sat in his room, looking wretched. Heneberry asked the obvious question: *What did the doctor say?*

Miller smiled sheepishly. He hadn't been to the doctor. He was too afraid of what his father would think.

Then Heneberry asked the next question that came to mind. Again, Miller shook his head. No, he assured Heneberry, it wouldn't affect his ability to play baseball.

The roar of the Scout was audible from a block away, as if a mechanical lion were descending upon the blocky yellow structure at Arrowhead trailer park.

Sweet hopped out of the car and busted in the front door.

"Hey, baby, your muse has returned!"

Jeanne turned and smiled. She was at the stove, cooking sloppy joes in bell bottom jeans and a blouse. Her straight brown hair, which she'd been growing out for months, now fell past her shoulders. A half hour earlier, she'd returned from Warrensburg-Latham High School, where she was teaching business classes such as typing and bookkeeping. It was a welcome change after six months of student teaching at a high school in Decatur, especially financially. After barely getting by for so long, the Sweets finally had dual incomes.

Sweet threw his bag on the counter and checked the fridge for beer. The trailer felt more like a real home by the day. There was a color TV in one corner, not far from the stereo, and a few of Sweet's novels were collected in one corner. Jeanne had even added a few decorative touches: a framed photo in the kitchen, a throw rug, some candles.

All in all, the couple was settling into Macon surprisingly well. Sweet was already encouraging Jeanne to apply for a job in the local school district. It would be romantic, he said—they could ride to school together every day, meet for lunch. In a few years, and with Jeanne minding the money, they'd have enough of a nest egg to buy a house and start a family.

"How's the team look?" she asked.

"Good," said Sweet. That's what he always said, though. In reality, he wasn't sure. He knew the team wasn't as talented as the 1970 squad, at least on paper. For starters, Tomlinson was gone. Tomlinson, who had pitched nearly every important conference game the previous two years, been both the team's best hitter and pitcher, and made up for any number of weaknesses by turning opposing hitters into statues. Not that losing Atteberry was much easier, as he'd hit a team-high .419 the previous season and provided valuable leadership.

In previous years, new talent had always filled the void. When a host of seniors graduated in 1968, Steve Shartzer stepped in. When ace pitcher Ray Martin and others departed in 1969, along came Snitker and Arnold, more talented than those they replaced.

There were no wonder freshmen waiting in the wings in the spring of 1971. Quite the opposite, Sweet had arrived at the first practice a week earlier to find a ten-year-old boy fooling around on the mound. Or at least that's what he looked like. Then Sweet learned that the ten-year-old was actually one of his freshmen, a dusty-haired kid with teapot-handle ears named Jimmy Durbin. Despite his best efforts, Durbin had to arc the ball just to get it from the mound to home plate. He might one day be a pitcher, Sweet thought, but that day was still years away. The rest of the freshmen, he soon discovered, were equally green. That left Sweet with only nine regulars coming into the season: Shartzer, Arnold, Snitker, Miller, Heneberry, Dean Otta, Dale Otta, Jeff Glan, and sophomore David Wells.

Sweet knew what many around town thought, including some of the parents: Macon had missed its opportunity. The boys might be good, but few expected them to match the 1970 season, much less surpass it. Too much had come together too perfectly: the dominance of Tomlinson, the depth of talent, the feel-good vibe of a new coach, and the providence that came with winning games like the one against Stew-Stras. Towns like Macon just didn't make it to the regionals very often.

Complicating matters, despite the 16–2 record in 1970 and the playoff success, McClard hadn't opened the school coffers, something that came as little surprise given the enmity between him and Sweet. So, as before, there was no stipend for hiring an assistant coach, even though that was the norm for football and basketball. The balls were the same sorry assortment, as were the bats. As for the uniforms, they now consisted of relics from three different eras. On some, MACON was written in large letters, while on others it was in small letters and still others featured only a purple M. As for the pants, they varied between featuring white pinstripes, black pinstripes, and being pure gray.

Lacking resources, Sweet had once again decided to get creative. The week after his reinstatement, he'd walked into a study hall and made an announcement. *Would any of you like to be the scorekeeper for the baseball team?*

Sweet then scanned the room for boys who might be interested. Before he saw any, an unexpected voice spoke up.

"Me! I'd like to do it."

Near the front, a small hand was jacked to the sky. Sweet looked down and saw not a boy but freshman Barb Jesse, eyes wide with hope.

Sweet looked at her. *Well, why not?* he thought. After all, just because no one had ever had a girl scorekeeper in central Illinois didn't mean it was illegal.

And thus, on the eve of the 1971 season, the Ironmen were complete: one coach, a girl scorekeeper, nine skinny kids who played, and five even skinnier ones who didn't.

12

Hippies, Tape Decks, and a Silent Infield

No one was more eager for the season to begin than Steve Shartzer. On March 31, the night before the first game against Pana, he lay in his bed in Elwin, visualizing his future. He imagined himself blasting a home run and dominating hitters on the mound the next day, then repeating the performance over the weeks and months to come. He imagined record-setting high school seasons and a standout college career and then, in four or six or seven years, sitting in a dugout in some midsized American city and being told to report to the manager's office, whereupon he would be handed a phone. A gravelly voice on the other end would say, "Good news. You've made the Show, kid." And only then would the journey be complete, the one Shartzer began all those years earlier while peering down at the older boys at Fairview Park and swatting balls in his backyard, the journey he'd planned on making from the time he was five years old, when he first began announcing to anyone who'd listen, "I'm going to be in the pros someday. Just you wait."

The Shartzer mailbox had already begun to fill with letters from college coaches, and Steve knew more were coming. How could they not? So far, his junior year had been one long athletic tour de force. He'd racked up yardage during football season by employing a "crash-and-go" approach—lowering his head and obliterating would-be tacklers to get to the outside edge, then turning on the jets. In the winter, despite being a six-foot center, he'd relied on his quickness, tenacity, and shooting touch to dominate on the basketball court, scoring forty points in one game, pulling down fifteen rebounds in another.

And now baseball season was finally here. Others might have doubted the prospects of the Ironmen, but Shartzer was not one of them. He intended to take the team, and the town, to new heights.

The following afternoon, under dark skies in Pana, he took the first step. He allowed one hit and struck out ten while blasting a two-run home run in a 13–1 win.

The next week, Shartzer drove in six runs in a win over Moweaqua. Not long after, he pitched another one-hitter. By the third week of the season, he was hitting over .500 and at the top of the conference in home runs and RBIs, facts he was acutely aware of. After each game, when Trusner tallied the stats to call in the box score to the *Herald & Review*, his phone invariably rang. "Read me what you got," Shartzer demanded.

"Three for four with two RBIs."

"And the strikeouts?"

"I have you at nine."

"Nine?! It was ten, Sammy. Make sure you get that right. Ten, got it?"

It got to the point where, as Trusner says, "I could set the clock to the phone call from Shartzer." While the fact-checking exasperated Trusner, as did all the ribbing Shartzer directed his way, it never dimmed his respect for his teammate. As Trusner put it: "You wanted to slap him in the face every day, but you wanted him on your side." It helped that the other players, especially Miller, gave Shartzer plenty of grief. "Steve, what's your average *now*?" Miller would ask during pickup games.

If the kids sometimes had to put up with Shartzer—Atteberry refers to him as "an amiable bully"—he made up for it with his fierce loyalty to friends and teammates, especially those he'd known for years. In the case of Jeff Glan, it was evident on the football field.

Midway through Shartzer's time at Macon, Jack Burns had seen him launching deep spirals during football practice and pulled him aside.

"Boy, you can really throw it. You're going to be my QB," Burns said.

"No Coach, I can't be," Shartzer responded.

"You can't? What in the *hell* are you talking about?"

"Coach, Jeff Glan has to be the quarterback. I can play running back."

Burns had glared at him, but as far as Shartzer was concerned, this was the only option. Growing up together in Elwin, he and Glan had pored over Chip Hilton books and fantasized about their athletic futures. The older they got, however, the clearer it was that the boys were born with different talents. Steve was tall, strong, and fleet-footed, seemingly good at everything that involved hand-eye coordination—the fastest shotgun draw, the best bowler, the most dominant Ping-Pong player. Glan, on the other hand, was small and neither quick nor strong. When it came to football, there weren't many positions he could play besides quarterback. So even though he possessed the stronger arm, Shartzer knew the only way his friend was going to be a high school starter was at quarterback.

That Shartzer was eventually able to convince Burns to consider the idea was not surprising, for he had a way of charming adults that bordered on magical. Despite being an average student, Steve was beloved by teachers, due in part to his wonderful manners. The same went for parents. In the case of Brian Snitker, all the usual family rules went out the window when he was with Steve. If Brian was going out with Shark he could do anything—miss curfew, drive to Decatur—it didn't matter. Says Snitker, "My parents thought he hung the moon."

Shartzer's combination of talent, confidence, and charm was not lost on the female population of Macon High. He was renowned for always having "the hot cars and the hot chicks," as friend Boomer Britton, son of Roger, puts it. Not surprisingly, Shartzer and Stu Arnold monopolized the attention of the girls, though in different ways. Arnold was an unusually sensitive young man, the kind who sang in the choir, considered some of his best friends to be girls, and saw no shame in discussing one's feelings. Steve was more elusive and brusque. When he was a sophomore, future homecoming queen Jane Metzger asked him to prom. Steve said yes, but it wasn't until he arrived at the dance that she truly believed he would show.

Then again, Shartzer had been warned. One day during football practice, a group of girls had congregated on the wooden bleachers, watching the team and giggling. Being teenage boys, the players puffed out their chests and acted as tough as possible. At which point Jack Burns—a man's man through and through, a Southerner by birth, and a footballer by trade—gathered them around.

"Now boys," Burns said, in his most paternal tone. "Those damn buzzsaws are going to mess you up. You better get away from them."

And then Burns walked over to the girls and told them, in no uncertain terms, to leave practice. When Burns walked back to the team, Shartzer spoke up.

"Coach, now I don't mean to sound ignorant," he said. "But why do you call them girls *buzzsaws*?"

Burns nodded gravely, paused, then started making a noise. "*Buh-buzzzzzz.*" As he did, he mimicked those wooden bleachers being sawed in half. Then he stopped. "Boys, those are buzzsaws because those girls' snatches are eating that board up. You can damn near see the wood chips flying out the back."

Burns looked around, as if addressing troops heading into combat. "Now I'm telling you, you don't want to mess with that. Because next thing you know, that buzzsaw is coming for you."

At the time, this struck Shartzer as a dire fate indeed, and he took the advice to heart. Girls were merely diversions from life's priorities. Basketball, football, and baseball were what mattered.

One cool morning that spring, a month into the baseball season, a man in a full-length doctor's coat walked into the senior English class at Macon High. If the students hadn't been so accustomed to it, they might have blanched. Then again, they knew it was just Sweet being Sweet.

Over the past school year, Sweet had become even more experimental in the classroom. He lived to provoke reactions, whether it was wearing the doctor's coat, encouraging the kids to be loud on certain days—he felt it important to learn to "concentrate amid chaos"—or passing out an excerpt from *The Prophet*, a book by the Lebanese poet and writer Kahlil Gibran that was popular in the counterculture movement. Titled "On Teaching," it touched on how, "If [the teacher] is indeed wise he does not bid you enter the house of his wisdom, but rather leads you to the threshold of your own mind."

The point, as Sweet saw it, was that he was a guide, not a dictator. As such, he believed every student needed guidance of some sort, even academic stars such as Jane Metzger, the pretty cheerleader who'd dated Shartzer. Active in numerous school clubs, Metzger had earned Macon's coveted "Gold Hall Pass," which was bestowed upon students who made the high honor roll or the National Honor Society and allowed its wearer to leave class without a teacher's permission. One afternoon, Metzger bragged to Sweet that, in four years of high school, she'd never once received a poor slip.

Not long after, Sweet called Metzger over after English class and, with a grim expression on his face, handed her an envelope. When she opened it, she was horrified.

In bold letters across the top, the paper read DEFICIENCY REPORT.

According to the sheet, Metzger was failing in not only English but also history, math, PE, study, and lunch. Her attitude, performance, lack of attention, and lack of effective motivation were noted. Sweet recommended after-school help five days a week, tutoring, and a conference with the teacher. Then, under COMMENTS, he'd written, "Jane is so stupid it's unbelievable—she has a poor attitude that makes things worse." Then at the end he added: "She has bad breath, too."

Appraising the slip, Metzger was paralyzed with fear. *My parents are going to be horrified!* Then after a minute she looked up to see Sweet wearing an enormous grin on his face. Finally, she exhaled.

The lesson was a simple one—*don't take life too seriously*—and Sweet reinforced it at every opportunity. One time, Metzger and some other students caught a ride home with Sweet in his Scout after an away basketball game. En route, Sweet detoured to the Steak 'n Shake in Decatur. When he did, Metzger noticed her white-haired, ultraconservative grandparents and their friends eating at a table next to one of the windows. At which point she made the mistake of saying, "Hey, there's my grandparents!"

Sweet perked up. "Let's go say hello!" he said, then drove the Scout up to the window and proceeded to honk the horn and wave like a goofball. When Metzger's grandparents looked up, they saw a strange-looking, long-haired hippie and four students grinning and waving wildly. Mortified, Metzger had ducked out of sight.

It took until the following week, when her mother relayed to her the story of some crazy man waving at her grandparents, for Jane to stop worrying about it. It took her years more to laugh about it.

When it came to the baseball team, Sweet saw no reason why he couldn't carry over his educational philosophy. So whereas many coaches might have responded to the unexpected success of the 1970 team by creating expectations and tightening the reins, by creating a *program*, Sweet did the opposite. He continued to let the boys run practice on occasion, encouraged them to make their own decisions in the field, and introduced elements such as "silent infield." Before certain games, he'd signal the boys and, as one, they'd stop talking: no chatter, no joking, no calling out bases. The only sound was the crack of the bat and the *thwap* of ball meeting leather. Sweet saw it as akin to a moment of meditation prior to the game. While the stillness could be unsettling to fans and opponents, the Ironmen players came to revel in it. It was one more thing that forged unity—that set them apart.

Indeed, theirs was a remarkable transformation. Two years earlier they'd been a bunch of country boys. Now, as Dale Otta says, by the day they "became more and more like Sweet."

The Ironmen's arrival at away games was particularly impressive—or peculiar, depending on your point of view. As the Macon bus pulled into the parking lot, the boys could be heard belting out "Yellow Submarine" at the top of their lungs. Then they piled out, one after the other, each looking stranger than the next. Craig Brueggemann, the center fielder for Mt. Zion, remembers seeing the Ironmen sprinting onto the field for an early season game with long sideburns while wearing hats that looked like they'd been purchased at a head shop. He remembers their coach, "who wore a Fu Manchu, dark sunglasses, long hair, and looked like Abbie Hoffman in a ball suit." And he remembers Macon's scorekeeper trotting out wearing a baseball hat, a uniform top, and shorts and only then noticing—what's this now?—that the said scorekeeper had suspiciously shapely legs, pretty eyes, and brown hair flowing out the back of her hat.

Witnessing it all, Brueggemann remembers wondering if the inmates had taken over the asylum over in Macon. At Mt. Zion there was a strict dress code. Students didn't have long hair; teachers *certainly* didn't; and coaches never, ever did. A few months earlier, one of the team's most talented players had decided to grow out his hair even though school rules decreed that a boy's locks could not reach his ears on the sides or the collar of his shirt in the back. Not long after, the boy had received a letter from the school. It read, in so many words: "In compliance with the school dress code, you are required to get a haircut or you cannot play baseball." The boy had decided to keep his hair. In return, he lost baseball.

But here came the Macon boys, looking like a bunch of country peaceniks—"field hippies" was the term Sweet enjoyed the most—and accompanied by a coach wearing aviator sunglasses who, as Brueggemann puts it, "had this look on his face like he knew all the secrets to the universe and was at peace with that."

It only got weirder from there. When Macon took the field for warm-ups, Brueggemann remembers hearing the strangest sound coming from the Ironmen bench. It couldn't be? *A rock opera?*

The eight-track tape deck had been Shartzer's idea. A gift from his father, it was the kind that split apart, with speakers that could be set on either side. At first, Shartzer brought it to practice just for the fun of it—and because he figured he could. Had he done so during football season, Jack Burns would have no doubt taken the stereo and heaved it over the fence, yelling "THIS ISN'T SOME DAMN PROM!"

But baseball was different. Not only did Sweet allow the tape deck but he appeared to enjoy its presence. This led Shartzer and Mark Miller to the next logical step: warm-ups. So for the first weeks of the season, the Ironmen had warmed up to the type of music opposing coaches tended to find distasteful, a fact that was not lost on Sweet.

At first Shartzer loaded up the box with Santana. Then one day Heneberry and Snitker were at church and their priest, a man known as Father Riick, introduced the class to a soundtrack called *Jesus Christ Superstar.* Around town, Riick was known as the cool pastor, and in *Jesus Christ Superstar* he saw an opportunity to reach the kids through music.

Snitker and Heneberry noticed one thing immediately: that music was catchy. Soon enough, they'd hooked their teammates. As Shartzer puts it, "If you took the words out, the damn music was great." He bought the album on eight-track and, from that day forward, his was the only tape the team used.

The scene during Macon warm-ups—of boys fielding grounders while singing about riding into Jerusalem, about being "obsessed with fighting times and fates you can't deny"—was made all the more surreal by the boys' hats, a number of which were embroidered with large white peace signs.

While they were a statement, the caps were also a necessity. Midway through the previous season, noticing that many of the boys had old, mismatched hats, a school parent named Dick Jostes who worked at Caterpillar had donated a box of CAT DIESEL hats. The Ironmen had worn them right up until the point that someone in the IHSA office caught wind and decided to ban the caps as advertising. Sweet thought this hilarious. A bunch of farmers' kids wearing hats in games few attended didn't strike him as the best advertising idea in the world.

Still, they were perfectly good hats. And, when you had $1.26 a month to buy supplies, as school records indicate Sweet received from Macon High that April, you didn't waste anything. So Sweet instructed the boys to cover up the writing as they saw fit. If they followed his lead and sewed a peace symbol rather than a Macon "M" over the CAT decal, well, who could blame them?

Beyond the music and the hats, what was most annoying to opposing teams, and especially opposing coaches, was the fact that the Macon boys were *good*. Even with no budget, no assistant coaches, and no bench, the wins piled up. By late April, the Ironmen were 6–2. By the second week of May they were 8–3–1. Arnold had emerged as a .500 hitter, Snitker was creaming the ball, and what the Ironmen lacked in depth they made up for with hustle, confidence, and a camaraderie forged through the success, and disappointment, of the previous season. They were a team of brothers now, and most everyone had his own nickname, from Shark to Goose (Heneberry's handle) to Dud (for Glan, due to his Dudley Do-Right chin) to Snik (for Snitker).

Most of the positions were unchanged: The slow-footed Snitker now manned right field full time, even if Shartzer still complained of having to pitch lefty batters away. In center field, it was the opposite. That's where Shartzer *tried* to get batters to hit it, "with a little air under it," because he knew Arnold would run it down. Left field was the domain of Dave Wells, a tall sophomore with a good arm. Wells' family owned a farm in the area, and he was the greenest of the boys in many respects. He'd begun the season wearing a hat his father had given him that read FS, for Farmers Service. Eventually, Wells had abandoned it when too many opposing fans mocked him, yelling out "Hey, does that stand for FARMER SISSY?"

Though Sweet lacked assistants, Bob Shartzer and Dwight Glan unofficially played the role. And with Heneberry now starting every game on the mound or in the field, the team needed a new first base coach. In Trusner, Sweet found the most serious one imaginable, a boy who appeared in the football team's yearbook photo wearing a jacket and tie. He took up his position in the box down the first base line with hands on knees, face in a grimace.

It was a tight group. Sweet rarely used more than nine players and relied primarily on two pitchers, Shartzer and Heneberry, whom he alternated every game, regardless of matchup or situation, with the other manning third base. A year older but still stick-skinny, Heneberry remained deadly when his off-speed stuff was breaking and inconsistent when it wasn't. As Maxine Glan said to him after one game: "Oh, John, I really like the games that you pitch. There's so much excitement and so many base runners. Not like Steve."

Indeed, Shartzer had developed into a force on the mound. At the time, the New York Mets had a young pitcher named Nolan Ryan who was renowned for doing two things: throwing high heat and not giving a damn what the batter thought about it. In many respects, Shartzer was the Nolan Ryan of central Illinois. Even more than in 1970, he relied on intimidation and power. He was wild when he needed to be, unafraid to brush back batters, and his fastball moved late, sinking as it approached the plate. Good thing, as nine out of ten pitches he threw were fastballs, and some games he never threw anything but "the ol' number one," as he called it. When he did unleash the rare curve, it had nice movement—it was really more of a "slurve," as much a slider as curveball—but he invariably telegraphed the pitch by emitting a prodigious grunt. Whether due to the speed of his fastball or the infrequency of his curve, opponents had yet to catch on.

By the start of the playoffs in early May, Shartzer had already thrown a one-hitter, a three-hitter, and a handful of shutouts. If he occasionally coughed on the mound, at times violently, few paid it much attention.

13

The First Step

The boys talked about it all the time. They talked about it while hunting doves, while drinking covert beers down at Mile Corner, and on nights they snuck an extra friend into the drive-in movie theater in Decatur by stashing him in the trunk of Otta's blue Impala. Theirs was a singular, unifying goal: Return to regionals and advance. Despite all the caveats—a thin roster, a young team, a weak conference—the boys were remarkably confident about their chances. "Maybe," as Shartzer says, "we were just too dumb to know better."

For the third year in a row the Ironmen had won the Meridian and now boasted a twenty-three-game conference winning streak that dated back three seasons. In truth, there was only one team in the area that worried them. As luck would have it, though, it was their first-round opponent in the district playoffs: Mt. Zion. Two of Macon's three losses had come at the hands of its rival, which seemed to grow stronger by the year. Buoyed by an influx of students from Decatur, Mt. Zion's enrollment now topped 500, and its sports teams were so dominant that it no longer played Macon in football and basketball.

Even so, the Ironmen were surprised to learn that Mt. Zion coach Ed Neighbors intended to start arguably his team's third-best pitcher in the district opener. Only twenty-three, Neighbors was a cocky, by-the-book coach who'd been named team MVP as a first baseman at

Millikin University. He was young enough to think he knew it all and talented and smart enough to back it up most of the time. He ran a tight program and didn't hesitate to lecture his players.

The contrast between the two teams could scarcely have been starker. Come game day, as Neighbors led his team through drills down the right field line, yelling to be heard over the Macon music, he looked over at the Ironmen bench and saw an entire lineup that wouldn't cut it at his school, beginning with the coach, who lounged in a chair wearing sunglasses and a bemused expression. From the stands, Neighbors heard the Mt. Zion fans. "Hey you hippies," they yelled, "turn off that damn music."

It was only the beginning of the pleasantries that were exchanged that day. Separated by only ten miles, Macon and Mt. Zion overlapped in many respects, giving the rivalry an internecine feel—had Jeff Glan lived one house to the east, for example, he would have attended Mt. Zion. The players knew each other from summer ball or working the crops; the fans knew each other from church or the taverns; and relatives sometimes split based on school allegiance. Fistfights were known to break out in the stands and, always, the animosity was palpable. As Jeff Brueggemann, the sophomore ace for Mt. Zion, put it: "If the Macon game was the only game you won in a year, that was OK for a lot of people."

Considering this, it was something of a risk for Neighbors to start lefty Gary Jones despite the fact that sophomore Jeff Brueggemann had better numbers and junior Rod Jones was equally if not more talented. Still, the move allowed Neighbors to save his best pitcher for the final and gave him the element of surprise, as both Brueggemann and Rod Jones had already faced—and, it should be noted, beaten—Macon that season.

It didn't take Neighbors long to regret his decision. By the fourth inning, Macon led 4–0. By the seventh, it was 8–2. Shartzer finished off the win in dominant fashion, then raised his hands to the sky. Most everyone was surprised. *Their players are bigger and badder,* Brian

Snitker thought as he jogged in from right field. *We had no business winning a game like this.* Meanwhile, Neighbors and the Mt. Zion boys slumped off, dejected. They'd wanted to not only beat Macon but destroy them. As Craig Brueggemann says, "We thought we were better, plain and simple."

That Macon crushed Blue Mound 10–0 the next day behind a Heneberry one-hitter to take the district title and advance to the regionals for the second time in two years didn't change Neighbors' opinion of the Ironmen. Macon had just gotten lucky. Small-town teams like that never went that far.

One of the umpires from the Blue Mound game, however, disagreed. After the Ironmen's win, as the team prepared to leave, he walked over and, after asking Sweet's permission, poked his head into the Macon bus. "Boys," he said. "I've umpired all year and you all are the best team I've seen by far. I'm amazed I hadn't heard anything about you." The boys tried not to look shocked. "Of all the teams at regionals," the ump continued, "I haven't seen any that should beat you. I'll be following you guys."

Four days later, Macon proved the umpire right and advanced again, routing Decatur Eisenhower, a big-city power and one-time state champion that had knocked off unbeaten MacArthur in the previous round.

A year later and against the odds, the Ironmen had returned to the regional finals. This time, there would be no disqualifications.

For the people of Macon, just this was enough. For years, the town's football team had played second fiddle to conference rival Illiopolis. The basketball team had lodged four straight losing seasons. When the Ironmen track team challenged for the conference crown in 1970 it ended up having to share the honor with Stonington. For the baseball team to not only win three straight conference titles but take down a big Decatur school at regionals? It was unimaginable.

Of course, the boys saw it from a different perspective. Every game was an elimination game now. Every game meant the end of the season and, for the seniors, the end of their high school careers. That the Ironmen were one win away from sectionals, and three from state, was never discussed. This was about doing what they'd pledged to do.

Sweet was of a similar mind. The night before the final, he sat at the table in his trailer, talking with Jeanne. Slowly, over the months, she'd become part of the fabric of the team. She came to nearly every game and spent weekend nights hanging out with the baseball parents at pig roasts and house parties. On occasion, she and Sweet hosted card games for the players at the trailer.

Now, she understood the stakes. After all, it was only a year earlier that McClard had called the boys into his office and ended their season, and only nine months since Sweet had been fired as baseball coach for being deemed a bad influence on the boys. Now, after all the anger and disappointment, followed by the resolve and preparation, the team—and Sweet—was getting a second chance, this time against Mt. Pulaski. Win and they'd advance further than any team in Macon history.

It was more than that, though. Win and the Ironmen would put Macon on the map. Win and they'd prove McClard and all those anachronistic parents wrong. Win and they'd create a legacy, the kind that can't be overvalued in a town as small and close-knit as Macon, where collective memory lives forever.

For a game of this magnitude, any sane coach would certainly want his best pitcher on the mound.

Instead, Lynn Sweet planned to send out John Heneberry.

The men were easy to spot on Wednesday afternoon at Warrensburg-Latham High, the site of the regional final. They came toting chair cushions and notebooks. They stood against the fence with fingers hooked through the wire. Older, with sun-wrinkled faces and leathery hands, they'd spent the bulk of their lives in search of hidden gems. They spoke the language of bat speed and sinking fastballs. Now they'd come to see the kid from Mt. Pulaski.

His name was Dennis Werth and he was a special talent. Three years later, he would be drafted by the Yankees, becoming the pride of Mt. Pulaski for generations to come. He would go on to play parts of three seasons in the Bronx. Decades later his stepson, a tall, fast boy by the name of Jayson, would be an All-Star for the Philadelphia Phillies and win a World Series ring.

For now, though, Dennis Werth was merely the baddest high school player in central Illinois. A senior, he'd started every game at catcher since he was a freshman, and opponents ran on him at their own peril. Teammates swear Werth gunned down three out of every four would-be thieves and, ten times a season or so, picked a runner off first with a snap throw, an exceedingly difficult thing to do. At the plate, Werth possessed the kind of natural power that can't be taught. As a skinny freshman playing in the regional finals against Lincoln High, he'd won the game by blasting a home run off a pitcher who was said to have entered the game with a 0.71 ERA. From that moment forward, Werth seemed destined for success. It didn't take long for the scouts to materialize.

On this afternoon, they received a surprise. The star catcher they came to see wasn't behind the plate but on the mound. It was a switch made out of necessity. Mt. Pulaski's top pitcher, John Jaggi, had pitched the first game in the regionals the day before and the team's number two pitcher and cleanup hitter, Mark Dannenberger, broke his collar bone toward the end of the regular season. It fell to Werth to take the mound.

It wasn't a huge drop-off. Though he possessed no off-speed pitches, Werth threw the ball as hard as any high schooler in Illinois. The same could not be said of the spindly boy who took the mound for the opposition, his shirttail spilling out of his belt.

As he peered in at Dean Otta, John Heneberry focused on one thing: starting strong. All season—his entire high school career, really—the first inning had been his weakness. His father could never figure it out.

"Why do we go through it?" Jack Heneberry had asked his son one night a month earlier, while sitting at the dinner table after a game.

"What do you mean?" John asked, even though he knew exactly what his father meant.

Jack rubbed his forehead. "Why do you have to walk the first two guys every game?"

"Well, you know, I didn't *try* to walk them."

"Maybe you should take a longer warm-up," Jack said. He was always looking for ways to remedy his son's wildness, certain there was a solution out there.

"But I did that."

Jack frowned. "Then don't do that. Try a shorter warm-up."

And on it went, Jack suggesting physical solutions to what was likely a psychological issue. *Move to the other side of the rubber. Watch where you stride and how far. Dig a deeper hole for your cleat. Do something, anything to get back on track.*

Now, just as Heneberry feared, his first pitch sailed wide. His second bounced in the dirt. *Oh crap.* He walked one batter, gave up a single.

Don't get in a hole, Heneberry thought to himself.

Crack! The ball soared into the alley for a triple. Hole dug. 2–0 Mt. Pulaski.

Outside the Mt. Pulaski dugout, the boys took vigorous warm-up cuts, all of them now eager to get a crack at Heneberry. Though Werth was the clear star, Mt. Pulaski was by no means a one-man squad. The boys played baseball in the fall (twenty-five games), the spring (another twenty-five), and the summer. The team was deep, well-coached, and took pride in its defense and pitching. Coming into the regional final, the players knew only that the Ironmen had an ace, a boy named Shartzer, and that they wouldn't have to face him. Now, up 2–0 in the second inning, and with Werth mowing down the Ironmen, they felt even more confident.

On the Macon bench, Sweet told the boys not to sweat the deficit. Werth may be a hell of pitcher, but if he was pitching it meant he wasn't catching. All the Ironmen needed were base runners. In the fourth inning, they got one. Werth lost control of a fastball and plunked Dale Otta. On the next pitch, Otta took off, swiping second. Moments later he scored when Shartzer's grounder snuck through the infield. With that, the floodgates opened. Stu Arnold doubled home Shartzer, Dean Otta doubled home Arnold, and David Wells singled home another run. Just like that, the Ironmen led the regional final, 4–2.

Now it was up to Heneberry to hold the lead.

With each at bat by Werth, Sweet held his breath. Yet time and again, Heneberry's curveball worked its magic. It had taken a while, but it was breaking again. Even Jaggi, who'd hit a first-inning triple, was stymied. Three times in a row he struck out.

Heading into the seventh inning, the score remained 4–2 in Macon's favor. Then, with two outs, the Ironmen took off running again. From the mound, Werth could only watch in dismay as the Ironmen circled the bases. By the end of the inning Macon had scored five runs—all with two outs—and stolen an astounding nine bases on the day, including a daring swipe of home by Arnold. In the bottom of the inning, after a rough stretch, Heneberry closed it out with one final curveball that dropped like an elevator that's had its cable cut. And with that, it was over; in a game they were expected to lose, the Ironmen had somehow won in a rout, 9-4.

Behind the backstop, the two hundred–odd Macon fans who'd made the trip leapt to their feet, arms upraised. Girlfriends shrieked. Grown men bellowed. Sweet beamed like a lottery winner. The players slapped hands, smacked gloves, and exchanged hugs. Even McClard looked pleased. Finally, they could say it: "regional champs!"

They were just boys. Fifteen-, sixteen-, and seventeen-year-old boys who did boy things. Mark Miller could pass gas on command. Dale Otta was fascinated by model rockets. Steve Shartzer loved comic books.

But somewhere in between the Mt. Zion game and beating Mt. Pulaski, they became more than boys. They became symbols of a town. Of many towns, really. Even over in Mt. Zion, the players were rooting for Macon, though of course they'd never admit it to the Ironmen. Strange as it may seem, the Macon boys were now heroes to many.

Scott Taylor was nine years old at the time and lived in Elwin, one house down from Steve Shartzer. His father was good friends with Bob Shartzer and went to nearly every Macon High game, no matter the sport. Bob Taylor rooted for the basketball team, helped fix pregame dinners for the football team, and came to every baseball game. One year at the Macon High athletic banquet the school awarded Taylor a plaque as MACON'S #1 FAN. It stayed on his mantel for decades.

His son was right there with him. To Scott, there was nobody on the planet more amazing than Steven Shartzer. Many an afternoon Scott sat on his porch, waiting for Steve to launch a Wiffle ball into his yard, just so he could return it and perhaps be invited to play.

It wasn't just Steve though. Scott looked up to all the boys on the team. He fetched foul balls at games. He sat on the end of the bench, mute, just so he could overhear the players joking and laughing. "Every once in a while," he says, "I'd even get to play catch with them."

During away games, Scott's father pulled him out of school and brought him along. He saw the boys' pictures in the paper; he read the articles. There was no pro team within easy driving distance of Elwin, just the Class-A Commodores in Decatur. In a world of three TV channels and one grocery store, being the star athlete at Macon High was about as big as it got. To Scott, the Ironmen were the closest thing in his life to celebrities.

Some of the players were oblivious to the power they now wielded; they were teenagers, after all. But not Shartzer. Blessed with talent and confidence, he was also cursed with self-awareness. He understood the stakes. This wasn't just about teammates and parents anymore. This was about all those folks at the Country Manor. It was about legacy and civic pride. It was about the Scott Taylors.

He didn't intend to let any of them down.

14

We've Only Just Begun

Would they even show?

All day the girls wondered. You never knew with those boys, after all. They might decide to go off fishing, or drinking beers. An impromptu game of over-the-line might take precedence.

Come 7 P.M. on Saturday, May 22, however, they were all there. There was Mark Miller, his blond shock of hair slicked down; and Heneberry sporting a powder blue tuxedo; and Dale Otta beaming as he escorted in the shapely junior Sherrie Dunmire. It may have been only three days before sectionals, but this was the Macon High prom. No boy with an ounce of testosterone would miss it.

One by one, dates on their elbows, the Ironmen ascended the steps of the Hotel Orlando, a stately, seven-story brick hotel in downtown Decatur. Across one wall the prom motto was written in big, happy letters: WE'VE ONLY JUST BEGUN. The theme came from a hit song by the Carpenters, but naturally the players saw in it a reflection of their baseball team's journey. Still, this was a night to dance. Over in the corner, Jeff Glan, hair parted just so, twirled around Jane Metzger, who'd long since split with Shartzer on agreeable terms—those being that Shartzer didn't want a girlfriend and Metzger didn't want a boyfriend who said he didn't want a girlfriend. If Glan's jacket looked a bit roomy as he danced, it was understandable. He'd sent his sport coat to the dry cleaners so it would be ready for the big night, but upon arriving to retrieve it had been told the coat was still being cleaned. Which is how, after some desperate beseeching, Glan came to spend his prom night wearing Roger Britton's double-breasted, two-button blue blazer.

It was an extravagant evening, at least by the standards of the boys, some of whom had never been to a hotel before. Dinner was served in courses—iceberg lettuce salad followed by roast beef with mashed potatoes and green beans and, for dessert, ice cream. Up on stage, Britton gave a little speech and senior class wills were read. Heneberry bequeathed "twenty pounds of excess weight to next year's football team," while Dean Otta bestowed his catching ability to Sam Trusner. Dancing was encouraged, though of course only with your date, and at arm's length.

Afterward, some of the boys headed to the site of the official post-party at the YMCA to play Ping-Pong and pool. Others, like Shartzer and Heneberry, headed home or out into the night. As Shark reminded them all, it was important to stay focused. They'd have plenty of nights to hang out in the years to come, but only one chance to prepare for the Illinois state sectionals.

Besides, they had a reputation to uphold now, at least if you believed that weekend's papers, whose sports editors knew a good angle when it showed up wearing a peace sign and a Fu Manchu. Suddenly, the Ironmen had become local media stars—and not just because of their success on the field. Under a large photo of Sweet in profile sporting those bushy sideburns and with his dark hair curling down his neck, the headline of the *Courier* of Lincoln, Illinois, read "Coaching Goes Mod," while an account of the game referred to the Ironmen as "Macon's Mod Squad." For its part, the Decatur *Herald & Review* ran a banner headline that read "Mod Squad Bids for State" above an article noting that "the baseball team loaded with players sporting long hair and wearing peace symbols" was set to play Potomac on Tuesday.

The media circus, and the game, would have to wait, though. On Sunday night the sky darkened. By dawn the next morning, it tore open.

Lynn Sweet
in his twenties,
before arriving
at Macon High.
Courtesy of Lynn Sweet

Steve Shartzer at fifteen.
Courtesy of Dale Otta/Macon High

Bill McClard
in 1968.
Courtesy of
Dale Otta/Macon High

Doug Tomlinson and Dale Otta, co-batting leaders, in 1969.
Courtesy of Dale Otta/Macon High

Jeanne Jesse in 1970, the year she began dating Sweet.
Courtesy of Jeanne Sweet/Delta Zeta Sorority

The Ironmen bench: Sweet (left, in black cap), Shartzer (next to Sweet), and the rest. Courtesy of Lynn Sweet

Mark Miller (left) and John Heneberry (right) showing off a fishing haul the day after the 1970 disqualification.

Courtesy of John Heneberry

Diane Tomlinson (left) and John Heneberry (right) before senior prom.

Courtesy of John Heneberry

Barb Jesse, the team's unlikely scorekeeper.

Bob Strongman/*Herald & Review*

Sweet on the bench during the 1971 season.

Ken Kiley/*Peoria Journal Star*

Sweet counseling Dean Otta, May 1971.

Herb Slodounik/*Herald & Review*

The 1971 State tournament program.

Courtesy of Lynn Sweet

Shartzer at the plate during the state tournament.

Bob Strongman/*Herald & Review*

Macon High students getting ready to leave for Peoria on June 4, 1971.
Courtesy of Dale Otta

Cliff Brown with the Macon flag at the Lane Tech game.
Bob Strongman/*Herald & Review*

The Lane Tech superfan and the drum he brought all the way from Chicago.
Bob Strongman/*Herald & Review*

The Ironmen and fans after a big win. Bob Strongman/*Herald & Review*

Dean Otta (foreground, left) and Heneberry (right) during the trophy presentation. Courtesy of Dale Otta

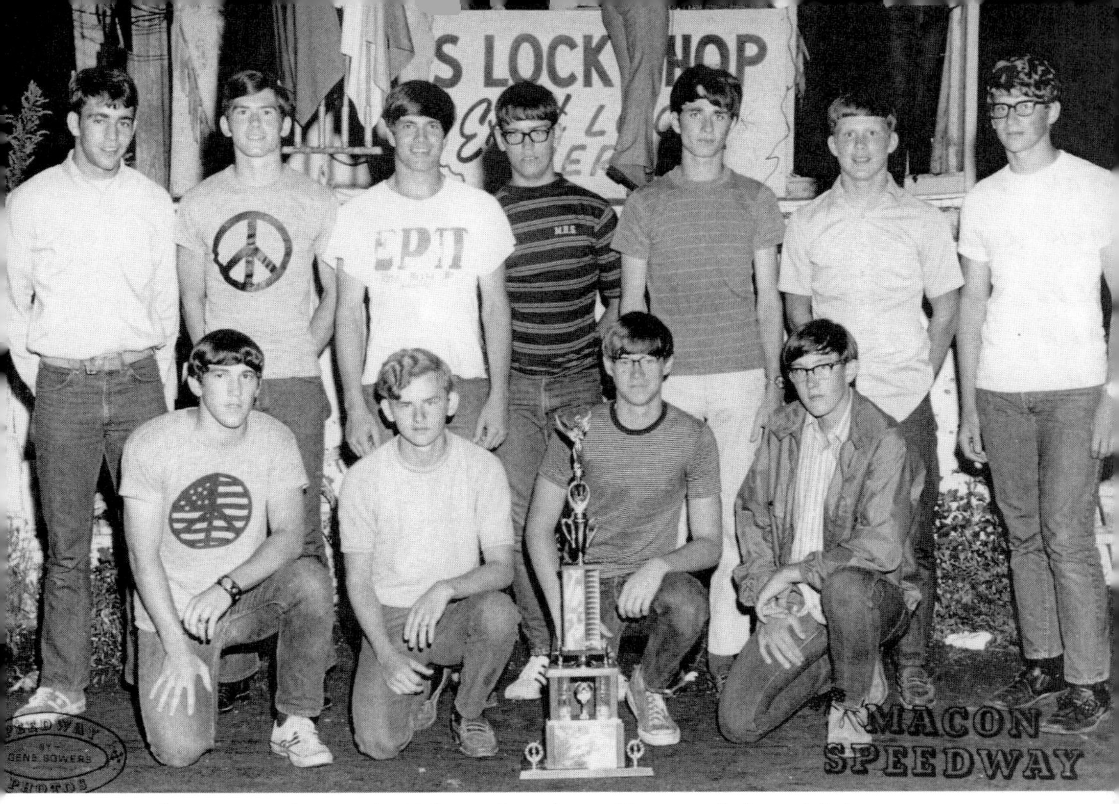

The Ironmen honored at Macon Speedway. Top row (left to right): Shartzer, Dale Otta, Arnold, Snitker, Heneberry, Glan, Buddy Morrison. Bottom row (left to right): Dean Otta, Jerry Camp, Greg Boggs, Stan Evans.
Courtesy of Dale Otta, from Gene Sowers/Speedway Photo

Lynn and Jeanne Sweet at Christmas, 1973.
Courtesy of Lynn Sweet

Sweet during his last year of coaching, 1976.
Bob Strongman/*Herald & Review*

Macon Ironmen in front of the Macon Water tower, 2010 (left to right): Jim Durbin, Dave Wells, Dean Otta, Lynn Sweet, Sam Trusner, Jerry Camp, Jeff Glan, Dale Otta, Barb Jesse Kingery, John Heneberry. *Sports Illustrated*

Steve Shartzer with his daughter, Anna.
Courtesy of Steve Shartzer

All day it rained in thick sheets. By midmorning, the first semifinal game between Matoon and Bloomington was called off. While the players cursed, the farmers rejoiced. After the dry spring of 1970 and a similarly dry spell in the early months of 1971, the deluge was especially welcome. Fortunately, the impact of southern blight had been less than expected, due in part to preventive measures. The manager of the grain elevator, a man named Jim Shaw, had flown to Georgia to learn about the disease, then returned to advise the farmers. Already, there was hopeful talk of a return to previous crop levels. It would be a busy fall at the grain elevator.

Tuesday morning, Sweet and the boys woke to more rain. That afternoon, word came that the Bloomington game was postponed again, until Wednesday afternoon. This meant two things. First, the field was sure to remain waterlogged for Macon's game a day later, a blow to the Ironmen's run-and-run-some-more style. Second, if the Ironmen did win the semifinal, they'd have to come right back and play the championship the next day while their opponent would benefit from a day of rest.

Those were future concerns, though. For the moment, the Ironmen prepped for Potomac, a small school from northeast of Champaign. All Sweet knew about the team was what he'd read in the papers, and most of that concerned ace pitcher Mark Carley, who carried a twenty-six-inning scoreless streak into the game. Of equal interest to college coaches and scouts, Carley was also batting .526 with eleven home runs in only seventeen games.

Naturally, Steve Shartzer viewed each of those home runs, and each of those scoreless innings, as a personal challenge. How dare there be someone as talented as him at sectionals.

On the eve of the sectional opener, Pat Shartzer fidgeted at the dinner table. She couldn't help it; she was excited for her brother. Tomorrow, he would pitch the biggest game of his young life.

Sandy-haired and pretty, with a raspy voice and a dry sense of humor, Pat was two years older than Steve. Marooned together in Elwin as children, they were often each other's only playmates. As a result, they'd brokered a deal of sorts.

"C'mon, play catch with me," Steve would say.

"I will," Pat would respond, "right after you play school with me."

"I hate playing school."

"Well I don't want to play catch, either."

And thus afternoons proceeded as follows: Pat sitting Steve down at the little desk on their screened-in back porch and playing the role of teacher, instructing him how to read and write. Or, if she was sick of playing school, Pat broke out her dolls and instructed Steve on how to play house. Then, an interminable time later (at least to Steve), the pair walked out into the yard, whereupon Pat wedged a sponge into her mitt for padding and Steve began pitching. Being a Shartzer, Pat didn't just wince her way through it. For years afterward, Steve measured all other catchers against his sister.

As Pat got older and started dating, it was Steve who found ways to turn the tables. "I think it's about time we go out back and play catch," Steve said on more than one weekend morning. "Oh really?" Pat responded. "Yeah," Steve said with a smile, "because otherwise I think Mom might like to know what time you got back last night."

Over time, Pat learned to see through her brother's ploys. Their mother was another matter. Short and proper, Georgianna Shartzer worked as a telephone operator at Illinois Bell. Like her husband, she had high expectations for Steve but it was obvious how much she adored him. In Pat's words Steve was "my mom's little prince."

Naturally, Steve took every opportunity to use this to his advantage. One time, when Steve was in the eighth grade, Pat was in the kitchen when she heard a shriek coming from Steve's room. She ran in to find her mother staring at a thermometer, face ashen.

"Steve has a fever of 106!" she said.

Pat looked at the thermometer, then looked at Steve, who was propped up in his bed. She knew enough about medicine to know that 106 was pretty serious, but Steve didn't appear to be seizing up. He wasn't pale, or sweating, or drawn. In fact, she thought he looked just fine. Then she noticed something unusual. Steve's bed had a lamp attached to the headboard, the kind with a clamp on the back, and it was turned on. This made no sense. Steve *never* read books. That's when Pat noticed something else: Steve was having trouble holding in, as she recalls, "the biggest shit-eating grin you ever saw."

"Well, Mom," Pat said. "If you turn off that lamp and don't let him stick the thermometer against it, I think he'll be fine."

As much as Steve enjoyed messing with his mom, he felt a great responsibility to his parents, especially his father. Bob Shartzer had been a Depression child. For the Shartzer family to have dinner each night when he was young, everyone had to work, even the kids. As a result, Bob was now driven to ensure his own children had a better experience.

Early on, he'd made a deal with Steve: As long as Steve played sports, he didn't need to work. This made him a rarity among his friends. Heneberry helped on his grandfather's farm, walking the lines of beans for $1 an hour and driving the tractor from the time he could steer it. Glan's father grew corn and soybeans outside Elwin while also working at the Pittsburgh Plate Glass factory, and Jeff was expected to help on the farm and rub down his father's legs when they got too sore from the long days. For their part, the Ottas worked weekends at the Country Manor, flipping burgers and sneaking bites of fried chicken in the back. But Steve never held an after-school job. Some children might have seen this as an opportunity to goof off. Steve viewed it as a responsibility. So when his parents said to him before a game, "We're counting on you, Shark, go out there and shut them down," he listened. As he says, "I took that shit serious. Very serious."

Thursday morning dawned blessedly clear. At 1 P.M., the boys fled class and headed for the bus, playing cards on the hour-long ride to Champaign Central High.

Located two miles from the sprawling campus of the University of Illinois at Urbana–Champaign, Champaign Central boasted the type of modern amenities a school like Macon lacked. What most impressed the Ironmen, though, was McKinley Field. Not just the bleachers and concession stands but in particular the sign at the gate. It read $2 ADMISSION.

Upon seeing it Mark Miller cracked up, as did Heneberry. "Two dollars? Really?" It was hard to fathom that people were going to pay to watch them play baseball.

But pay they did, and by game time a large, raucous crowd was on hand. Plenty rooted for Potomac, but it felt like even more roared for Macon. One whole section of the bleachers appeared to consist solely of Lynn Sweet fans. There was his buddy Fred Schooley and one of his high school teachers and a bunch of his friends from his Champaign days. And, just down from them, a sturdy man with gray hair standing next to a pretty, older brunette.

Sweet was surprised to see his parents, especially his father. Though the two men were friendly, they shared little in common. Had you met them together, you might not have guessed they were even related.

Lynn Sweet Senior was a true American hard-ass. He grew up in Williamsport, Pennsylvania, the black sheep of seven siblings in the family. He left home early, enlisting in the Army right out of high school in 1933, in the midst of the Great Depression. When he got out, he worked in a shipyard and then enlisted again in early 1943, during World War II. While in charge of a relief convoy, Sweet was sent to the Battle of the Bulge in Belgium. When the front lines broke down, he found himself manning a machine gun in the most deadly American battle of World War II. It is said the average life span of a machine gunner in that battle could be measured in minutes. Sweet survived unscathed.

Three years later, he rejoined the military and eventually shipped out to Korea, after which he remained in the service as a quartermaster. In 1963, he retired with the rank of Master Sergeant. To his children's friends, he became known as "Sarge."

As Sarge saw it, life consisted of a series of tests, each of equal importance, regardless the context. This manifested itself in myriad ways. One day while Lynn was in college in Champaign, he and some friends were playing a game of tackle football in a city park when Sarge showed up. It was snowing and the grass had turned white, six inches deep with powder in places. "Mind if I play?" Sarge asked. He was almost fifty years old and had lost some of the muscle that once made him so intimidating. Figuring they'd be nice about it, the boys said yes.

On the first play of the game Sarge charged up the middle with astonishing speed, eluded a would-be blocker and laid out the ballcarrier. On the next play, he did the same thing. The college kids were stunned. What they didn't know was that Sarge grew up playing football in the coal towns of eastern Pennsylvania before briefly joining a semipro team. To him, there was no such thing as a friendly afternoon of tackle football.

When the game was over, the elder Sweet leaned on a nearby bench, wheezing. "Boys, I think I'm too old for this," he said. Without hesitation, they all agreed. None of them wanted any part of Sarge, ever again.

His son, of course, had no choice. From an early age, the two had butted heads. Sarge was given to absolutes, and it didn't help that he was a hard-line conservative while Lynn grew to become an outspoken liberal. To Lynn Senior, it must have seemed a failure of parenting to have brought up his only son on a succession of military bases, instilling in him the virtues of service, and then have the boy turn out to be, in Junior's words, "a total peacenik." As a result, there were arguments. Sarge wanted Lynn to embrace the military ethos, and became frustrated when Lynn Junior spent his time in the ROTC playing elaborate pranks on his instructors.

Even when Lynn Senior found his niche in civilian life, retiring from the military and working as the business manager for the theater at the University of Illinois, his expectations remained. Through Lynn's time in high school, college, and beyond, his father made clear his disappointment. Lynn in turn made clear his disappointment in his father's disappointment.

And yet, now the son was on the verge of doing something impressive. Not in teaching, or writing, or some other pursuit of the mind, but in athletics, a language his father was fluent in, even if he'd never been much of a baseball man.

Down by the bench, Heneberry was the first to notice. In the two years that Sweet had been coach, it was the first time he'd seen Sweet's dad at a game. Heneberry knew enough to realize it was an important moment. Quietly, he passed word to his teammates.

As expected, the game began as a pitching duel. Then, after three scoreless innings, Dale Otta stepped in. All season, Shartzer and Stu Arnold had received the bulk of the attention. They were the ones who crushed home runs, who the pretty girls in tight tops flocked to. Each was outgoing and, in his own way, supremely confident. But Otta had been nearly as valuable to the team, if not as flashy. Organized and conscientious, he was, as Heneberry says, "often the closest thing we had to an assistant coach."

So when Otta broke Carley's scoreless streak, naturally it was not with a booming shot over the fence but rather a clean, hard single. It landed just deep enough for Miller to scamper home from second. Moments later, Stu Arnold blasted a fastball over the 320 sign in left field for his seventh home run of the season. Macon led 3–0.

Behind the backstop, the scouts waited for Carley to turn it on, to bring his team back. Instead, the ornery kid from Macon with the peace sign on his hat kept striking Carley out. In fact, that ornery kid kept striking out everybody. Not until the sixth inning did Potomac manage a hit off Shartzer, and he squelched that rally immediately. Meanwhile, Carley was struggling. The Ironmen added another run in the fifth and five more in the seventh. By the time Shartzer finished off a dominating, 9–0 two-hitter with his tenth strikeout, the scouts could be forgiven had they migrated to the other side of the backstop.

Afterward, as the Macon players and fans celebrated, Lynn Sweet Senior descended from the bleachers and made his way over to the Macon bench, where his son was busy talking to a reporter.

Between a different pair of men, hugs might have been exchanged and a son's heart may have swelled. The Sweet men were not given to sentimentality, though. So instead, when Lynn Junior turned to face him, his father said, "Good win. Hell of a pitcher you got there." And Lynn responded, "We'll try to get one more tomorrow." They talked about a couple plays in the game, about the opponent that awaited. Then Lynn Sweet Senior patted his son on the back and headed off. It wouldn't be until years later, after his father had passed away, that Sweet would come to appreciate the importance of the moment, how in some respects it signaled his father's first sign of approval of the man his son had become.

Not far away, another father stood, arms crossed, trying hard not to look too proud. Bob Shartzer had spent years preparing his son for moments like this. And now he knew what was needed. Not congratulations but a new challenge. When Steve walked over, Bob sized him up. "That was a good win but we got more hay to mow," he said. "Time to start getting ready for Bloomington."

"David Meets Goliath" wrote the local papers, and with good reason. Bloomington High had as many students, twelve hundred, as the town of Macon had residents. A year earlier, the Purple Raiders had won the sectionals behind the hitting and pitching of a strapping junior named Robin Cooper, advancing to the state tournament before falling in the first round. Now Cooper anchored a deeper, more talented team. Despite playing in a tough conference, Bloomington entered the game 21–6.

If that weren't enough to dampen the optimism of Macon fans, word leaked out after the Potomac game: Sweet wasn't going to start Shartzer. It seemed a risky strategy to the reporters on hand. Sure, Shartzer would be throwing on back-to-back days, but he was Macon's star and grittiest competitor. If you had one chance at the biggest game in school history, wouldn't you want your best player on the mound?

Sweet smiled when asked about it. You folks must not understand how we do things in Macon, he said. If he needed a big out, or someone for a relief appearance, Sweet assured reporters he "wouldn't hesitate" to use Shartzer. But he was going to start Heneberry. All season he'd alternated pitchers. What kind of message would it send to the players if he stopped doing it now?

That night, in a mobile home six miles south of Macon in Moweaqua, Bill McClard packed an overnight bag.

It had been weeks since McClard had confronted Sweet. There had been no snide comments, no dark stares. Sweet had begun to wonder if McClard felt he'd broken him. Later, he came to wonder if it was the other way around—if maybe it was he who had broken McClard, or in some way helped change him. Because he had changed.

In his early years at Macon, McClard had gone out of his way to be an enforcer. Not long after arriving, he expelled a student named Charles Dalluge for, as the school board minutes recorded it, "complete disregard for the rules and regulations." Then he'd fired Guy Carlton. Back then, as math teacher Carl Poelker remembers it, McClard served as "the perfect combination with Roger Britton. Britton took into consideration the kid and the background, while Bill would nail anybody's butt to the wall."

As the years passed, however, McClard had become more lenient. There had been fewer paddlings, more stern talks. Eventually, he began to question his role as a disciplinarian. In high school, he'd been a poor student himself—"never took a book home, just barely got by," according to his wife, Vi. He'd always been a dreamer, though, a chaser of windmills. For years, he wondered if he'd missed his calling as a psychologist. He felt he understood kids and that he knew what was wrong with education. Discipline, he came to believe during his time at Macon, was only one part of the equation.

So, in the fall of 1970, McClard had started filling out applications for graduate programs. In the spring of '71, he learned he'd been accepted into Ball State's education program, which is how he came to walk into Roger Britton's office and tender his resignation in March. For the sake of continuity, the move wasn't announced, and only a handful of people knew beyond Britton and the board. Sweet was not among them.

Now that McClard was moving on, perhaps he came to a realization of sorts. What was the point of staying mad at a guy like Sweet? Why should he be the only one who didn't get to have fun? Besides, McClard was a baseball man. He'd coached the game earlier in his teaching career, and had to admit, if grudgingly, that Sweet was doing an impressive job with the players. It was time to enjoy the ride.

So McClard packed up his stuff for a road trip. Macon's team—*his team*—was going to the sectional finals. He planned on being there.

15

Big Coop

On Friday, May 28, the Bloomington team arrived at McKinley Field with the full force of its thousand-strong student body, the members of which soon realized they faced a wonderful dilemma: Make fun of Macon for being hicks or for being hippies? In the end, the Bloomington fans chose both. From their bags, they pulled cowbells, which they rang incessantly. They taunted the Ironmen as "country rednecks" and shouted at Heneberry, "Where did you learn to throw that curveball, out behind the barn?"

The Ironmen had heard it all before. The difference this time was that, as against Potomac, the roar was almost as loud on their side. There in the bleachers were Bob and Scott Taylor and the regulars, now surrounded by roughly 150 of Macon High's 250 students. It sounded like every one of them was cheering.

On the far side of the diamond, the Bloomington players warmed up. As they did, one boy stood to the side, long-tossing. The ball exploded from his hand. Behind the Macon bench, Bob Shartzer squinted.

Son of a bitch.

Shartzer watched a moment longer, then checked the lineup cards. He couldn't believe it. That was Robin Cooper. The same Robin Cooper who'd played for the Bloomington American Legion team against his son's Decatur Legion team the last two years and almost single-handedly beat it. One year Cooper pitched a shutout and hit a mammoth shot for the game's only run. And here he was, *still* in high school. It didn't seem possible.

Bob Shartzer knew what he needed to do. He made a beeline for John Heneberry.

Down the first base line, Heneberry was warming up and, as he was prone to doing, overthinking. He looked up in the stands and saw his uncle and his cousin. A little farther down, he recognized three other familiar faces. When Mike Atteberry heard the Ironmen had made the finals, he was working a summer job pouring concrete. After begging his boss to let him off work, he joined Brad Roush for the hour-plus drive in Brad's Dodge Polara. Standing next to them, back from Kaskaskia College, was Doug Tomlinson, smiling and clapping.

No, Heneberry thought, *no pressure at all.*

Just when Heneberry had worked himself into something resembling a nervous wreck, Bob Shartzer appeared in front of him, looking agitated.

"You can't pitch to this kid."

Heneberry looked at him, startled. "Which kid?"

And then Bob Shartzer explained about Big Coop, about how he'd killed Shartzer's American Legion team, which meant that Steve hated him with a deep passion, though that was beside the point. The point was that John absolutely couldn't give the kid anything to hit. "And whatever you do," said Bob Shartzer, "don't throw him a fastball."

Heneberry nodded. He might have been nervous before. Now he was both nervous and scared.

As he walked to the mound, Heneberry had the same thought as before the Mt. Pulaski game, the same thought he always had: *Don't start slow*. He dug a little divot to the right of the mound, kicking out the dirt. He adjusted his hat. He waved out Dean Otta and, in that slow drawl, said, "I need you to set up just a little more on that outside corner for me now; you set up out there, I'll thread the needle, baby." He looked at his father in the stands and nodded. Then he peered in at Bloomington's leadoff batter, centerfielder Brian Burd, knowing the one thing he couldn't afford to do in a game of this magnitude, with all those people counting on him, was start the game off with a walk. He fired one right down the middle.

Crack! Burd smacked a single. Then he stole second. Heneberry retired Bloomington's number two hitter, but now he faced Big Coop with a man in scoring position and the cleanup hitter, Mike Abfalder, on deck. Heneberry had planned on following Bob Shartzer's advice and pitching around Cooper, but now he was in a tough spot. If he walked Cooper, then Abfalder would come up with two men on and only one out.

Heneberry decided to try to start on the outside corner with an off-speed pitch. Only the ball drifted toward the middle of the plate, as if struck by a sudden gust of wind, and Cooper smacked it for an RBI single to left. Moments later, Abfalder doubled to bring in Cooper. Just like that it was 2–0 Bloomington. Heneberry trudged off the mound at the end of the inning, despondent. He'd done it again: put his team in a hole.

Compounding the situation, none of the Ironmen could get around on Bloomington starter John Adams' fastball. One batter after another went down: Miller, Arnold, Shartzer. Through three innings, the Ironmen remained hitless. Then, in a fitting metaphor for the afternoon to date, Macon's best bat, the thirty-four-inch Mickey Mantle, cracked under the weight of an Adams fastball in the third inning. It was the Ironmen's third shattered bat of the day.

For most teams, this would have been an annoyance. For Macon, it bordered on a crisis. Despite the team's success, the Ironmen were still operating on a tiny budget. Balls were hard enough to come by; bats were an endangered species. Since they cost five or six dollars each, the team generally had only three or four at a time, and usually at least one of those was donated by the parents. In hopes of preserving the team's lumber, Sweet had tried everything, including telling his hitters to hold the bat so that the burned-in trademark symbol—allegedly the weakest part of the bat—faced up when swinging. Thus the trademark ended up protected on contact with the ball. No one knew if it actually helped but, hey, it sounded good.

Usually, the Ironmen broke one bat per game. But never three. Now, one Mantle and two Nellie Fox bats were toast. All that remained was the second Mantle. Sweet turned to Trusner at the end of the inning.

"Sammy, I need you to get us some bats."

"Me? But I'm the first base coach."

Sweet mulled this for a moment, then looked down the bench. "Hey, Jimmy," he yelled toward the end of the dugout, where Jimmy Durbin, the timid freshman with the jug ears, sat with hands on knees. "How do you feel about coaching first base?"

Jimmy looked around, as if there might be another, more experienced Jimmy sitting somewhere behind him.

"Yeah you, Jimmy," Sweet said, smiling.

Jimmy nodded, if slowly.

There was another problem, though: Trusner needed a ride. Sweet walked over to the stands and explained the situation.

When he was finished, an unlikely voice spoke up: "I'll go."

Standing there, sweating in the sun in his dress shirt and slacks, his hair a bit rumpled, stood Bill McClard.

Sweet nodded. "Sam, you know what we want, go with him."

So off they went, Trusner and McClard, in search of bats. In the meantime Sweet told the Macon hitters to make a big show of taking their lone bat back to the dugout, then pretending to assess an unseen stock of choices before pulling the same one out of the bag, a subterfuge they took to with great enthusiasm. The last thing they needed was the Bloomington players knowing they owned yet another advantage.

By the fourth inning, Heneberry had settled down. His curve was snapping and his fastball was back under his control. Instead, it was Adams who now struggled, as if Heneberry's shakiness had been a communicable disease transferred between innings. In the fourth, with Bloomington leading 2–1 and Heneberry stepping to the plate, Adams loaded the bases. Sensing danger, Bloomington coach Bob Spahn signaled to his ace.

Over at first base, Robin Cooper nodded and jogged to the mound. In the on-deck circle, Heneberry watched as Big Coop sent one sizzling warm-up pitch after another into his catcher's mitt. If Cooper was worn out from pitching the semifinal two days earlier, he didn't show it.

Finally, Heneberry stepped in. It was the kind of opportunity boys either dream about or dread: two outs, bases loaded, one run down in the biggest game in school history. As Cooper looked in from the mound, it's safe to say he wasn't worrying about Heneberry's bat the same way Heneberry did Cooper's. No doubt Cooper would have been even less concerned if he knew the skinny kid at the plate was using a bat two ounces too heavy for him.

Around the same time Heneberry stepped in, Trusner and McClard raced through Bailey & Himes Sporting Goods store in downtown Champaign. At the time, sporting goods stores competed with hardware stores, and Bailey & Himes did its best to set itself apart with service. So when Trusner spoke to the clerk, a man named Rob Carlson, he told him the circumstances and exactly what the Ironmen needed. As Carlson hustled off to find the bats, Trusner worried that McClard might skimp on the bats. When the clerk brought out four, McClard eyed them up as only a former baseball coach can: a 35 Mantle, a 34 Mantle, and a pair of 33 Nellie Foxes.

"We'll take 'em," McClard said. "Let's go."

Trusner smiled. "All four?"

Aware of the situation, the clerk hustled them out the door, promising to send a bill to McClard. The total, paid out of school coffers later that month, was $20.40. It was the most the administration had spent on the baseball team all season.

The first two pitches from Cooper to Heneberry were pure gas. Heneberry fouled one off and watched the other go wide for a ball. From the bench, Shartzer yelled at him. "Keep it steady, Goose! Keep it steady!" When Cooper came back inside with another fastball, Heneberry took a shallow breath, cocked his elbow, and let it rip.

To his surprise, he made contact. The ball shot past the second baseman and into right field, deep enough to score a run. In the stands, the Macon students yelled as one. Tie game.

At the end of the fourth, the boys jogged back to the dugout, the game still tied. There, they were met by the smiling face of Trusner. He stood at the lip of the dugout brandishing four brand-new bats, including Shartzer's favorite, the Mickey Mantle K55.

As proud as Trusner was, one man appeared equally so. Behind the bench, McClard stood, arms crossed, wearing something the boys were unaccustomed to seeing on him: a smile.

With Heneberry on the mound, no inning was an easy one. In the bottom of the fourth, with the score tied 2–2, Abfalder came to the plate with runners on first and third and two outs. Instead of trying to jack one out of the park, though, Abfalder hit a perfect swinging bunt down the first base line. Glan charged the ball and, with no play at the plate, turned and threw as hard as he could to first. Unfortunately, Mark Miller had been playing deep at second and had to race to get to the bag, meaning the ball, Miller, and Abfalder all arrived at almost exactly the same time. Miller lunged for the bag while reaching back to spear the throw bare-handed. As he did, Abfalder, a rock of a boy who played fullback for the Bloomington football team, hit first at full speed. Instantly he transferred all that force into the small body of Miller. On the bench, Sweet cringed. In the stands, the Macon fans held their breath as Miller shot into the air and flew backward. Only, in a remarkable feat of coordination Heneberry would recount for decades afterward, rather than crashing to the ground, Miller somehow executed a perfect backward somersault and emerged holding the ball aloft in his right hand. The ump looked, paused, and then, with what Heneberry swears was extraordinary gusto, shouted "YERRRRR OUUT!" Macon was still tied.

Now it was the Ironmen's turn. In the top of the fifth inning, with Dale Otta on second base, Shartzer grabbed the K55 and strode to the plate. During two seasons of battling each other in American Legion summer ball, he'd come to detest Cooper for being so talented and confident. Now he stepped in and tried to time Big Coop's fastball. No luck. Cooper got two quick strikes on him. Shortening up on the bat, Shartzer fouled the ball off to stay alive, then fouled off another and another. He scowled out at the mound. One thought stuck in his mind: *That big bastard isn't striking me out.*

Cooper must have been tiring by now. Still, he unleashed another heater, and Shartzer got around on this one. The ball soared to the bottom of the left field fence. Otta tore around third to score and now, suddenly, the Ironmen had a 3–2 lead. In the stands, the Macon fans yelled, louder than Sweet had ever heard them. In the front row, Bob Shartzer and Dwight Glan couldn't believe it. *Six outs to go.*

After another scoreless inning from both teams it came down to this: the bottom of the seventh. Three outs for state.

Would Sweet call on Shartzer? Behind the backstop, a man wearing slacks and a short-sleeved button-down shirt and carrying a pencil and notebook watched and wondered. After two years of covering Macon over the phone, Joe Cook was only now seeing the Ironmen in person. Looking out at Sweet wearing what appeared to be a tie-dyed hat, he finally understood the grumblings. Ever since the end of the 1970 season, when Macon began winning, Cook had heard Decatur coaches complaining about Sweet. A conservative group, they thought it ridiculous that he allowed his players to have long hair, and more ridiculous that Sweet himself had it. "He's just a hippie with a bunch of farm boys," they told Cook. And at first, Cook had nodded along. Now, though, he wasn't so sure. After following Macon's route through the playoffs, and watching the team in action, he thought maybe the hippie coach knew more than he let on.

In this situation, though, Cook thought Sweet had to go to his ace. After all, Bloomington had already done so—what was stopping the Ironmen from doing the same? What's more, while Macon batted in the top of the seventh, Sweet had sent Shartzer down the right field line to warm up. Surely the coach would bring him in now, with so much at stake.

Instead, with a pat on the shoulder, Sweet sent Heneberry back out to the mound. Sweet didn't need to say anything; he knew he'd already sent the most powerful message he could. He'd warmed up Shartzer.

In two seasons under Sweet, Shartzer had never relieved Heneberry, just as Heneberry had never relieved Shartzer. Some boys might have itched to enter the game in the late innings, to ride in for the chance at glory, but that's not how it worked with the Ironmen, or with Shartzer and Heneberry. Each took pride in finishing what they started, and pushed the other to do the same.

Now Shartzer walked over to the mound and looked his friend in the eye. "Goddamit, suck it up and get this done," he said to Heneberry. "I don't need to come in and do your job, just like you didn't come in and do mine."

Heneberry nodded. This is how the boys had talked to each other for years. When Shartzer got in trouble in the past, it was Heneberry who sidled over to the mound. "Sharrrrk, your goddam fastball looks like a beach ball coming in there," he'd say. To which Shartzer would retort, "Good, you skinny bastard, I'm going to throw it in and let them pull it right at you." And of course Heneberry would then smile and said, "Yeah, baby, send it my way."

This was different, though. This wasn't some podunk game on a crappy field against a bunch of farm boys. This was a chance to go to state. Still, Shartzer was right. This was no time for overthinking. *Just suck it up and get this done.*

Bloomington sent up the top of its order in the seventh. Heneberry responded with a fusillade of curveballs. Down went lead-off hitter Brian Burd. *Just suck it up and get it done.*

Then, solid contact. Bloomington had a man on second base. *Shit.*

Up strode Cooper. Heneberry heard Bob Shartzer's voice in his head. He knew what he was supposed to do: Pitch around him. Instead, Heneberry unleashed a big, beautiful curveball. Strike one!

Cooper had been ahead of the pitch but he was too good a hitter not to adjust. *No way I can get three in a row by him*, Heneberry thought. He looked in and, behind the plate, Dean Otta was doing something unusual. Between his legs, Otta had put down two fingers. He was calling a pitch.

Heneberry shook him off. Again, Otta put down two fingers. *Throw the curve.* Again, Heneberry shook him off.

And so, with a man in scoring position, Heneberry came set and threw a fastball right down the pipe. Cooper wasn't fooled. He reared back and swung for the fences. There was a loud *crack*. Heneberry felt sick to his stomach. Only, instead of soaring over his head, the ball shot into the backstop. Cooper had been dead on it and barely missed the pitch, fouling it straight back.

Now Heneberry knew what to do. This is what he'd spent all those afternoons in the backyard preparing for. At 0–2, he knew Cooper would expect him to waste a pitch. Heneberry looked over at Sweet. Sweet nodded back at him.

In the back of his mind, Heneberry heard Bob Shartzer: *Don't pitch to him.* In the front of his mind, unavoidable, he heard Steve Shartzer, who was standing near third and of a different mind than his father. "Finish him right now, Goose!" Steve yelled. "Finish this big bastard off!"

Heneberry kicked and delivered. The ball hung and then dropped out of the sky. Cooper unleashed a mighty swing. *Strike three!*

Behind the Macon bench, Jack Heneberry nodded and clapped. All his boy needed was one more out for state.

On the Bloomington bench, the players watched as Abfalder walked to the plate. A different thought no doubt ran through their minds: *One big swing and we're headed to state.*

Heneberry started out nibbling at the edge of the plate again and soon it was 2–2. *One strike away.* With a runner in scoring position, Heneberry didn't want to take any chances; he had to end it on a strikeout. He went to his best pitch, a curveball that would tail inside to the left-handed Abfalder.

Heneberry rocked, kicked, and fired. The ball tailed, just as it was supposed to. Only Abfalder did something he wasn't supposed to. With an inside-out swing, he pulled the ball, crushing it on the ground toward right field. At first base, Glan dove but couldn't get a glove on the ball. Heneberry's heart sank. Once the ball got to the outfield, the Bloomington runner, already on the move, would score. He'd been one strike away and blown it.

And then from out of nowhere darted the form of Mark Miller. To this day, Heneberry has no idea how his friend covered that much ground. Out of respect for Abfalder's power, Miller had played the slugger exceptionally deep, standing on the edge of the outfield grass. Now, moving to his left, he speared the ball in short right as if snagging a passing bullet. Turning to throw to first, he encountered one small issue: No one was there. Glan lay prone where his dive had taken him, a plume of dust encircling his head. Meanwhile Heneberry, caught up in the moment, was standing like a statue on the mound. *He'd forgotten to cover the base.* All the while, Abfalder steamed down the line. With no other choice, Miller sprinted toward first.

For the second time in the game, the two were on a collision course. Abfalder lunged. Miller leapt. Years later, Shartzer would call the sequence "one of the top three plays I've ever been on the field for." Considering Shartzer's career, that would count as high praise indeed.

By the slimmest of margins, Miller beat Abfalder to the bag, then slipped past him. Then, like a running back seeing daylight, Miller kept right on going as chaos erupted around him, sprinting through a hole in the fence all the way to the team bus.

Heneberry followed, running as hard as he could, the roar of the Macon fans trailing him. Vaulting up the bus stairs, Heneberry saw Miller, who was standing in the aisle grinning, the ball still gripped in his right hand. Miller lifted it up and stuffed it into Heneberry's right hand while grabbing his friend's shoulder. "State, baby, state!" he shouted.

Back on the diamond, the Macon fans were going nuts. Students rushed the field, swarming around Sweet. Parents walloped each other on the back, legs still shaky from the back-and-forth drama. Dick Jacobs, a Macon Little League coach, turned to his fifty-eight-year-old father, Myrtle. "Dad," Dick said. "You got any more of those heart pills?"

His father looked at him, surprised. "Why?"

"I think I need one."

On the Bloomington bench, coach Bob Spahn slumped, disbelieving. Macon had finished with only four hits but still managed to win. On the field, the remaining Ironmen leapt and hugged and woo-hooed as only sixteen-year-old boys can. All except Shartzer, that is. He stood gripping his left wrist and grimacing. The injury had occurred in the fifth inning. After his RBI double, Shartzer tried to score on a single to the outfield. Halfway down the line, he realized he wasn't going to beat the throw. So he did what any super-competitive athlete would: He tried to vault the catcher.

Hurtling through the air, Shartzer had turned in an attempt to reach back and touch home plate. Before he could, he was tagged out. Then, milliseconds later, he'd landed and felt a sharp pain. In breaking his fall he'd fractured a bone in his left hand.

There was no time to worry about that, though. Out of the seven hundred high schools in Illinois, Macon was one of only eight that were now headed to Peoria.

It was a bus ride they'd remember the rest of their years. Shartzer sat in the back, hand clenched to his side, whooping like a pirate. Sweet was right there with him. The boys clapped, laughed, and roared. And then, somewhere along the hour-long drive, Stu started singing.

In a bus full of giddy boys, the sound cut through the air, high and pure. Stu was the lead in all the plays and sang in choir. Decades later, his son would front a rock band, his voice just as sweet and melodic as his father's.

They all recognized it instantly: the first song from *Jesus Christ Superstar*. Within seconds, Stu had company. First it was Jeff Glan, his voice almost as pure as Stu's. And then the rest of the boys joined.

It was their song now. So when the line "You really do believe this talk of God is true" came on, the boys instead sang, "You really do believe this talk of state is true." And instead of, "When do we ride into Jerusalem?", the boys sang "When do we ride into Peoria?" Soon, they were joined by the tape player, situated in the middle of the bus as always, where Trusner was in charge of operating it. When "King Herod's Song" came on, Shartzer yelled "Take it away, Sam!" and Trusner leapt into the aisle to play the meanest air piano you've ever seen. And on it went, the bus rumbling through the gloaming of an Illinois spring night, a chorus of voices rising from the open windows. In the midst of it all, a dark-haired man who'd never intended to be a baseball coach closed his eyes for a moment and smiled.

16

Riding into Peoria

News travels fast in a town the size of Macon. By the time the players returned it seemed everyone knew: *The Ironmen were going to state!* Meetings were interrupted, card games stopped middeal. A small cheer went up at the Country Manor when the news was announced. This was big—*real* big. Macon was the kind of town where, when the fire siren on the water tower went off, it was common to see a good portion of the townspeople grabbing their kids, hopping in their cars, and following the fire trucks to witness the blaze themselves, even if it was the middle of the night. Usually, the height of excitement every year was the Macon Playday, held every summer in the small park across from Wiles Grocery Store and featuring food booths, Dunk the Dummy, a parade, and a Little Miss Macon baby contest. But going to state? As Jack Stringer would later say, "That was the most exciting thing to hit Macon that anyone could remember."

The team had nearly a week to savor the feeling before leaving for the tournament the following Wednesday. On Sunday, the Decatur *Herald & Review* named Steve Shartzer the area Player of the Year. His stats were impressive, even by high school standards: a .412 batting average with forty-seven RBIs in nineteen games. As a pitcher he was 8–1 with a 1.74 ERA and eighty-one strikeouts in sixty-one innings. The Coach of the Year came as more of a surprise to some, especially the old coaches in Decatur. His name was Lynn Sweet and, according to the *Herald & Review,* his mod style was "a topic of conversation."

Sweet marveled at how popular he'd suddenly become. All those parents who'd disapproved of his methods, all the school board members who thought him too rebellious, too wild, too different? Now they patted him on the back. "Good luck at state!" they yelled in his ear. "Way to go L.C.!" they roared while offering to buy him beers at the same bars they'd chastised him for frequenting only months earlier. A different type of man might have taken the opportunity to turn a cold shoulder, to exact verbal revenge. Sweet? He accepted the congratulations and patted back. He drank the beers and bought the next round.

As the week wore on, Shartzer's hand continued to swell. Concerned, his parents took him to a local doctor, who confirmed what Steve already knew: His hand was out of commission. Treatment was discussed but Shartzer would have none of it. "What are you going to do, rub out a broken bone?" he asked.

The way he saw it, since the injury was on his nonthrowing hand it was irrelevant. He'd be fine to pitch, and could make do in the field. Hitting might be a challenge, but one he was certain he could overcome. After all, he had no other choice.

Across town, another member of the Ironmen dealt with a different diagnosis. All week, Brian Snitker had kept tabs on his father, who remained under observation at St. Mary's hospital. The heart attack had occurred on the night of the Bloomington game. While the kids rode back on the bus, Dick Snitker drove the same road in the family station wagon, his wife, Catherine, beside him and Brian's two younger sisters, Angela and Andrea, in the backseat.

Halfway back to Macon, Dick had complained of shooting pains in his arms. Upon returning home, he'd gone straight to bed while Catherine called their doctor, who hurried to the Snitkers' two-story house on West Hight Street in southwest Macon. Upstairs he found

Dick Snitker lying in bed, looking pale but claiming to be just fine. He just had some chest pain, that was all. The doctor disagreed: "We need to get you to a hospital, Dick."

The next morning, Dick Snitker got the news. He'd suffered a minor heart attack and would need to stay in the hospital for a week, maybe longer.

Dick was not pleased. Over the course of the season, the Snitkers had grown especially close to the team. With the rare exception of when Dick was on the road for work, they'd attended every game, and their home had become the Ironmen's unofficial hangout. Almost every evening, Brian brought home teammates to eat his mom's cooking—spaghetti one night, fried chicken and fresh corn from the Wells farm the next. It got so the boys didn't even knock on the Snitker front door, they just ambled in. Stu Arnold even said "Hi, Mom, hi, Dad!"

While the boys came for Catherine's dinners, the baseball parents came for the company. Dick was personable and took entertaining seriously, as any man who's worked for Jim Beam and Pabst might. His refrigerator was always thick with beer and one wall of his garage constituted both his work inventory and the largest liquor cabinet in central Illinois. Over two seasons' worth of drinks and meals, the Snitkers had come to view the players and their parents as one big extended family. The fact that Dick had helped engineer Sweet's return to coaching only cemented the bond.

And now the doctors were telling Dick that he had to stay in the hospital during the tournament. Even though his own son would be playing. Even though only eight teams in the entire state of Illinois made it. Even though no one in their right mind ever expected a team from Macon to go this far.

At 5 P.M. on Tuesday, the eve of the Ironmen's trip to Peoria, the phone rang at the Heneberry house. When Betty Heneberry answered, she looked surprised. She told the caller to hold on, then walked to the backyard, where John and Dean Otta were playing a lazy game of catch.

"It's for you, John."

John tossed the ball to Dean and jogged in, expecting to hear one of his cousins from Decatur on the other end of the line. But when he picked up the phone, he heard not a Heneberry but the scratchy voice of an adult.

"John, this is Joe Cook from the Decatur *Herald & Review*. I'd like to talk to you about the state tournament."

Heneberry froze. He'd played three sports at Macon for the better part of four years, but this was the first time anyone from a newspaper had wanted to talk to him. Hell, not even the *Ironmen Scene* had interviewed him. He had, he realized, no idea what to say. Should he try to sound like the athletes he read about in the paper? Should he mimic Shartzer, whom he'd seen interviewed once or twice? Or should he just answer the questions to the best of his ability?

After a moment of indecision, he settled on the final strategy. So when Cook asked, "Do you think you can play with the bigger schools up at state?" John answered as honestly as he could. And when Cook followed that up with, "You mean you think you can win the state championship?" John answered that one best he could, too.

Then Heneberry hung up and walked back out to the yard, confident he'd acquitted himself well.

The following day, the Ironmen walked out of the Macon High gym toward the bus and, to their surprise, found a receiving line waiting for them. One teacher after another clasped their hands and patted them on the back, wishing them good luck. Then came a row of administrators, each as serious as the next, hands extended. Dale Otta remembers being taken aback, because the administrators *never* shook their hands. He felt like he was going off to war.

One by one, they climbed up into the bus. At the wheel was Phiz Adams, a honest-to-goodness actual bus driver. As he pulled the bus onto 51 headed north, it was joined by a succession of cars. From the air, it must have looked like a motorcade. Otta looked out the rear window, marveling at the sight. There was Bob Shartzer's white Ford Fairlane and Britton's sedan and Bob Taylor's car, his son Scott wedged into the backseat. Ironmen flags ruffled out windows, horns honked. It looked like an entire town just got married.

From Macon, the bus headed through Decatur and then continued northwest toward Peoria, cutting through a landscape of fledgling cornfields. On the drive, the boys talked about the teams they might face and bragged about the suitcases they'd brought, for this was the first time many would stay overnight at a hotel. With some prodding, Jeff Glan stood up and did his best imitation of Burns imitating Patton. Then, it was on to reciting lines from a speech by legendary University of Illinois football coach Ray Eliot.

"If you think you're beaten, you are," Glan bellowed, addressing the back of the bus. "If you think you dare not, you don't. If you'd like to win but think you can't, it's almost a cinch that you won't."

Glan paused, looked around, raised the volume. "Life's battles don't always go to the stronger or faster man. But sooner or later the fellow who wins is the fellow who thinks he can. It's all a state of mind."

Glancing around the bus, Sweet thought about how close the boys had become. A few rows behind him, Heneberry did the same. As one of only five seniors, he felt the weight of the trip more than most. Sitting there, watching endless green rows of soybeans slide past, he thought about how he'd probably never wear a uniform again. He thought about how much he loved the boys around him, this team, and being a baseball player. He thought about how when he hung up his uniform it would be time to go get a job, and how some of his older friends were already talking about draft numbers for the war. And, as he had before the season, he thought of how it was, as he says, "my last time to be a kid."

A more majestic sight they'd never seen.

It was as if Phiz Adams had pulled that old yellow bus off the highway and right into the driveway of Shangri-La. The façade towered over them, lights shining down, a peaked turret piercing the sky. JUMER'S CASTLE LODGE, it said. All David Wells could do was stare.

Wells had grown up on a farm near Macon where electricity was sporadic and hot water nonexistent. He'd never been to a city like Peoria. To say Jumer's blew his mind would be an understatement. It was not only the first hotel he'd ever checked into, it was one of the grandest buildings he'd ever entered.

Even the handful of Macon boys who'd stayed in hotels were in awe, for Jumer's was not a hotel so much as an experience. Opened a year earlier, it featured Bavarian architecture, high-class service, and all manner of unusual antiques. A giant stuffed black bear, arms upraised and teeth bared, greeted visitors in the lounge. Uniformed members of the hotel's four hundred employees hustled by. Hallways led off in seemingly every direction, leading to the hotel's 168 rooms. Sweet had to hand it to Britton and the rest of the administration—they'd finally come up big for the baseball team. By the end of the tournament, Macon High's coffers would cover $653.50 in lodging, meals, and other expenses at Jumer's.

The Ironmen arrived at 5 P.M. At six, Wells was still in the shower, reveling in the exotic stream of warm water. Meanwhile, the Otta twins explored the grounds, for neither had ever spent a night in a hotel. Trusner stood in the gift shop, horrified by the prices it was charging for seemingly mundane items such as a comb or a bag of peanuts. Nearby, Sweet found his own Shangri-La in the large, roomy bar where, he'd received word, the coach's drinks would be paid for by the school.

Eight miles down the road, seven baseball teams gathered at 7 P.M. at the Heritage House, a buffet-style restaurant. Quincy was there, as were Nashville and Rockford West, along with Waukegan, Piasa Southwestern, Kankakee Eastridge, and, for the second year in a row, Lane Tech High of Chicago. Dozens of baseball players wearing blazers and ties filed into a large room and took their seats, quietly sizing each other up. Peoria mayor E. Michael O'Brien welcomed the boys, then turned the microphone over to the tournament managers and, finally, featured speaker Johnny Klippstein, a former big league pitcher who now scouted for the Tigers. Dinner was served, speeches were made. The boys fidgeted in their seats.

Off to the side, one table was conspicuously empty.

The welcome banquet was only one of numerous scheduled tournament events. There was a barbecue Thursday night after the games and, for the players, a continuous loop of World Series highlights at the Holiday Inn. The Illinois High School Baseball Coaches Association was holding an annual golf tournament and a smoker. For the press, there was a reception at the Ramada. And of course there were all manner of unofficial parties. For many, the tournament was as much a social event as a sporting one, and coaches and fans came from around the state just to be part of all the activities.

Sweet intended to participate in as few as possible. He didn't see any reason to intimidate the boys right off the bat. He knew the other teams would be full of tall, talented kids. He knew they'd have two dozen players each. He knew they'd wear nice clothes and talk about big-city things and past appearances in the sectionals and at state. He didn't see much his boys could gain from that experience.

That's why he'd booked Jumer's Castle Lodge instead of the preferred tournament hotels. Here, the boys could stay in their bubble. Here they could maintain their optimism. And here, Sweet could drink beers at the bar without having to talk to any hard-ass coaches who would undoubtedly question his hair, experience, and acumen. It seemed an easy decision.

While the other boys checked out the swimming pool and played cards, Shartzer gripped the bed in his room. His breath came in short bursts. His face was red, his eyes watered. He tried to force air down his throat.

The coughing fits began when he was a boy. When he was six years old, his parents carted him to a top hospital in St. Louis. "Your son has a bad case of asthma," the doctors said.

It seemed unfair to Steve. His whole life revolved around sports, around being the strongest, the most indomitable. And here he was, felled by a stupid cough. The attacks hit at the worst times. He could be on the mound or at a football game, and then, suddenly, he felt like he was suffocating.

When Primatene Mist came out in 1963, it was a godsend, and as he'd gotten older the attacks became less frequent. By high school, he was sure he'd grown out of it. Yet every once in a while the asthma flared up. Sometimes it was dust, or the humidity.

After what seemed like hours, the air trickled back in. Slowly, he regained his wind. And then, moments later, it was sucked right back out again. By the time he rolled out of bed in the morning, Shartzer had slept only three hours.

Mark Miller walked in at breakfast, grimaced, and handed a copy of the Decatur *Herald & Review* to John Heneberry.

John unfolded the sports page and scanned it until he saw Joe Cook's mugshot, the lank brown hair combed over his forehead. The headline on his column read "Macon Players Supremely Confident." John began to read:

> *Macon and Nashville, opponents this morning in the opening game of the Illinois state high school baseball finals at Peoria, aren't exactly strangers. At least the seniors on the clubs aren't. Kaskaskia Junior College of Centralia, in a recruiting venture, invited the upperclassmen of both teams to visit its campus Monday.*
>
> *The players wasted little time in sizing up each other. Macon pitcher* John *Heneberry said afterward: "I don't think they [Nashville] were impressed by us and I know we weren't impressed by them. The one thing they have going for them is size."*
>
> *The Macon boys are confident. In fact, you wonder if they might be taking Nashville (14–9) too lightly. "I know we'll beat Nashville," said Heneberry, "and I think we'll win the tournament. I don't know the other teams in the tournament, but I know mine."*

Heneberry finished reading, then looked back up to see Miller shaking his head. "I can't believe you said that, John."

Reading it again, Heneberry couldn't either. He'd just answered honestly. He didn't mean it to sound like that.

If the Ironmen were supremely confident in their chances, they were the only ones. At the press reception the night before, the Peoria *Journal Star* had asked twenty-six writers, baseball luminaries, and radio and TV reporters who they thought would win the state tournament. Not one had picked the Ironmen. Judging by the votes, only a handful thought they'd even win one game.

Here's how it broke down:

1971 State Tournament Poll by Illinois Sports Writers
(Number of first-place votes in parentheses)

Chicago Lane Tech (19)	... 200
Waukegan (2)	... 148
Rockford West (1)	... 148
Quincy (3)	... 130
Kankakee Eastridge (1)	... 112
Macon	... 88
Nashville	... 60
Piasa Southwestern	... 45

So unexpected was the Ironmen's tournament appearance that even the organizers appeared to be caught off-guard.

The official tournament program was a handsome booklet. It cost twenty-five cents, was forty-one pages long, and was chock-full of photos. Inside, there were portraits of IHSA administrators, each as serious and clean-cut as the next. There were scorecards and tournament records and pages and pages of ads. Peoria Motors hawked a car called the Pinto, advertising it as "for the Young at Heart," while the Ramada Inn offered "Resort Atmosphere in Downtown Peoria."

Nearly every tournament qualifier had its own page, complete with a team photo and a roster listing each player's height, weight, position, age, and batting average. Except for Macon, that is. For the Ironmen there was only a half a page of information and no team photo or stats. The players' heights, weights, and ages were listed, but a casual reader could be forgiven for thinking that the school had mistakenly submitted its jayvee roster. The team boasted more underclassmen (eight) than upperclassmen (seven) and had no one over six feet or 160 pounds (and only Shartzer at both).

The rest of the tournament field was littered with figurative and literal heavyweights, teams with twenty-plus players, a handful of whom were built like men at six-foot-one or six-foot-two and 180 to 200 pounds. Quincy High entered the tourney with a 25–9 record and boasted a six-foot-five, 195-pound catcher named Craig Kroeter who'd hit .365. Rockford West was 25–4 and had an enrollment of 2,750. Waukegan High was making its eighth appearance at the tournament, and its photo looked more like a class reunion than a baseball team; including coaches there were thirty faces staring back.

Piasa Southwestern, Kankakee Eastridge, and Nashville were all making inaugural trips to the tourney, but their lineups were stacked. Eastridge had a junior ace named Jeff Scott who sported an ERA of 1.69 and had already pitched four shutouts, two no-hitters, and a perfect game during the season. Nashville had one of the top five major league prospects in the state, a speedy center fielder named Rick Keller. And then of course there was Lane Tech, which was now tied with Peoria Manual for the most trips to state, with ten.

If Tech won, it would continue a staggering run of dominance for Chicago-area schools, which had triumphed in twenty of the thirty-one years the IHSA had held the tournament. Across Illinois sports, the Chicago stranglehold had become even more pronounced of late. Of the twenty-six state titles in all boys' sports over the past three years, only three had been won by teams outside the Chicago metro area.

By most any measure, Macon got lucky in the first-round draw. At 405 students, Nashville was the second-smallest school in the tournament, though it still had nearly twice Macon's enrollment. The two teams were scheduled to face off in the tournament opener, at 9:30 A.M. on Thursday. The winners of the four first-round games would advance to the semifinals Friday morning, from which two teams would survive and battle for the state title at 4:30 on Friday afternoon.

For two days, the eyes of Illinois would be upon Peoria.

It was already warm when Sweet headed out to his car at 7:30 A.M. on the morning of Thursday, June 3. Outside Jumer's he met up with a bleary-eyed Shartzer and the two headed to the campus of Bradley University. Tournament officials required that Shartzer get his hand taped prior to the first game.

Not that the mandate did much good. Within half an hour Shartzer had cut off the tape and gauze with a pocketknife, a move he would later explain to tournament umpires as necessary because the tape was "restrictive."

Later in the day, when Lane Tech took the field, the stands would fill with fans and the scouts would come out en masse—twenty-two from major league teams as well as fifteen college coaches. Meinen Field would take on the air of a college game. At 8:45 A.M., however, it was still relatively quiet, the grass still dewy from the night before.

Upon arriving, the Macon boys walked out and, much as they had a year earlier at Fans Field, took a minute to revel in the surroundings. The infield was combed dirt, the outfield flat and well-groomed. Bleachers lined either foul line, and stanchions of lights looked down on the field. The fence was deeper than any they'd played on all year and seemed miles away: 337 feet in left, 373 feet in center, and 335 in right. Appraising it, sophomore left fielder David Wells turned to Stu Arnold. "Hey Stu, how far are we supposed to play from that fence?"

Arnold peered out, thought for a moment. "I don't know. I think I'm going to play back. It's easier to run in than out."

Fifteen minutes later, at a little after 9 A.M., the sounds of *Jesus Christ Superstar* filtered into the morning. It was almost time.

They kept coming. As gametime approached, cars pulled up, honking as they unloaded friends, parents, and siblings. Even though it was a workday, more than two hundred people had made the drive from Macon. As always, Dale Otta scanned the faces from his position at shortstop. And, as always, he hoped to see his father.

In Dale's entire playing career, from Little League to his senior year, his father had never attended one of his and Dean's games. Dwight Otta worked on commission as a milk truck driver for Meadow Gold, leaving before 6 A.M. every morning and returning around 8 P.M. At night, he'd sit at the kitchen table for another hour punching away at his adding machine, making sure the day's receipts totaled out. On weekends Dwight worked all day on Saturday and spent the bulk of Sunday sleeping. In his free time, he also managed to be a pillar of the Macon community. He served on committees, joined the city council, and was later elected mayor and, after that, town fire chief, which required him to sleep at the firehouse every other night (because someone needed to answer the phone). One thing he never found time for, however, was his youngest sons' games.

Dale had never played catch with his dad, or talked baseball, or pored over a scorecard together. In the mornings, his mother made breakfast and then he and Dean walked to school from their house on Front Street. If it was winter, they trudged through the snow in the dark. When they needed a lift somewhere, or someone to teach them to throw a curveball, they looked not to their father but to their older brother, Ron. When Dale went sledding, it was on an old car hood that Ron hooked up to his bumper and pulled around town, and Dale still proudly displays the chipped tooth he got when he once went sailing off the sled. As much as his brothers took care of him, though, Dale saw the roles the other fathers played and tried not to be disappointed. He knew his father was a busy man.

Now, Dale looked up and recognized teachers, townspeople, and a handful of Macon students, and then he saw him, sitting in the back of the bleachers and wearing a dress shirt. Dwight Otta had asked for a day off from Meadow Gold, apologized to his customers, and left the house early to make the two-hour drive from Macon. His sons were in the state tourney. He needed to be there. He smiled at Dale, who smiled back, nearly bursting with pride.

On the mound, Shartzer slipped on his glove, wincing as he did. He thought about keeping the glove in front of him to knock down balls if he needed to. He thought about the asthma attack the night before, worrying that it would drain his stamina. He thought about the fans. And then, as he always did, he cleared it all out of his mind and thought about one thing only: *Here it comes boys, the best that I got.*

Eighty miles from Peoria, Dick Snitker lay propped in his hospital bed, a transistor radio tuned to the game. Two hours later, at exactly 11:30 A.M., the nurses at St. Mary's heard a strange noise coming from Mr. Snitker's room. It sounded like . . . cheering.

He had good reason. In the first round of the state tournament, propelled by a two-for-three day at the plate from a sophomore named

Brian Snitker, Macon had defeated Nashville by a score of 5–0. The Ironmen were headed to the semis.

In Peoria, Shartzer walked off the mound. Teammates and parents swarmed, patting him on the back. He'd thrown seven masterful innings, allowing four hits and striking out eight.

As elated at the other boys were, Shartzer felt more relieved than anything. His fastball had been off all game, so for the first time in ages he'd had to rely on his curve, telegraphed grunts and all. Despite his injured wrist, he'd been able to field the ball and even gotten one hit. He'd made it through.

While the players gathered their gear, an IHSA official shepherded Sweet to a makeshift tent area for a postgame press conference. The state tournament was big news in Illinois, and treated as such by the media. Papers from across the state sent reporters, as did radio stations. It wasn't uncommon for results to merit banner headlines in the sports sections, even in papers as large as the Chicago *Tribune*, which regularly put tournament stories ahead of Cubs games.

As Sweet began taking questions, a cluster of reporters gathered around—Charles Chamberlain from the Associated Press, Phil Theobald from the Peoria *Journal Star,* and a half-dozen others. It took only one quote to start them furiously scribbling.

"I guess you could say I'm more of a sponsor," Sweet said when asked about his coaching strategy. "I'm not a coach, and I don't intend to stay in coaching." Asked about his background, he claimed that he had "watched a lot of baseball on TV."

The hair? "If the kids want long hair, I let them grow it," he said. "We're a team of individuals and I don't see that we have to look alike. I don't see what long hair has to do with playing baseball anyway."

The scribbling became more frantic.

What about fundamentals, someone asked.

"We don't emphasize fundamentals," Sweet said. "We just let

them have fun. There is really not much I could tell them. They've all played a lot of baseball and know the game as well as I do."

And on it went, Sweet covering his personal style: "Yes, I've had some static about my long hair and mustache. Not everybody understands." His team's chances: "Actually, we had a better team last year because we had more pitching. But this one will do. We may be living on borrowed time, but we're not scared of anyone." His attitude: "I don't like the win or die attitude. We set our goals to have a good time and learn some baseball." His disciplinary style: "I would never bawl out a boy for making a mistake. I've seen coaches chew a kid out right in front of the fans. I don't go for that."

Normally, a postgame presser lasts only a few minutes, but in this case the reporters only crowded closer. This was gold. For his part, Sweet appeared to be enjoying himself. His teaching style? Why, yes, he had something to say about that. "It's a carryover from my classroom procedure. I can't make a kid do anything, but I can suggest an alternative."

"Has there been any backlash?" one of the reporters asked.

"Sure, I've gotten a few letters from some of the members of the community," Sweet said. "Let them talk about how we look, but I don't think they could find one kid on this team that doesn't have around a B average and isn't aiming to go to college. It's all theater to us. We're togetherness."

And, finally, the line that really cracked up the players the next day, in response to how the farm boys from Macon practiced: "I'll come out and say, 'I think we ought to have a practice today,'" Sweet said. "If there are six or seven kids who don't want to practice, we call it off. Most of the time, though, they want to practice. It isn't that the kids are lazy or anything. But somebody might have to go to the dentist or somebody else's pigs might be out. So we'll go chase pigs."

A pig-chasing coach? The reporters couldn't get back to their typewriters quick enough.

While Sweet entertained the media, a number of the boys lingered at the field to watch the start of the Lane Tech game. This turned out to be a poor idea. In the span of twenty minutes, the boys witnessed two things they'd never seen before in high school. First, during warm-ups, the Lane Tech right fielder, a boy named Richie Coleman, unleashed a throw from deep in the outfield that sailed so far it put a dent in the top of the backstop at Meinen Field. Then, on the first pitch of the game, Lane's John Rockwell crushed a home run to left field that soared over the fence and onto Highway 74, the road that arced around the field. Those present later estimated the ball traveled more than 400 feet. Heneberry remembers watching it and thinking he'd never seen a ball hit that far in high school. He remembers feeling like Macon might be in deep shit. And he remembers realizing that, if Lane did win, he would be the one to face Rockwell and company the next morning.

A few minutes later, the boys and their parents headed back to their respective hotels to get some rest. As they did, a thin, quiet man carrying a small yellow notepad stayed behind. He had work to do.

Back at Jumer's, Trusner was on the move. Going room to room he collected and marked each player's uniform, then rode the elevator to the lobby, headed for the Laundromat.

As he stood in the elevator, a bundle of dirty uniforms in his arms, a woman stared at him. It was one of the Lane Tech mothers.

"Why don't you just wear your other set of uniforms?" she asked.

Trusner looked at her. "Ma'am, we don't have another set. This set doesn't even match."

It was true. That they even matched as closely as they did—the colors a pastiche of purple and other hues—was due to Trusner's last-minute run to the sporting goods store before the tournament to pick up more pants with black pinstripes. He figured those looked the most purple.

Across town that same afternoon, Bill McClard no doubt couldn't believe what had happened. He'd finally jumped with both feet into this baseball thing. He'd driven up to Peoria on Wednesday and stayed at a hotel along with Burns, Stringer, and a bunch of others. (Though he'd made sure to charge the twenty-four dollars in travel to the school expenses under "principal travel, baseball tourney.") He'd slugged back beers and talked and laughed. Then he got up early Thursday morning and headed to the Nashville game where, to his great surprise and delight, the Ironmen actually won. Caught up in the moment just like the rest, McClard cheered and rooted as he sweated right through his dress shirt. And then it must have hit him: The win meant the Ironmen would play again the following morning in the semis. If by some miracle the boys won that game, they would play in the finals at 4:30 on Friday, June 4.

This would be wonderful. It would bring glory to the school. It would also give him a headache. A week earlier, when planning Macon High's end-of-the-year school schedule, McClard had slated graduation for the evening of June 4 at 8 P.M. At the time, he couldn't imagine any possible conflict.

Now, he began to worry. That is, until he received the news: As expected, Lane Tech had won its first game in the tournament over Piasa Southwestern, which meant Macon would be facing the best team in the state of Illinois in the second round. Graduation would not be an issue.

17

The Baseball Factory

In home after home in Macon, people began packing and making calls: "Macon is playing Lane Tech!" If you didn't know better, you'd have thought a hurricane was bearing down on the town, so frenzied was the activity. Those who hadn't already gone up to Peoria started finding ways to do so. Farmers closed up their barns, business owners stuck CLOSED FOR TOURNAMENT signs in their windows. Cathy Schley, who worked as a nurse at a hospital in Decatur, started thinking of what excuse to use when calling in sick for work the following morning. After some thought, she decided on diarrhea. No one argued with diarrhea.

To the students at Macon High, Lane Tech was so exotic-sounding it might as well have been the capital of a foreign country. A school in Chicago with fifty-two hundred boys? Who knew such a thing existed.

Indeed, the two schools could scarcely be more different. Founded in 1908 as a training school for boys, Lane Tech at first offered courses in cabinetmaking, foundry, and welding. By the twenties, it had broadened its curriculum considerably. Its music program was designed by Chicago Symphony Orchestra director Frederick Stock, and the Lane print shop turned out a daily four-page paper and a monthly fifty-six-page magazine. By the late thirties, Lane had moved to a new campus, and at nine thousand, the student population was so vast that classes had to be held in shifts.

From the start, Lane dominated Chicago sports. To walk its halls is to see row upon row of plaques, the spoils from hundreds of city championships in a variety of sports. Its most famous athletic alum was Johnny Weissmuller, who won five gold medals over the course of two Olympics, set sixty-seven world records, and later went on to star in the Tarzan movie series. Lane's football program turned out pro players, including Fritz Pollard, who was later inducted into the NFL Hall of Fame as the league's first African American head coach. The athletic department's crown gem, however, was baseball. The program produced over twenty major league players, won dozens of city titles, and was a regular at the state tournament.

Whereas only a handful of new players came out for the team each season at Macon High, baseball was survival of the fittest at Lane. In the spring, prospective players were judged like prime livestock, run through a variety of tests under the watchful eye of the seniors. The competition was staggering. Greg Walsh remembers being handed a tag that read 431 when he came out as a freshman. Next to him, a boy named Richie Coleman received 432. Walsh was taken aback. He turned toward the man doling out the numbers. "We thought these were only freshman tryouts," he said.

"These *are* freshman tryouts," the man responded.

As opposed to Macon, where the boys grew up together, the Lane Tech team was essentially a Chicago-land All-Star squad pulled from a host of feeder schools, and most players had never met until the first day of practice. If it was too wet to go outside, the players ran in the hallways, which were so vast that the track team was said to occasionally hold the 4×100 relay inside.

Lane's head coach was Ed Papciak, a large bespectacled man with a pendulous gut. Though able to both instill fear and command respect, Papciak was not the most strategic of coaches. He had only one sign, a brush down his left arm to tell a player to steal. (At one point, one of his players said, "Coach, maybe you want to mix it up, use an indicator," prompting Papciak to do just that. But since he still only had the one sign, only now preceded by an indicator, opponents eventually figured it out and began pitching out upon seeing the indicator.)

Not that it mattered. With so much talent, Papciak didn't need to employ much in the way of strategy. So dominant was Lane that it routinely won city league games by a dozen runs. Even so, Papciak was a notorious griper—about his field, his players, and his resources.

There wasn't much for Papciak to complain about in 1971, though. In this, Lane's record-tying tenth trip to the tourney, the team was as talented as ever. Its lineup was full of major league prospects, all of whom were excellent dead fastball hitters, their timing honed from summers playing on semipro teams. Ranked first in Illinois entering the year, Tech had started slow, going 6–4 to open the season. Then team captain and star pitcher Mark "Wronk" Wronkiewicz held a players-only meeting, after which the team went on a tear. By the time of the semifinal against Macon, Lane boasted a 32–5 record.

Now, after an unexpectedly tough 2–1 win over Piasa Southwestern that had infuriated Papciak—"we hit like a bunch of minis out there today," he told reporters—Lane was two games from fulfilling its destiny. The only team the players viewed as a threat was Waukegan, which was in the other bracket. It's fair to say that Macon, with its hippie coach, tiny roster, and number two pitcher slated to take the mound, did not. Even that hippie coach appeared to know what he was in for. As Sweet was quoted as saying in the Thursday afternoon *Herald & Review*: "Lane Tech will have to go to sleep for us to beat them."

It was not the only time Sweet appeared in the papers that afternoon and the following morning. The Tech-Macon semifinal may have been a monumental mismatch, but that only made it irresistible to reporters, who couldn't get enough of Macon and, in particular, Sweet. Phil Theobald of the Peoria *Journal Star* wrote that Sweet "wouldn't stand out in your local commune." Another scribe said that Sweet "picked up his coaching methods from the L. C. Sweet Coaching Manual, with contributions from Dave Meggyesy, Rennie Davis, and Timothy Leary." Another went even further, describing Sweet as "a pinch of a bad Mexican hombre, a fun-loving Joe Pepitone, and a collegiate peacenik," as well as a "liberalized, long-haired, mustachioed thinking pinko" who if he "ever got too close to a police van at a protest mop-up . . . would find himself in need of a lawyer." Others just ran a virtual transcript of Sweet's comments the previous day.

Sweet read the coverage and smiled. He was amazed at how well his little press conference had gone over. His immediate goal had been to draw attention away from the players. He didn't want them bothered, becoming anxious about the media or having to answer for the hats and hair. He also knew that all the ridiculous coverage—and the feelings it engendered among rival teams and coaches—would galvanize his kids.

On a larger scale, Sweet delighted in using this relatively grand stage as an opportunity to tweak the coaching establishment. Just as he'd thrown out the English curriculum at Macon High and been successful with his own methods, now he had a chance to prove that there was more than one way to coach a successful high school team. He looked around and saw fifty- and sixty-year-old war vets with flattops who ran their teams as if they were still in the Army. Sweet was pretty sure that regimenting young men to the point where they're not thinking for themselves wasn't a good way to get the best out of them. Though he was too modest to say it, he really thought what he was doing was in some small way revolutionary. He'd gone into the hardest, most doctrinaire corner of the scholastic experience and proven that a team didn't need a dictator to win, that a coach could put the emphasis on the experience—on fun and cooperation and the kids—and also win.

While most of the press was having a ball mocking Sweet, one reporter had caught on to what he was doing. It was Bob Fallstrom, the *Herald & Review* editor who'd received Sweet's survey all those months earlier. Now he penned a column for Friday's paper that had a different tone. Called "Sweet Ignores Coaching 'Rules,'" it compared Sweet to Vince Lombardi. Wrote Fallstrom:

> *Many high school coaches try to imitate Lombardi. After all, winning is just as important on the prep level—unfortunately. It's win or look for another job—in most cases.*
>
> *I've often thought that prep athletics are being spoiled by this "must win" approach. Ruined because the fun of competing is being squeezed out of existence, replaced by relentless pressure to succeed.*
>
> *Then along comes L. C. Sweet. And his team, without coaching, without haranguing, without discipline, is successful . . .*
>
> *Most of the coaching fraternity regard Sweet as a freak.*
>
> *But there is no denying that the Macon players are relaxed, having fun. Having a ball, instead of being uptight about losing.*
>
> *Is having fun so unorthodox in high school athletics? Do coaches have to be a combination of Vince Lombardi and Gen. Patton?*
>
> *Sweet doesn't think so. I'll back him up.*

How to prepare for the biggest morning of your life? That was the question that faced the Ironmen on Thursday night. In one room, Heneberry and a half dozen others huddled around the color TV and watched as Cubs ace Ken Holtzman mowed down Cincinnati Reds batters. Others played games of Pitch, the unofficial card game of Macon.

Throughout, one boy was conspicuously absent. Earlier in the evening, Shartzer had been spotted in the lobby with Mark Miller, briefly conferring with a few female Macon students, but now he was nowhere to be found. No one went looking for him, though, as Steve had asked to be left alone during the tournament. Down one of the long halls, he lay on his bed, staring up at the white perforated ceiling tiles.

Tonight, there was no asthma. His hand throbbed but he didn't think about that, either. Instead, Shartzer thought about how many people were driving up from Macon, and how they were all counting on him. He thought about how far the team had come, and how important it was for him to lead them now. He thought about how, as he later said, "No one elected me to carry the flag, but I took the damn thing and wasn't going to fall on it."

18

The Drums

The Macon High students couldn't believe it. SCHOOL CLOSED TODAY read the sign on the front of Macon High. It was like having a snow day in June.

Not that any of the kids planned on goofing around. The student bus left the parking lot for Peoria at 6:30 A.M. and it was joined over the course of the morning by enough cars to fill three parking lots around Meinen Field. Flags fluttered from windows and pennants twirled. One Macon fan used duct tape to plaster the side of his white sedan with: #1 MACON IRONMEN YEA.

Jane Metzger was one of the students on the school bus and she remembers the giddy excitement of the morning. For two hours, Tim Cook, the diminutive former junior high baseball coach, led a series of Ironmen cheers. In the back, a student had tuned a transistor radio to WLS-AM 890 out of Chicago. At one point the DJ, Larry Lujack, began talking about the state baseball finals and mentioned that some tiny school from Macon had made it. Lujack then cracked that he'd never heard of Macon, and had no idea where it was.

For Metzger, it was one of the first times she realized just how small her town was.

Three hours north in Chicago, hundreds of thousands of people awoke and opened their *Tribune* to see that same small town on the front of the sports page. Above a story reading "Top 2 Draft Choices Sign Bear Contracts" and another about the Cubs with the headline "Santo Has Sympathy for Bench" ran a banner headline: "Lane Tech Wins State Opener, 2 to 1." Just below, in large letters, it read: "Macon to Provide Next Test."

Friday morning dawned hot and muggy. Sweet rose not long after sunrise after spending part of the previous night at the bar talking with Jeanne about ways to keep the team loose. Sweet was proud of how independent the boys had become. He wanted them to forge their own identity, to realize the world wasn't that big and that Macon wasn't that small. Now, as the Ironmen were poised to make another tournament run, he wanted outsiders to see the team as self-sufficient, to give the boys credit for their success, not the coach or some "program." Most of all, he wanted the boys to keep it all in perspective.

So far, his strategy had worked. His stunt with the press had gone over as well as he could have hoped and his decision to shelter the team at Jumer's was also paying off. Now he'd restricted all access. He didn't want the boys overthinking the game; he just wanted them to play.

It was time for one final gambit. He gathered the Ironmen at breakfast in the hotel restaurant. The boys looked up, wondering if Sweet had prepared a speech. Instead he looked them over and, in a very serious voice, said, "Guys, now you've heard that these Lane Tech guys are just like us. They put their pants on one leg at a time." Sweet paused and scanned the room again. "Well, they're not. They jump into them two feet at a time!"

At one end of the table, Jeff Glan watched his teammates' reactions, the way they begin giggling, almost against their will. He'd heard Sweet refer to himself as a "sponsor" before but Glan saw his coach as more of a psychologist. He'd never had a teacher or coach who understood moods and motivations like Sweet. What Sweet possessed, Glan would later realize, was what people called emotional intelligence.

After breakfast, Jack Heneberry approached. After asking Sweet's permission, he walked off to the side of the room with his son. Looking John in the eye, Jack told him how it would be asking too much to win this game. He told him how the Ironmen had had a great season, how *John* had had a great season, and how he was so proud of him for that Bloomington game. Then he told him that it was OK—no one expected him to win this one.

Then Jack Heneberry pulled out a crumpled piece of paper and handed it to his son. "But this might help," he said.

By 8:15 A.M., when the Macon bus left for Meinen Field, the players were already sweating. Though warm on Thursday, it had been pleasant enough—nearly perfect baseball weather. Now the heat hung like a wet blanket over Peoria, as if the whole river town awoke to find the banks had overflowed and taken to the air.

As the bus pulled up, the boys were shocked to see spectators already lining the bleachers. By 9:15, they overflowed onto the grass. One Lane Tech fan with sunglasses and prodigious muttonchops had brought a large snare drum. You could hear the *BANG! BANG! BANG!* from a quarter of a mile away.

The Lane Tech contingent was impressive but paled in comparison to the crowd on the other side of the diamond. There had never been, and likely never will be, a Macon away crowd like this one. As he looked around, Heneberry recognized one face after another: Britton, McClard, Poelker, Burns, the entire Otta extended clan. There was Jane Metzger and Diane Tomlinson, screaming like the cheerleaders they were during basketball and football season. Around them swarmed a horde of students already chanting for the Ironmen, the cheers led by a handsome, dark-haired senior named Cliff Brown, who stood waving a large, purple Ironmen flag. There were kids from Blue Mound and kids from Moweaqua, relatives from Decatur and Champaign. There were babies in sun hats and mothers in big dark glasses fanning themselves. Little boys ran in circles behind the bleachers; others like Scott Taylor sat rapt, watching. Heneberry tried to count all the fans but could only guess at their number. A thousand? Two thousand? One thing was sure: Of the twelve hundred residents of Macon, the vast majority were in Peoria on this day.

Farther down, the scouts huddled with their arms crossed, whispering to each other. Heneberry had never seen so many at a game. There was one in a Kansas City Royals shirt, and another with a Yankees hat. Over to the side he recognized Itchy Jones, the coach at Southern Illinois, the biggest baseball power in the state.

Heneberry was supposed to be warming up, but he couldn't help himself. He had to take it all in for a minute. Either way, win or lose, he knew this was the last game of his high school career; if Macon won, Shartzer would pitch the title game. Heneberry thought about how crazy and wonderful it was that on the last day of his athletic career he got to pitch for a chance to reach the state championship. He tried to soak up the moment, to freeze time, to scan the crowd and imprint each face into his memory.

Then, before he took his first throw, he pulled the small, yellow piece of notepad paper from his back pocket one last time. John knew his father lacked traditional baseball training, but Jack had seen enough of his son's games to know the type of hitters he could and couldn't get out. So while the other parents had headed off to celebrate the previous afternoon, ecstatic just to have won one game, Jack had stuck around to watch Lane Tech. Immediately, he'd noticed one player, the Kid with the Big Black Bat, as he described him—Mark Wronkiewicz. "He can really hurt us," Jack scribbled in a notebook.

"Don't even pitch to him." He wrote the same thing about John Rockwell, the leadoff hitter who'd tagged the monster shot on the opening day of the tournament.

The best piece of advice, though, was one of the last things Jack said before he handed his son the piece of paper. "Son," Jack had said, "they really looked terrible against the pitcher's curveball in the first game. Now, this guy's a better pitcher than you are, but when he went to his slow curve, they looked sick"—and here he'd placed his hand on John's shoulder and smiled—"and you have a better slow curveball than he does."

Nearby, Joe Cook and Bob Fallstrom stood and watched, incredulous. Cook had seen Shartzer pitch a number of times, but neither of the men had seen Heneberry in person. Now, as Heneberry sent a succession of floaters toward Dean Otta during warmups, Cook couldn't believe what he was seeing. *This* was Heneberry? The kid couldn't break a windowpane. He was, as Cook remembers, "just sort of lobbing it in there."

On the other side of the diamond, Wronkiewicz was also warming up. Like everyone on Lane Tech, he sported a bright green and gold uniform and he looked, as Cook remembers, "like he just came out of a showroom." Tall and muscular with a strong chin, Wronkiewicz threw one fastball after another, popping the mitt on each. Presently, Fallstrom turned to Cook.

"Well, this doesn't look like much of a game."

Cook had to agree with him. *This is going to be a disaster,* he thought. *Why are we even up here?*

As the first pitch neared, the two men headed to the small press box behind the backstop. It was farther from the field than either was accustomed to. Whereas at most fields in central Illinois the backstop was only fifteen feet or so behind home plate, at Meinen Field it was closer to sixty.

As always, Cook kept score. Quickly, he scribbled down the lineups:

MACON		LANE TECH	
Mark Miller	2B	John Rockwell	2B
Dale Otta	SS	Jim Iwanski	1B
Steve Shartzer	3B	Jim Flammang	LF
Stu Arnold	CF	Mark Wronkiewicz	P
Dean Otta	C	Walt Kryklywec	C
David Wells	LF	Richie Coleman	RF
Jeff Glan	1B	Dale Wietecha	3B
Brian Snitker	RF	Rick Wachholder	SS
John Heneberry	P	Nick Owcharuk	CF

When he finished, Cook checked his scorebook. For some reason, Lane had inserted its backup catcher, Kryklywec, into the lineup rather than the usual starter. At the time, Cook didn't think much of it.

All that preparation, all those dreams and this is what happens?

At 9:30 the state semifinal began and the Ironmen promptly forgot how to hit. For three innings, all the Macon boys did was go down swinging. Working from a windup, to the sound of the drums going *BANG! BANG! BANG!*, Wronkiewicz blew away one batter after another, striking out six straight Ironmen at one point through a combination of fastballs, sliders, curveballs, and forkballs. For the season, his record stood at 10–1, with 104 strikes in seventy innings. That he'd nearly gone his entire high school career without pitching was hard to believe. As it was, only when a scout saw Wronkiewicz whiffing batters during a summer semipro league and mentioned this fact to Papciak did the old coach get the idea that maybe he, too, should put the kid on the mound.

As for Heneberry, he took the mound as concerned as ever about walking the first batter. What's more, that batter was Rockwell, and

Heneberry remembered all too well what he did to the first pitch in the quarterfinal game. So Heneberry rocked, unwound, and looped in a curve that appeared headed right for Rockwell's head. Acting on instinct, Rockwell took cover. He was sitting in the dirt, on his butt, when the umpire said "Strike!"

Inside, Heneberry felt a prickle of excitement. *I've got my good stuff.* Of course, the good stuff only worked if his defense backed him up, and in the second the Ironmen ran into trouble. A pair of errors was followed by a sacrifice fly to give Tech a 1–0 lead. *BANG! BANG! BANG!* went the drum.

As the Macon players jogged back to the bench, Sweet stood up to meet them. But rather than ripping into the boys after the errors and telling them to get their heads in the game, he smiled. "Alright, hand me your gloves. I'm going to have Sammy here sew up the holes in between innings."

Then he patted Mark Miller on the back. "Now I think we've let this big kid get his fill of strikeouts for the day. How about a hit?"

Next to the bleachers a handful of the coaches from the other teams in the tournament watched in disbelief. Who was this guy? For two days they'd read about Sweet, with his peace signs and hippie-dippy approach to the game, and they were sick of it. When Charles Chamberlain, the AP reporter, ambled over between innings, he got an earful. "If Macon wins the state championship," one of the coaches told him, "it will set back Illinois high school baseball ten years." Another—of course asking to remain anonymous—called Sweet "a disgrace to the profession."

On the field, the disgrace gathered his players near the bench. "Guys, run if you get on base," he said. "It's awful hot out here and I think those city boys are having trouble with it. Let's see if they can catch you."

Sweet was right about one thing: The weather had become a factor. Though only a little past 10 A.M., the temperature had soared past 90 degrees and the humidity was extreme. In the field, Lane shortstop Rick Wachholder was already having trouble. He could feel the heat shooting up through his metal spikes, searing the soles of his feet, and he waited as long as possible to head out to the field each inning. Once there, he counted the seconds until he could get back to the bench, where the Lane coaches had a cooler filled with cool, wet towels, which the Lane players draped over their heads between innings. Shartzer looked over and was no longer envious of those thick, pretty uniforms.

It wasn't much better in the stands. The heat was so intense that the generator providing power for the hot dog stand had broken down before the end of the first inning. This being the age before sunscreen and bottled water, the fans had no choice but to pull their hats down and sweat it out. Metzger's hair had long ago shot out into a halo of frizz, and one man from Macon named Marvin Lash ended up going to the hospital with heat stroke. Superfan Cliff Brown had doffed his shirt and now wore only a wide-brimmed hat, sunglasses, jeans, and a bandanna tied around his neck. Around him, other Macon boys followed suit, shifting restlessly, waiting for some reason to cheer.

In the top of the fourth, Dale Otta finally gave it to them. Once again, as he'd done against Mark Carley earlier in the playoffs, Otta broke the pitcher's spell. This time it was a single to center to halt the string of six strikeouts. Once on first, Otta didn't hesitate: It was time to test the backup catcher's arm. Moments later he was at second. With the Macon crowd roaring, the rally continued. Four hits and another stolen base later, Macon held a 2–1 lead.

Now it was up to Heneberry to hold the line, and for three more innings he worked his magic. Just as Jack Heneberry had surmised, the Lane players continued to hack away at fluttering curves in the dirt. Each time they swung at one, Heneberry figured he should throw another in the same spot. By the fifth inning, Lane's assistant coaches were yelling "TAKE SOME PITCHES!"

Still, Heneberry was concerned. His pitches were certainly breaking but he didn't feel like he had great control. If Lane just made him throw strikes, it could get ugly. Every once in a while, just to make sure his dad saw, he pulled out the paper and looked at it, but he no longer needed a scouting report. It was going to be all junk, all the time.

Heading into the top of the seventh, Macon clung to that one-run lead. Then a strange thing happened: Mighty Lane Tech, not Macon, cracked under the pressure. Of all people, Jeff Glan laid down a perfect bunt to start the inning, right off the third base line. Kryklywec, the reserve catcher, got to it in time but launched the throw past the first baseman, allowing Glan to reach second. Then Wronkiewicz uncorked a wild pitch, prompting Papciak to stalk to the mound. He signaled to a relief pitcher, Jim Iwanski, but Iwanski fared no better. Again and again, the Ironmen ran.

Poor Walt Kryklywec. Not only was he unaccustomed to playing this much, but after two hours in that heavy catcher's gear in the thick heat, he was absolutely gassed. Wild pitches in the Chicago city league merely caromed off the backstop ten feet to the rear; here at Meinen Field they skittered to the distant collegiate backstop. When Kryklywec did catch the pitches, it seemed a runner was always going. Three times he made throwing errors trying to nail all those dancing, sprinting Ironmen. As he did, the runs started to pour in: 3–1, then 4–1, now 6–1! All Heneberry needed to do was shut down Lane Tech in the bottom of the seventh to send Macon to the state final.

There was only one problem: Now it was Heneberry who started thinking about the magnitude of the moment. He plunked a batter with a curve that never curved, gave up a double, then walked a batter. Soon Lane Tech was down only 6–3. Worse, the bases were loaded and there were no outs. The time had come for Sweet to make the long walk to the mound.

Slowly, head down, he strolled out. The crowd stared, Heneberry stared. Sweet reached his pitcher and cleared his throat. "So, everybody's looking at me like I'm supposed to come out here," he said. "So here I am."

After a moment, Sweet patted Heneberry on the shoulder and walked back to the dugout. Then motioned not to Shartzer but to Jimmy Durbin, the tiny freshman with the jug ears who hadn't pitched the whole season—the kid who could barely get the ball to home plate on a straight line. "Get up and start throwing in the bullpen," Sweet said.

Durbin's face registered shock, followed milliseconds later by fear. *Me?*

So, dutifully, Durbin jogged down the right field line to begin warming up. Behind him, 1,971 fans watched in astonishment. Sweet was thinking of bringing in another pitcher and it was *this* kid? Where was Shartzer? What in the name of all that was holy was this hippie coach thinking?

Back on the bench, Sweet grinned. More important, with every looping warm-up pitch Durbin heaved, so did the Ironmen players. For Sweet, moments such as this were both the most difficult and most crucial times to reinforce his ethos. Otherwise, it was easy to succumb to thinking that the game was more important than it was and lose one's identity.

On the mound, Heneberry stared in disbelief. *Durbin?* Then, as he watched the kid tossing lollipops, Heneberry realized the message Sweet was sending: He had the utmost confidence in him. With that, Heneberry felt a surge of energy. Rather than trying to muddle through, he decided to go for broke.

Climbing back on the mound, Heneberry proceeded to unleash a half-dozen gorgeous curveballs—the kind that peak near a batter's ear and then plummet to the dirt. He allowed one run but, more important, struck out two batters on 3–2 called strikes. And thus the moment—*his* moment—arrived. With the score 6–4 he faced left-handed first baseman Jim Iwanski, who was 1–3 on the day.

Heneberry wound and kicked, his arm out at that familiar three-quarter angle. At the plate, Iwanski tensed his body. He knew what was coming—everyone at Meinen Field did. It didn't make it any easier. Iwanski had been taught not to swing at curveballs until there were two strikes, for the best that could happen was you hit it hard on the ground. But with Heneberry, he knew all he was going to see were curves, and anyone who's played high school baseball knows the sweating nightmare that is hitting a vertiginous curveball. Someone with professional-quality heat has a reputation that precedes him, allowing batters to stand farther back and choke up. But a curveball pitcher is a terrorist who can come from anywhere.

So even when Iwanski saw Heneberry's hand fall from behind the pitch, seeing the magic trick before it was performed, he still had to override his instincts. The ball was floating in high and outside but he knew it would not end up there. Iwanski needed to stay back, to swing at a place where the ball was not. Gathering his strength, he took a mighty cut. The pitch had dropped so far, however, that his bat caught only the very top of the ball on its descent toward his knees. Slowly, the ball bounced toward first base, right at Glan. He caught it with his left foot already on the bag.

There was the briefest of pauses, a millisecond during which a profound shift occurred for the boys in the Macon uniforms. Lives tilted, expectations were altered, legacies formed. After this, nothing would ever be the same again. Then, Meinen Field exploded. Out they came, streaming onto the field: girlfriends in short shorts and parents and teachers and shirtless students tossing their hats in the air, the mad, crazy rush of a small town that suddenly felt big. Circling them all in great arcing loops, like some crazed valence electron, ran Cliff Brown, the giant purple M of his flag ruffling through the air.

When it was over, Stu Arnold's four stolen bases had tied a record set by a boy named Lou Elke of Streator High back in 1942, and Lane Tech had tied a tournament record with five errors in one half inning, three charged to Kryklywec and two to Wronkiewicz.

Papciak was steamed. He grumbled and grimaced. When a reporter from the *Journal Star* asked him what happened, he said, "I don't know if it's Lane or me, but we never seem to come through in the clutch." Later, the players heard that Papciak said he felt the team had "let him down."

On the field, the players lined up and shook hands. Knowing Lane's reputation, Heneberry expected the players to be bitter or perhaps complain about how *we should have beat these sumbitches*. They weren't. Instead, a couple of the boys said "Great game." Another said, "We're hoping you guys win the title."

Then the façade cracked. As Lane center fielder Richie Coleman walked off, he couldn't help himself, breaking down in tears. When Wronk saw him, he began crying, too. He didn't care that the scouts were watching. It was prom night that evening back in Chicago but Wronk wouldn't attend. Neither would he say a word during the three-hour drive back to Chicago. It wasn't supposed to end like this.

For most of Macon, this was enough: this moment. Now the radio DJs would know where Macon was. Now there would be a story to tell the kids, and the grandkids, about how *I was there the day Macon beat mighty Lane Tech*. There was reason for optimism and celebration. There was a reason to be proud of being from Macon. As Fallstrom of the *Herald & Review* would later say, "That really felt like the championship game right there."

As the students belted out the Ironmen fight song and reporters crowded around Sweet, ecstatic about the underdog story they'd just witnessed, one boy watched in horror, the elation seeping out of him. *Ah fuck*, Shartzer thought to himself, *now it's on me*. He looked at all the people going crazy over the win, at all that jubilation, and he worried. This wasn't the championship. Why were his teammates and the fans acting like it was? *How*, he wondered, *are we going to get channeled and focused and ready for the title game?*

19

One Shot

It was time to regroup. Back at Jumer's, the players showered and stayed as close as possible to the AC, under strict orders from Sweet to remain inside. Meanwhile, Maxine Glan and Georgianna Shartzer hurried to the Laundromat with the uniforms.

At 1 P.M., the team gathered for lunch in the hotel conference room. Mark Miller, normally the loosest of the boys, was so anxious he could only nibble at his food. The same went for Dale Otta. Presently, a skinny man with brown hair walked in. Most had met him before: It was Fred Schooley, Sweet's buddy from Champaign. Schooley was a savvy baseball man who'd played in the Eastern Illinois semipro league. A few weeks earlier, he'd driven down to Macon to help the team with situational fielding.

On this afternoon he came to offer information. Earlier that morning, Schooley had volunteered to scout Waukegan, which had whupped Rockford West 10–0 in six innings in the other semifinal, the only tournament game called on account of the mercy rule. Now he stood at the front of the room and looked at the boys. He wasn't going to lie to them.

"You ain't going to beat them," Schooley announced. "There ain't no fucking way you can beat them."

The boys stared, shocked.

"They're like a minor league baseball team," Schooley continued. "They'll take the Commodores two out of three. Their catcher is a first-round pick for the Pirates." He turned toward Sweet. "L.C., he completely eliminates your running game."

Sweet looked sick to his stomach. Everything his friend said may have been true, but it should have been relayed in private. A few feet away, Shartzer stared in disbelief. He liked Schooley, and respected his baseball knowledge, but the guy clearly didn't know anything about communicating that knowledge. For one, he was selling the Ironmen short. Second, even Shartzer knew better than to say something like that in front of a bunch of young boys. Looking around, Shartzer saw that some of his teammates looked pissed. Others looked scared.

Sweet cracked a joke, trying to reassure the boys, but the damage was already done.

Delivery aside, Schooley was right: Waukegan *was* a powerhouse. While Lane Tech may have been the most talented team in the tournament, Waukegan wasn't far behind, and no one was better prepared.

A factory town of eighty thousand or so in the northern suburbs of Chicago, Waukegan was a conservative place, and the high school sports teams reflected that. A two-year ROTC stint had long been mandatory at the school and most of the players' fathers fought in World War II. The head baseball coach, a man named Jack Mallory, believed in structure and discipline. A tall, lanky man with a grandfatherly affect, he was both patient and persistent. His goal was for his players to become so well versed in the game that they never had to think, but instead reacted on instinct.

To enforce this, Mallory scheduled practices down to the minute: Bunting at 3:12 P.M. in the northwest corner of the field, then pickoffs for pitchers at 3:17. The routine changed daily, and Mallory expected everyone to hustle between stations. He placed particular emphasis on situational plays. He wanted the boys to know exactly where to throw the ball in any given scenario, and split batting practice into multiple sessions—focusing on skills such as hitting the opposite way to advance runners.

The system worked. Waukegan was a perennial power that came within one game of the state final in 1967. Even so, the 1971 team may have been Mallory's most talented squad yet. Four players were named All-State, including star catcher Mike Uremovich. The son of a Marine sergeant, Uremovich had the whole package. He hit the ball a mile, ran well, and could throw a football sixty yards. He was in every way the team leader. Uremovich was the one who penciled in "Waukegan State Champs" when Mallory tacked a 1971 postseason schedule on the wall at the start of the season. He was the one who called the guys at home and got them to the field on the rare Sunday Mallory didn't schedule practice. He was the player who had the crispest uniforms and the straightest edge to his pants leg, the one who taught his teammates how to sew elastic bands from old garter straps into the bottom of their pants legs to hold up their sanitary socks and stirrups, a trick his mother had discovered.

In the eyes of the pro scouts, Uremovich was one of two or three surefire prospects at the state tournament, and his teammates had long since grown accustomed to seeing up to a dozen scouts at their games. These men loved Mike's size and power, and what *Journal Star* columnist Phil Theobald described as "the howitzer hanging from his right shoulder." They also loved his attitude—not just the leadership but the intensity. In the conference playoffs, Uremovich had broken a bat with his bare hands after striking out.

Mentally, Uremovich had prepared for the chance to play Lane Tech. Then, on Friday morning, one of the coaches came into to his room, where he and a few teammates were watching TV. "I've got some news," the coach announced. "Lane Tech lost to Macon." The boys were shocked.

All Uremovich knew about Macon was that they were a tiny school and their team had "speed in centerfield, the big hitter, and the pitcher." He'd learned long ago never to take an opponent for granted, though. There would be no giggling about peace signs so long as he was on the Waukegan bench.

By the time Macon and Waukegan took to the field at 4:30 P.M. for the state final, the Ironmen had gone national. Charles Chamberlain of the Associated Press filed a story entitled, "At Macon High School Baseball's a Happening."

Chamberlain referred to Macon as a "dot in Central Illinois," noted that they became the smallest school ever to reach the finals in thirty-two years of Illinois high school baseball, and described the boys as "a bunch of rock music lovers with long hair." He also mentioned Barb Jesse, the team's official scorer, "who sits on the bench wearing a pony-tail."

While Chamberlain was preparing his story, the Macon fans had continued celebrating. With five hours to kill before the final, the teachers and parents did what any sane Maconite would do on such a heady day. They made straight for the cool interior of a bar.

By the time they returned to Meinen Field, they discovered that the 4 P.M. heat was even worse than the 11 A.M. heat. Keeping their energy up was going to be a challenge. Even so, most of the fans were alert enough to notice that, with only half an hour to go before game time, Macon's coach and star player were nowhere to be found.

Not far away, Sweet and Shartzer fidgeted in Bradley University's training room. That morning's trip to wrap Shartzer's wrist had been a snap. This time, however, not only had the duo showed up late, but the process was taking longer.

Still, Shartzer wasn't too concerned. He didn't need long to get warmed up. As the minutes ticked by, though, he began to worry about how the delay would affect the perception of Sweet. As the season went on, Shartzer had begun to feel protective of his coach. Sweet could laugh it off when people mocked him, but Shartzer took it personally. He knew everything Sweet did to help the team. How he understood which players to boost up and which to take down a peg with a well-placed joke. How he invited the team over to play cards at his trailer, and how he took them hunting and fishing, making them feel not like boys but men. How when one of the freshmen got scared on an overnight trip and came to Sweet's door, the coach had invited him in to sleep in his room even though Jeanne was there and it was probably the last thing he wanted to do.

When together, Shartzer and Sweet never talked of bigger picture topics. Still, slowly and subtly, Sweet pushed the boy. When Shartzer had gotten sick of basketball and decided he didn't want to play, it was Sweet who took him for a walk, leading him down to the gym, where he pointed at Arnold and Glan and the others. "These are your teammates, Shark. They need you. Now get out there." Peer pressure didn't work on Shartzer but this was different. This he understood. He rejoined the team that day.

Over time, Sweet and Shartzer had become closer than most in Macon knew. Now they had a chance to do something special. Just so long as the doctors finished the damn tape job.

At Meinen Field, the minutes ticked by. Now it was 4:10. Now 4:15. And still, the Area Player of the Year and Coach of the Year were nowhere to be seen. What's more, Sweet had all the gear in his car. With no other choice, the Macon boys borrowed a couple of baseballs from a kid who lived nearby. Finally, fearing the worst, Jack Heneberry walked over and told his son he should probably start getting loose.

John's arm was shot from that morning's game, and he doubted he could get the ball over the plate with any snap, but he dutifully started preparing. Dale Otta, the most organized and conscientious of the boys, became particularly agitated. *This was the state finals, where was their coach?* Behind the bench, the parents fretted. It was decided that Bob Shartzer would take over as coach if necessary.

Finally, with only five minutes to spare, Sweet pulled up outside the field in the school van. Next to him, Steve Shartzer jumped out of the passenger seat carrying a crumpled-up ball of athletic tape, the remnants of the trainer's work.

With a quick hop, Shartzer made for the mound. Around him, the Macon fans rose by the hundreds in the heat and began cheering. Their hero had arrived.

From the press seating, Joe Cook watched and wondered if he'd been wrong. What if this kid *could* do it? By this point, Shartzer had pitched four consecutive shutouts in tournament play. Granted, he'd thrown seven innings only a day earlier and his left hand appeared to be bothering him, but Cook had learned not to underestimate the boy.

Then again, Waukegan had an ace of its own on the mound. Tall and with dark, Hollywood looks, Paul Waidzunas had pitched a five-hitter in the tournament opener and was 7–0 on the season. Though not overpowering, the junior reminded teammates of Orioles ace Jim Palmer, a pitcher who could move the ball around and hit his spots. He had a good fastball, a curve, a slider, and a changeup.

As Cook began to jot down the lineup, he got word that one of the Waukegan players, a boy named Frank Gaziano, wasn't playing due to heat stroke. It was going to be a rough one.

When Cook finished, the lineups for the thirty-second Illinois High School State Baseball Championship looked like this:

WAUKEGAN		MACON	
Jim Davila	LF	Mark Miller	2B
Joe Rajcevich	1B	Dale Otta	SS
Mike Uremovich	C	Steve Shartzer	P
Hal Hollstein	3B	Stu Arnold	CF
Bert Bereczky	SS	Dean Otta	C
Jack White	RF	David Wells	LF
Jim Dietmeyer	2B	Jeff Glan	1B
Joe Mirretti	CF	Brian Snitker	RF
Paul Waidzunas	P	John Heneberry	3B

The game began and Shartzer felt it from the first pitch: Something was off. He walked the leadoff hitter, who then stole second base. The next batter, Rajcevich, singled and stole second as well. The Ironmen weren't accustomed to this. Usually they were the ones stealing bases. Behind the plate, Dean Otta smacked his glove in anger. On the mound, Shartzer, usually so proud of his pick-off move, stewed. Then Uremovich drove in a run with a ground ball: 1–0, Waukegan.

Up stepped third baseman Harold Hollstein. A dead pull hitter, Hollstein was a big, lumbering boy—"slow as the devil on the basepaths," according to teammate Joe Mirretti—who could hit it a mile. Even so, he proceeded to do the most unexpected thing: He squared to bunt. Heneberry and Glan were playing a mile back at the corners and Shartzer was caught off guard. *Who puts on the suicide squeeze with their cleanup hitter?*

What Shartzer didn't know was that, unlike so many teams that had taken Macon for granted, Waukegan had scouted the Ironmen. After the semifinal that morning, Waukegan assistants Rick Mowen and an old coaching friend of Mallory's, Tommy Correll, returned with two pieces of advice: You can run on them, and you can bunt on them.

This wasn't a big surprise. At the time, bunting was a common tactic in Illinois high school ball, and often an effective one. Given uneven diamonds, pitchers who were unsure fielders, and third basemen unaccustomed to making throws on the run, just getting the ball down often led to an error or a base hit. Whereas this was indeed a good strategy against Heneberry, who had limited fielding range (and who had pitched the semi that Waukegan had scouted), Shartzer was another matter. Not only did his fastball tend to rise, making it difficult to get down a good bunt, but his defensive range was such that when he played third, as Mt. Zion coach Ed Neighbors says, "It was like the kid was also playing short." Put Shartzer on the mound and he could cover the whole middle of the infield.

So when Hollstein sent a bunt trickling down the third base line, it normally wouldn't have been effective. But now not only did the big Waukegan kid own the element of surprise, but Shartzer was hobbled by a bad glove hand. Charging the ball, Steve knew his only play was at first, and another run scored. Now it was 2–0 Waukegan.

An inning later, it got worse. Uncharacteristically, Shartzer lost control of a fastball and plunked a batter. A stolen base and a passed ball later, Waukegan had another run. Macon was in a 3–0 hole.

Meanwhile, just as in the early innings of the Lane Tech game, the Ironmen were listless at the plate. Unlike against Lane, however, there was no midgame rally. One Ironman batter after another hit weak grounders, due in part to the sinking motion on Waidzunas' pitches. Making matters worse, Macon received no help from the Waukegan defense. Without many walks or errors, the Ironmen couldn't get on base, and without base runners they couldn't create havoc. When they did have one opportunity to run, Uremovich had unholstered that howitzer and gunned down the would-be thief with ease. It wasn't until the fourth inning that Mark Miller singled for the Ironmen's first base hit, but his teammates couldn't bring him home.

Then, in the top of the sixth, Waukegan struck again. Uremovich singled to right for his sixth hit in ten tournament at-bats, a two-day hot streak he later called "The best hitting days of my life." A wild pitch sent Uremovich to second and then Shartzer, to his amazement, was called for a balk. No one called balks in the Meridian conference. With Uremovich on third, all it took was a lazy sacrifice fly to bring him home. The scoreboard now read Waukegan 4, Macon 0.

In the stands, the Macon fans sat looking glum. They'd used up so much energy earlier in the day, and it was so hot, that the slightest exertion was draining. Even Cliff Brown, with the giant flag, was listless. Only one inning remained in Macon's fairy-tale season and this was how it would end?

And then, in the bottom of the seventh, a glimmer of hope: Shartzer crushed a pitch to deep left that barely curled foul, and then, unfazed, he stepped back up and stroked a single. An error, a wild pitch, and a groundout later, Shartzer tore home to score Macon's first run. Moments later, Wells singled to drive in another, prompting Mallory to yank Waidzunas in favor of Rick Haapanen. Wells greeted him by stealing second. Now the Ironmen were down only 4–2 with one out. Better yet, Jeff Glan, who was leading the Ironmen in batting average during the tournament, walked to the plate.

In the bleachers the Macon fans rose. The purple flag whipped through the heat. As it did, it was joined by an unusual but familiar sound: *BANG! BANG! BANG!* Shirt unbuttoned to his navel, shades on, muttonchops thick with sweat, the Lane Tech drummer was now on the Macon side of the bleachers. He'd been so impressed with the Ironmen in the morning that he'd decided to stick around. Maybe they'd need his help. So now he slammed on the drum as, around him, parents and students and little kids roared with him. All afternoon this is what they'd waited for: one more shot.

In center field, senior Joe Mirretti readied himself. He knew Glan didn't have a ton of power, so he played in a bit. During long summers of American Legion ball, Mirretti had played on plenty of impressive fields but Meinen was the finest he'd ever set foot on. The grass was perfectly groomed, like a warm green carpet. He crept in even farther, knowing the ball wouldn't take any strange bounces. Then, on the third pitch to Glan, he heard a crack.

Standing off second base, Wells heard the same noise and saw enough to know Glan had muscled an inside fastball and that it was headed toward left center. Head down, Wells took off for third. Tall and lanky, he was one of the fastest players on the team. As he approached third he looked up, unaware of where the ball was. All he saw was Sweet waving him home.

Down the first base line, Glan rounded the bag in time to look up and see two things happen at once: Wells tear around third and the center fielder field the ball cleanly. It would take a good throw, Glan thought, but he could get him.

Seeing the ball soaring toward him, Mirretti had charged it hard. After scooping it up, he did what he'd been taught to do for so many years: Don't think, just react. So he came up firing, aiming to throw the ball right through the chest of the cutoff man, as Mallory taught all his outfielders.

Behind the plate, Mike Uremovich watched it all play out. The soft liner, the big kid taking off from second, Mirretti scooping it up. When he saw the Macon kid round third, Uremovich gauged the distance to Mirretti and began yelling at his shortstop. "DON'T CUT IT! DON'T CUT IT!" This one needed to come all the way home.

In center, Mirretti heaved the ball and watched it soar. Back in Waukegan, the school's field sloped downward from home plate toward the outfield, so he was accustomed to throwing slightly uphill. At Meinen, however, because of the way the field's drainage was planned, it was the opposite—now he was throwing down toward the plate. Mirretti knew it would give him a touch more power on his throw. Once he'd released the ball, all he could do was watch.

From the stands, Jack Heneberry followed the arc of the ball, his breath wedged in his throat. Outfield throws at the high school level were a risky proposition, especially without a cutoff man. Often enough, they ended up off line, or skidded to the backstop. Surely, Heneberry thought, the kid must be feeling the pressure.

Decades later, when the local paper ran a story about the greatest moments in Waukegan High sports history, number two on the list would be "Mirretti's great throw." Those on hand say they've seen few better. The ball came in, straight and true, bouncing once between the rubber and home. Later, Sweet would say: "It had to be on the money. If the kid had to do it ten times, we're going to score seven or eight times." As it was, Uremovich caught the ball a few feet up the third base line. Seeing Wells coming in standing up, he did what he'd been taught: He hid the ball behind the glove, reached up with both arms, and leveled his opponent in midstride. Wells went down and the ball stayed with Uremovich. The umpire looked, paused, and then yanked back his fist. "He's OUT!"

And just like that, the Macon magic evaporated. Had Wells scored, it would have been 4–3 with one out and a runner in scoring position. Instead, it was 4–2 with two outs. The Macon fans settled back into the bleachers in disbelief.

It seemed a formality when the next batter, Brian Snitker, sent a chopper down the third base line for the final out.

The Ironmen didn't have much time to grieve. No sooner had they finished shaking hands with the Waukegan players than the boys began receiving congratulations. Moments later, they were summoned to the infield.

There, IHSA executive secretary Harry Fitzhugh held aloft the second-place trophy. It wasn't as large as Waukegan's and was silver rather than gold. A shiny miniature batter crouched on top, frozen in midswing. "And now," Fitzhugh said into a corded PA system, "I give the second-place trophy to Coach Smith and the Ironmen!"

If Fitzhugh noticed that Coach "Smith" was trying to stifle laughter as he accepted the trophy, he didn't let on. Immediately, Sweet passed the trophy to the players, who gathered around him in dirty uniforms, sweat streaked down their faces. One by one they raised the trophy over their heads, to the cheers of the Macon faithful.

The crowd was still going when, a few minutes later, Waukegan was honored. Mallory complimented the Ironmen players and then said, "I would like to commend those fans seated right over there." Then he pointed toward the Macon horde, hundreds of whom had stayed and continued to cheer.

Off to the side, a wide, powerful man stood taking it all in. Itchy Jones, the SIU coach, hadn't come to see Steve Shartzer, but he sure as hell was glad he had. To Jones, Shartzer looked like a kid who could play at the big-time Division One level.

Shartzer wasn't the only one being scouted. Lakeland College coach Gene Creek was also on hand, attending his sixth straight state tournament. Creek was different from many of the old-school coaches of the day; he was younger and sported his own set of bushy sideburns. After the game, he sidled up to Joe Cook. "Does Sweet have a master's degree?" Creek asked. Cook said he didn't know. Creek nodded. "If Sweet can inspire the kids to play that well, I should hire him as an assistant. I'm serious."

A few minutes later, when Cook mentioned this to Sweet, the coach smiled. "Nice of the man to say," Sweet said, but he couldn't talk right now.

A night like no other awaited him.

20

June 1971

Had you walked past Route 51 on the evening of June 4, 1971, you would have been forgiven for thinking Macon had won the state title.

The caravan began in Peoria, fifteen or twenty cars long. After dinner, the Ironmen stopped at Millikin University in Decatur, honoring a pregame promise Sweet made to a local radio station and the parking lot turned into an impromptu pep rally. The asphalt was clogged with friends and family, as well as kids from local high schools and small-town people who, as Trusner says, "just wanted to be part of something." The players streamed out of the bus, accepting the hugs and high fives.

All except one, that is. During the ride from Peoria, as his teammates peered out the windows of the bus, soaking in the sight of the caravan of cars, Shartzer had hunched in the back, lost in himself. The guy who'd pitched two games with one good hand—who'd vowed to pick up that damn flag, who'd spent all season galvanizing his teammates—blamed himself. *How can we have this celebration when we just lost?* he wondered. When the bus reached Millikin, Shartzer remained on it, wedged into his seat.

Finally Bob Shartzer climbed the bus stairs and walked to the back. He didn't say anything at first, just sat there for a moment. All those games of checkers that Bob wouldn't let Steve win, all those lessons taught on the living room rug, all those years of repeating his mantra of "Concentrate, goddammit"—now he needed to impart a different lesson.

"Son, did you do your best?"

Steve looked up. "Yeah, I did." He paused. "Well, no, I didn't. I made some mistakes, and it hurts."

The father looked at his son. He put a hand on Steve's shoulder.

"Whether you're happy with it or not, you've got to learn to live with the good and the bad," Bob said. "Now it's time to come on out. There's a whole damn town out here that thinks you're a hero."

Slowly, Steve Shartzer rose and walked down the stairs, out into the madness that awaited.

Millikin was only a warm-up, as it turned out. By the time the team hit Elwin, five miles north of Macon, fire engines joined the caravan. Soon enough, a police escort arrived to lead the bus and what the paper later estimated was three miles of cars. Horns honked, townspeople ran out of their houses to wave, kids who'd been allowed to stay up late whistled and screamed.

The bus rolled into town, past the Arrowhead Tavern and the grain elevator, rumbling by churches and homes, then finally came to a stop in front of Macon High. Since it was close to 11 P.M., many of the players expected to go to bed. Instead, they were directed to the school auditorium, on the double.

There, waiting in the thick summer heat, were the rest of their classmates. Senior graduation had been set for 8 P.M. Perhaps the most formal event in Macon, it included a processional, an invocation, a clarinet solo, and a presentation of awards. Pre- and postgraduation parties were planned at the houses of parents around the town. When word came that the team would be arriving late, some of the parents had urged the school to get on with it. The senior class, however, had voted to wait.

So for three hours on a humid 90-degree day in a gym without air conditioning, dozens of boys and girls, many of whom had rushed back from Peoria to shower and change, waited in their finest. And when the Ironmen finally burst into the gym just after 11 P.M. with robes thrown on over their uniforms and cleats still on their feet, there was a roar that could be heard for miles, across 51 and out past all those cornfields. The five seniors on the team tore down the aisle carrying Sweet on their shoulders as he hoisted the second-place trophy for all to see. McClard thought of stopping them, of trying to retain a shred of formality to the occasion. But as he told the newspaper, "I would have been trampled to death if I had tried."

To the graduating seniors who watched, some of whom would never see Sweet again, it looked like he was riding a wave of joy toward the stage. So that's how they remember him now, thrust up in glory, smiling that wild smile, a man carried into the light by a bunch of boys.

Part Three
Ghosts

Baseball was such an experience in my life that, ten years later, I have still not shaken it, will probably never shake it. . . . It's as if I decided at some point in my life, or possibly it was decided, that of all the things in my life only that one experience would most accurately define me. . . . Yet it never seemed to end properly, neatly, all those bits and pieces finally forming some harmonious design. It just stopped, unfinished in my memory, fragmented, so many pieces missing.

—Pat Jordan, *A False Spring*

COURTESY OF DALE OTTA

Heneberry in the aftermath

21

Never the Same

Macon, Illinois, Spring 2010

It is almost fifty years since Lynn Sweet first drove from Chicago to Macon. To make the same journey today is to leave behind the concrete overpasses of the city and burrow into a heartland that still feels as if it's from a different era. The central Illinois landscape is one of American flags on porches, blinking radio towers, Baptist churches lit up like beacons in the night, oversized John Deere tractors creeping down the side of the road, general stores with neon Budweiser signs, silver grain silos, and endless green fields of soybeans and corn. Turn on the TV during the fall and chances are at least one station will be covering the IHSA football playoffs; flip to the FM dial and you'll hear the game play-by-play.

Arrive in Macon and the high school baseball diamond is visible from the bypass, its presence advertised by the giant green H-A-W-K-S letters planted in the grass. It is a proper, well-groomed field now, with a scoreboard and a batting cage. Behind it, the school—now renamed Meridian High after the merger with Blue Mound—resides in the same brick edifice on South Wall Street. If the district ever gets the funding, the plan is to erect a new school, but it's tough with the state budget crisis. For now, the money has moved up the road to Mt. Zion, where white flight from Decatur has turned the town into a bustling community of restaurants, McMansions, and a gleaming new school.

There is little gleam to Meridian High, though there is reason for pride. Inside the glass double-doors, visitors are greeted by a floor-to-ceiling trophy case honoring the Meridian basketball team, which won the state championship in 2009. A twenty-foot-long photo banner of the players dressed in shiny green uniforms is visible farther in, on one of the gym walls. Triumphant news clippings from the Decatur *Herald & Review* are pasted on office doors. "PRIME MERIDIAN," they read.

There is an invisible asterisk attached to the banners and trophies, though. There are now up to eight classes in Illinois high school sports, including four in baseball and basketball. In 2009 Meridian competed in Class 1A in basketball, the lowest. To win a state title, the Hawks didn't have to play any Lane Techs, Waukegans, or Decatur Eisenhowers. They didn't even have to play Mt. Zion.

As for the long-time pride of Macon, the shelf where the Ironmen's second-place trophy used to rest is now occupied by a plaque commemorating the 1995 Meridian girls' softball team. In all, there are nine trophy cases lining the school's front hall, stretching almost the length of the gym. Everything from the dance team to the scholastic bowl is represented. There are no reminders of the school's days as Macon High.

By the same token, a visitor can walk the linoleum-tiled halls, peek into the classrooms, and examine the framed photos on the walls. But nowhere is there any mention of a teacher and coach named Lynn Sweet.

Sweet is not an easy man to find these days. This is how he gives directions to his house outside Moweaqua: "Take a left at Casey's store, go two-and-a-half miles, and when you see the church signs, take a right on the unmarked road. Go a mile or so and I'm the big farmhouse."

The house, which Sweet bought in 1982, sits on twenty-five acres surrounded by miles of cornfields. He calls it his "enclave," a former corn farm that he has transformed into an animal refuge under a state program called Acres for Wildlife. It draws quite a crowd: pheasants, turkeys, coyotes, whole families of deer. Sweet plants blueberries, strawberries, and raspberries; tends to cherry trees; and stocks his three-acre lake with bass, crappie, and bluegill. His barn is thick with the trappings of a life lived outdoors: a hulking John Deere 4020 tractor, five mowers, a wagon, a bevy of bikes.

The old coach now spends much of his time in his living room. Here, with windows on three sides, he can sit in his armchair, watch the wildlife, and read. The shelves are lined with an eclectic collection of books: Ford Maddox Ford's *The Good Soldier*, *The Embezzler* by Louis Auchincloss, *Field Guide to Eastern Birds*. In a small den there is a photo of his daughter Leslie with Barack Obama, when she was a delegate at the Democratic National Convention. There are also photos of Jack Burns and Mark Miller, laughing and eating, and one of Lynn and Jeanne at the Great Wall of China.

What's left of Sweet's hair is white, and his goatee is an ashen stubble, but the big hazel eyes remain young. At sixty-eight, long retired, he spends most of his time with Jeanne. They visit their daughter in Sacramento, drink wine in Sonoma County, try to get to Chicago when they can. As Sweet puts it, "We don't have a lot of friends, but we know a lot of people."

He didn't intend to stay in the area; it just sort of happened. They bought a house in Dalton City, ten miles east of Macon, in 1973. Soon Jeanne was pregnant. They had two daughters, Lindsay and Leslie. As the girls got older, both began to realize the power of the family name. Leslie, the older of the two, remembers how people were drawn to her when they learned she was a Sweet, and how it made her feel like a celebrity at times. As she says: "I wasn't royalty based on wealth or power but based on my parents being good people."

Even so, after that '71 season, things were never the same for Sweet in Macon. At first the Ironmen were riding high. The Macon city council passed a resolution of congratulations to the team (addressed to L. C. Sweet at "Arrowhead Mobile Home, Macon, Illinois"). The Illinois Legislature went one step further, declaring June 14, 1971, "Macon Ironmen Baseball Day" and including in the proclamation a passage that read, "We particularly compliment Coach L. C. Sweet for his outstanding leadership."

In 1972 the Macon booster club financed overnight trips and the team finally got a full-time bus driver, as well as handsome new purple uniforms. Sweet declined an offer to be an assistant coach at Lakeland Junior College, and Joe Cook wrote a column daring the big-city schools to add tiny Macon to their baseball schedules, though none took him up on it. Behind the trio of Shartzer, Snitker, and Arnold, who all hit over .500, the Ironmen romped through their schedule, winning games by scores such as 26–0, 21–4, and 18–0. They entered the regionals with a string of seven consecutive shutouts, then lost to MacArthur despite entering the seventh inning with a three-run lead. Even so, the team had become a local dynasty.

There were expectations now. By most standards, Sweet met them. Over the next five years, Macon extended its streak of consecutive conference victories to fifty-eight while winning numerous district titles, though the Ironmen never got back to the state tournament. By 1976, Sweet's last year of coaching the team, some of the joy had drained out of the job. He'd grown his Fu Manchu into a bushy beard, and his dark hair flowed past his shoulders. "Sometimes I just wish we could go back to that first year," he told a reporter at the time. "It was just twelve or thirteen guys, and all we had was a bunch of baggy uniforms and a lot of fun."

The 1976 team finished 16–9, beat Taylorville to win the district, and then lost to MacArthur again, Sweet's last game. Just like that, he quit (in a show of solidarity, so did Jack Burns). Sweet had had enough of the culture of sports and the endless focus on winning. "Games were invented as a way to accommodate leisure time," he explained to a reporter. "Now they've become a semi-religion . . . A lot of other people give baseball more importance . . . especially in high school and amateur sports. The pressure, God, they make you a hero when all you're doing is playing baseball."

What really got to Sweet were the parents. Teaching their sons how to enjoy life and grow into free-thinking men wasn't enough anymore. The parents wanted college scholarships and trophies. Sweet couldn't take it. "The parents were yelling at me too much," he says. "They wanted it to be like it was. We'd always win more than we'd lose, but they all expected to go to state, the elusive state . . ." He trails off, looks out at the window at the birds in his yard.

Sweet moved on. He coached girls' track and, naturally, the team flourished. One of his runners became a state champion, and the Ironmen won several sectionals. Soon enough, Bob Fallstrom was writing stories in the *Herald & Review* titled "It's a Sweet Repeat," about how the girls were inspired by their coach. Still, it wasn't the same as baseball. Nothing ever was.

Teaching changed, too. Sweet got a master's in secondary English from the University of Illinois in 1974, and added another master's ten years later, but he grew weary of how his legend preceded him in Macon. "I'd walk into a room and people would say, 'Oh, you're Lynn Sweet. Well, be Lynn Sweet.' I ran out of gas to be me." Then, in 1994, when Macon High consolidated with Blue Mound, Sweet was expected to teach a standard curriculum, with an emphasis on grammar drills and passing standardized tests. No longer could he have students read *Macbeth* twice or stock the shelves with *Popular Mechanics*. Four years later he retired. He didn't fit in the new teaching environment. "I was happy in the '60s and '70s," he says. "The world made sense."

Sweet doesn't hold on to memories of that '71 season. There is only one photo of the team in his house, in an upstairs room, and precious few mementos. He shows up at the annual benefit in memory of Mark Miller, who died of cancer in 2006, but other than that he doesn't see "the kids," as he calls them, too often. Asked about that season, he says,

"I know it's a good story. I lived with it. You know why it's a great story? It can never happen again."

The more Sweet talks, though, the more he seems perplexed. Even if he tries to let go of that season, he finds he can't. "Why does it mean so much?" he asks out loud at one point. "I don't know. It means a lot to me but I don't dwell on it all the time. You can't do that. I'm not defined by that. I don't know . . ." He pauses, looks at the table, looks back up. "Some of them, maybe they still are."

The man who answers the door is still trim, with neatly parted white hair. He is wearing glasses and a crisp white button-down shirt that he has carefully tucked into his jeans. Thirty-nine years later, Dale Otta still looks eerily similar to the boy who once played shortstop for the Ironmen.

His modest home—where he lives with his high school sweetheart, Sherrie—sits less than a mile off Route 51 in Macon. After graduating from Macon High, Dale played one year at Kaskaskia Junior College in central Illinois. He intended to become a coach and a history teacher, but then got a job at Caterpillar and never had a good reason to leave. Now fifty-seven, he has worked there thirty-five years and hopes to retire when he turns fifty-nine.

Dale's feelings about Macon have changed. From his backyard, he can see the water tower and the grain elevator. If he wanted, he could drive to town in under five minutes, but he rarely goes in anymore. "Back then, you knew everybody there," he says. "Now I hardly know anybody."

On his dining room table, Otta has spread out mementos of the 1971 season: newspaper clippings, a peace sign, yellowed photographs. On his TV, he's cued up a video he made about the team, with footage of the old ballpark in Stonington where the postseason run began. He can get lost in the memories, and often does. He is jarred back to the present by the ringtone on his cell phone. It is the chorus of John

Cougar Mellencamp's "Small Town," in which he sings of being born in a small town and intending to die in one—of expecting that a small town is "prob'ly where they'll bury me."

Dale excuses himself. There on the table, the faces stare back: Glan and Shartzer and Heneberry and Snitker. Presently, Otta returns and apologizes. The call was about tonight, he says. The group is getting back together again.

Whit's End diner is easy to find. The only restaurant in Macon, it occupies the building where Cole's Arrowhead Tavern used to be, in the heart of town, and offers prime rib dinners on Friday night and cold Bud Lights for $2. Just in back are the railroad tracks and, shadowing them, the grain elevator. Up the road are a couple vacant storefronts where the Country Manor once stood.

Other than a few families near the front of Whit's End, the gray-haired men are the only ones in the diner on this night. They sit around a long table in collared shirts, jeans, and denim jackets. A stack of gray-and-purple T-shirts that read MACON: 1971 STATE RUNNER-UP rests nearby, next to a signed baseball.

It's the first time some have seen each other since Sweet held a reunion at his house, nearly twenty years ago. That afternoon, they stood around drinking beer and telling stories until someone convinced Shartzer to put on a glove and air it out a bit. So Dean Otta wedged himself into that familiar crouch and Shartzer, being Shartzer, couldn't help himself. He started rocking and firing and pretty soon he had sweat running down his forehead. There's still a dent in Sweet's barn from where one got away from Shark.

Even after all this time, most of the players are easy to pick out. Heneberry looks remarkably like his high school self, still lanky, with combed-down hair that's now slate instead of brown. He played a little at Kaskaskia as well, married, and took a job as a salesman at a lumberyard, where he's been for thirty-six years. He lives seven miles south of

Macon in Moweaqua, just down from the Dollar General store and across from a field of soybeans, in a small one-story house with aluminum siding. These days he can't throw a snowball without his arm throbbing. "It's OK, though," he says. "I wouldn't trade that season for anything." Sitting next to him, wearing a baseball hat and drinking a Bud Light, is his father, Jack Heneberry, who is still going strong at eighty-five. All those years of walking eight miles a day on his mail route paid off. He's the last living father of the Ironmen.

The men settle in, ordering $3.50 burgers and sharing stories. As they do, the lives unfold. They talk of how Barb Jesse ended up being cast in an orange juice commercial that ran on national networks, how cranky old Ed Neighbors went on to become a coaching legend at Mt. Zion, how Dave Wells grew into a star pitcher at Macon. They talk of Doug Tomlinson's dental practice, and the change in Bill McClard—how he got his degree at Ball State and ended up at Lincoln High a different man, popular and well liked by the students, before later becoming a proponent of educational reform. They talk about how Jeff Glan was the only one of the starting nine who didn't play college baseball, instead getting an English degree from Millikin with the intention of becoming an English teacher and coach, just like Sweet, only to wind up as a contractor for an agribusiness in Clinton, Illinois. And, in due time, the story comes out about how Miller, Heneberry, and the Ottas gathered around a transistor radio while at Kaskaskia, listening to the lottery results for the military draft. Almost immediately, Heneberry drew 112, prompting the rest of the boys to break into Army songs until Miller, who'd been the most amused by Heneberry's new "career," drew 4 himself. In the end, Miller traveled to St. Louis for a physical but that's as far as it got; none of the Ironmen players deployed.

The tone changes when the topic turns to Stu Arnold, who as much as any of the boys seemed destined for greatness. Arnold attended Millikin, where he was a three-time All-Conference centerfielder and set a single-season record for punt return yardage that stands to this day. As the story goes, he tried out for the Dallas Cowboys as a punt returner but didn't make the team. "He was going to be successful at whatever he did," says Heneberry, and, indeed, Arnold ended up in Indianapolis, a well-off stockbroker. Then one afternoon Arnold was coming home from work and, for reasons no one will ever know, his car crossed the center line and collided head-on with a semi. It was over in an instant, the impact propelling the steering wheel through his chest. The boy Sweet once called "the most graceful person I ever met" died at forty-one.

All the players who could make it to Arnold's funeral in Bloomington, Illinois, did. Mitch Arnold, Stuart's then-teenage son, saw how hard the loss hit his father's teammates, as if something integral within them was lost. He remembers seeing the pain in their eyes and how when they looked at him they saw Stu. "I could tell by the way they put their arms around me, by the way they shook my hand, that they'd lost a best friend," says Mitch.

As the night continues and the old names come up, there are surprises: Jim Durbin, the tiny freshman, sprouted up and pitched a one-hitter to help Macon win the conference championship over Niantic-Harristown in 1974. Others struggled with alcohol. There were DUIs, lost licenses. There's one former teammate that none of them have heard from in years. He's somewhere in Decatur, the men say. Even his Alcoholics Anonymous friends can't find him.

Some ended up doing exactly what you'd imagine. Sammy Trusner sits at the end of the table with a shaved head and a goatee in an Under Armour shirt, talking in a serious voice. The equipment manager at Millikin, he was previously an assistant equipment manager at the University of Illinois and has twice been a finalist for a national award in his field. For ten years Trusner wore around his neck the silver baseball each member of the Ironmen received for finishing second at state. Then one night he lost it. "It's still a sore spot for me," he says.

Nearby, stooped and white of hair, Bob Fallstrom trades stories. At eighty-three, he still writes for the *Herald & Review* and is occasionally in touch with Joe Cook, who ended up in Kansas City and finally retired after forty-one years as a newspaper man. Both men say that in all their years, they never saw a more improbable, unlikely outcome than Macon versus Lane Tech.

Indeed, the '71 season follows the Ironmen. Dean Otta, thinning of hair and still built like a catcher, talks about how he was recently at a dinner party and a guest became excited upon learning that Dean was on *that* team. "Around here, people follow high school sports more than college or the pros," Dean says. These days when he does business or goes to church he still sees the boys from Mt. Zion and Blue Mound and the other teams he played against, and they still talk about that season. Like many of the Ironmen, he remains in many ways defined by who he was, and what he did, when he was seventeen.

There is one player from that team who validates the story of the Ironmen. He is the one the others point to. His success is their success.

It is an overcast spring day in 2010 and he walks through the Braves clubhouse. "Wanna do it here?" he says, pointing to a couple of chairs.

Brian Snitker's face is brown from the sun and he still has the build of the slugger he once was. He hit over .500 his final two seasons in Macon, then played at the University of New Orleans before being signed by the Atlanta Braves in 1977. He climbed the ladder from Single-A to Triple-A and then, in 1980 at the age of twenty-four, his career stalled. Snitker was a savvy player, though, and possessed unusual warmth. "Ever think of coaching?" his bosses asked. So again he started at the bottom and moved back up, from Single-A Durham to Double-A Greenville and Triple-A Richmond to, finally, in 2007, the big leagues, where he is now the third base coach for the Braves. There is talk, during the early days of this 2010 season, that Snitker may be next in line when Atlanta manager Bobby Cox retires.

As Snitker talks, the Braves players walk by on their way to batting practice—there is Chipper Jones and Jason Heyward. Sntiker does not notice them. He, too, gets lost in the past. He says he tells the story of the Ironmen to other major league coaches, as well as some of the ballplayers. He talks about how his experience in Macon formed the way he views life and treats people, how it allows him to keep things in perspective. "When you have that many good memories it stays with you," he says. "It's hard to articulate it, but the thing I had growing up is something that I've never heard anyone else have in all my years since in college and professional baseball. I don't hear people talk like that and have the relationships and the friendships that we had. We cherish those."

Snitker doesn't get back to Macon often, but he makes sure to see his old teammates when he's on the road. He leaves tickets and invites them into the dugout to take snapshots with the Braves and then meets up after the game for drinks. Snitker sees how much the other Ironmen cherish that one season. He does as well, but not in the same way. "It was a great time in our lives," he says. "The experiences in that little town were unbelievable. I don't remember a lot and I remember a lot, if you know what I mean."

After forty-five minutes, Snitker gets up. He has to prepare for batting practice. Before leaving, he stops to ask a question. There is one teammate he grew to be closer to than any other, and he thinks about him often but rarely sees him. "How's Shartzer?" he asks.

It all happened so fast after that junior year. As a senior, Shartzer led the conference in scoring as a running back, averaged 28.6 points for the basketball team, ran a 10.3-second 100-yard dash, and threw no-hitters while batting over .500 on the diamond. The letters poured in. In all, more than twenty schools were interested: Missouri, Colorado, The Citadel. Some wanted him to play football. Others wanted him to star in three sports. Eventually, Shartzer signed a letter of intent with Arkansas State to play football, then changed his mind when Itchy Jones at Southern Illinois offered a baseball scholarship. In the end, Shartzer says the decision was easy: He just loved baseball more.

From his first day on campus, Shartzer was a star. He finished second in the country in batting as a freshman and hit .348 during his three seasons at SIU. He led SIU to a third-place finish in the College World Series in 1974; twice led the team in home runs; and was drafted after his junior year by the St. Louis Cardinals, who projected him as a second baseman with twenty-home-run power. When it came time to negotiate a contract, Shartzer leaned on Sweet for advice. Once the negotiating was done and it was time to sign, he brought not a lawyer or an advisor but his father. Bob Shartzer, a lifelong Cubs fan, walked into the office of Cardinals president August Busch wearing a Cubs hat and said, "I'll never cheer for the Cardinals but I'll be a Steve Shartzer fan." Busch appraised him, nodded, and said, "Well, Mr. Shartzer, that's fair enough." At which point Bob Shartzer looked around and said, "OK. You got any beer around here?"

After signing with St. Louis for a good bit more than $20,000, Shartzer headed to Rookie League ball. He married a girl, rode buses, moved up in the system. Then one day during his first year of Single-A ball he decided he'd had enough. Just like that, he quit the game. He went back to school and became a college professor and coach. Years later, when his students asked him what happened in the minors, he always answered, "Obviously I wasn't good enough, or I wouldn't have to be standing here teaching you people."

But it wasn't really that. By most accounts Shartzer had the talent but might have cared *too much*. To him, the game was sacred. What he couldn't overcome was the idea that when he came to the park every day, he was arriving at his job. He was a commodity being paid for his talents, surrounded by other commodities, some of whom didn't care about any one game or the team. He was supposed to pace himself, to think about the long term, to look out for number one. He couldn't do it.

Still, the game stayed in his blood. He went on to tour the country playing fast-pitch softball. He coached baseball for fifteen years, first at Huntingdon College in Montgomery, Alabama, then at Berry College in Mount Berry, Georgia, and later led a girls' softball team to the state final. They lost that one, too.

Along the way Shark got divorced and fell in love with another girl. Her name was Melanie and she was younger, full of life. They had a daughter named Anna. Eventually, Steve and Melanie split up, too, while Anna grew up to become a star softball player at the University of West Alabama. Now, sometimes when he watches her play, so willful and aggressive, Steve sees himself. There's only one difference: Anna can let go of the losses.

It is the spring of 2010 and Shartzer's feelings about Macon remain complicated. Unlike his teammates, who revel in what they accomplished, he can't stop thinking about what they did not. "Probably the biggest disappointment in my career is losing the damn state championship," he says. At fifty-six, he has a halo of gray hair and the hint of a paunch, but he retains that old intensity. More than any of his teammates, he can remember every pitch of that game, every opportunity missed. He remembers the ball he hooked just foul in the seventh inning, the one that would have been a home run—who cares that the reason he hooked it was probably the injury to his top hand or that he went on to hit a single in the same at-bat. He remembers those wild pitches, the balk.

He remembers it all even though he's been trying to forget it for forty years. The process began in the summer of 1971, not long after the state tournament, when he and Heneberry drove down to Virginia to go fishing on Wards Creek, off the James River. The two boys stayed at an old fishing camp with no power, running water, or bathroom, spending their days drinking beers, braving torrential thunderstorms, and, as Shartzer puts it, "catching the shit out of the fish." On the last day, Shartzer decided it was time for a ceremony of sorts. His old eight-track tape deck, the one that had been on all those bus rides and on the bench for all those games, that had become the totem of their state tournament run, needed to be retired. So the duo rowed out to the middle of the creek and Shartzer stuck in the *Jesus Christ Superstar* soundtrack, cued it to the first song, and cranked it up as high as it would go. Then the two boys grabbed the tape deck—and with it all those memories—and they stood up and heaved it as far as they could out into the creek. Shartzer remembers how the stereo arced through the air, how it hit with a splash and gurgled for a moment, then disappeared forever.

And yet here he is, half a lifetime later, and the memories continue to surface. Even now, Shartzer still can't bring himself to face the people of Macon. In the last forty years he has been back three times: once for the reunion and twice for funerals. "My daughter is on me real hard," he says. "She wants to go back this summer and meet John Heneberry and see these places and meet some of these people." He pauses. "It's hard, though. They expected me to win that championship game, and I just didn't get it done. In a lot of ways I still feel like I let them down. There's a lot of people who probably think I could use some professional help, but I felt that strongly that I could win that game. I had the ball in my hands . . ." He trails off.

At first Shartzer hesitated to even discuss that season. He knows it's strange, but he doesn't want to constantly replay that game. "It's in my heart and soul," he says. "And it will be to the day I die. I'd like a rematch." He pauses. "I guess I'm still upset that we didn't win, and I'm not sure how to resolve that. Maybe old Coach will help me one more time."

22

The Return

"Forty years later and he's still worried about some game?"

Mark Wronkiewicz shakes his head, blows a puff of steam into the cold Chicago air. "C'mon man, get over it."

A year has passed and now it is the early months of 2011, nearly forty years to the day since the state semifinal. Wronkiewicz is on his way to the annual Lane Tech baseball reunion. This year it's at an Italian joint on the north side of Chicago, where Wronk joins fifty-odd Lane alumni from as far back as the class of 1949. They eat pizza off red-checked tablecloths and drink pitchers of beer and Coke. When talk turns to the Macon game, some of the men have a hard time placing it.

"Was that the state tournament in '71 or '72?" asks one player.

"I think it was 1971," says Jim Iwanski, the first baseman on that team. The confusion is understandable. After all, Lane Tech made it to the state tourney three years in a row. After losing in the quarterfinals in '70 and to Macon in the semis in 1971, the 1972 team went 27–2 and again arrived at the tournament as strong favorites before losing 1–0 to Kankakee.

Much of the 1971 Lane Tech team is on hand for the reunion. There's John Rockwell, the leadoff hitter who was drafted by the Royals out of high school. Next to him, talking loud and patting everyone's back, is Rick Wachholder. Short and wiry and full of life, he's the one who organizes these reunions, who keeps everyone coming back.

And then there's Wronk. At fifty-eight years old, he is tall and handsome, with a strong chin and great hair. He looks like a politician or the father on a TV show. After high school, he went to Illinois State, led the team with a 2.12 ERA in 1973, and pitched against Shartzer when the latter was at SIU. At twenty-four, while playing in the low minors, Wronkiewicz was cut. "It broke my heart," he says, looking down into his beer. "I was paid the least and had invested the most." His downfall? He never did adjust to the curveball.

As one beer leads to another, the Lane players' memories start to come back. It turns out they do remember the Macon game, quite well in fact. They especially remember what happened to their starting catcher. He wasn't injured, like most people thought. Rather, the poor bastard got too drunk the first night of the tournament and Papciak, forever old school, decided to punish him by benching him against Macon. Papciak thought he could "get by" Macon with his backup catcher, as the players remember it. What he didn't count on was the distant backstops of Meinen Field and the speed of the Ironmen. Even with all the errors, though, Wronk doesn't like to make excuses. "To be clear, they were better than us on that day."

After the reunion winds down, the core of the '71 team moves to the Har-Hig pub at the corner of Harlem and Higgins, a small neighborhood bar where the regulars pay for beers with poker chips. Soon enough, shots of Jameson are sent down gullets and the Irish is rising in the boys. There is talk of going down to Macon, busting into the gas station, and liberating the trophy in order to reengrave it. To which Wronk quips: "Why would we want it? It's a second-place trophy."

As the lighthearted boasts continue, it becomes evident that these men are not that much different from those down in Macon, at least not in the ways that matter. They still love each other and the game. They feel a sacred bond to what happened when they were seventeen and feel that bond is worth holding on to, no matter what it takes. They are teammates.

Finally Greg Walsh, a reserve outfielder on the '71 team and the most gregarious of the bunch, raises his beer and sends a message. "Tell the Macon boys we'll come down there and kick their fucking ass in a rematch," Walsh says. Then he smiles. "And if we don't, then we'll drink beer with them."

C'mon man, get over it.

Shartzer is trying. Still, he remains conflicted. Preparing to talk about that season again, near his house in Foley, Alabama, in February of 2011, he calls Sweet for advice, expecting to hear how they're going to spin the media on this one. But instead Sweet says something strange: *It's OK, Steve. It's time to come to terms with this.*

So Shartzer gets up early, shaves meticulously, and puts on his matching softball jacket and hat. Then he heads to the local Waffle House, where he stations himself in a booth. Over the years, his body has betrayed him; he is now thick in the middle and walks gingerly. "I sit sometimes and I think where are those son of a bitches at now that told me how good I was, with two bad shoulders, a bad hip, and a bad knee," he says, staring into his cup of coffee. "We didn't know what a damn concussion was. Burns would say, 'Go out and ring that bell for me' and, buddy, we did, or we got our bell rung."

After his second divorce, Shartzer bought a beach house in Gulf Shores, Alabama. Four hurricanes and a market crash later, he can't bring himself to sell it so far below value. He doesn't want to stay here, doesn't want to die in Alabama. But when it comes to Macon, as he says, "It's pretty hard to go back, those days are gone . . ."

Just talking about the team is still difficult. More than once he says he's only doing so "because Sweet and Anna got me to." They told him to "have fun with it," that everything doesn't need to be "serious and negative," that he was a "positive force for a lot of people." That he *deserves* it. Shartzer shakes his head. "Deserve what? We lost the damn game. Anna says, 'They wouldn't have even been there without you.' But we were there. See, they missed that. We *were* there. And I let down all those people." He pauses. "I know them boys are having a ball reliving this. I just don't."

Sweet has been urging Shartzer to come back to Macon. So far, he has resisted, but he knows he must at some point. "I just really need to get over that thing," he says. "I don't know why. I really don't. I don't have all the answers, I need to find them, though."

A month later, in March of 2011, word comes from Sweet. It took some prodding, but Shartzer is on his way back home.

The following Saturday afternoon, there they are, just like in the old days: Goose, Shark, and Sweet, all sitting around Sweet's large wooden dining room table. Shartzer is once again wearing his softball hat and jacket, and is in the process of rapidly evacuating a can of Bud Light. Sweet sips a Sam Adams from a plastic mug. Heneberry drinks only water, though not for lack of effort on the part of Shartzer, who made a spirited attempt to get his friend to imbibe that ended only when Heneberry finally made it clear, after repeated hints, that he'd given it up years ago.

The men settle in, talking about kids and jobs and, eventually, the 1971 season. Here, amid friends and outside of town, Shartzer is comfortable. Told that the Lane Tech players want a rematch, he roars in approval. "Tell them I said we'd beat them again," he howls, slamming his Bud Light onto the table. "They couldn't beat Goose. They'd never beat me. Their ass!"

There is laughter. No, he is told, the Lane Tech guys are *serious*. They actually want to play. Now Shartzer frowns. "Maybe we got to split the game up," he says, thinking of his bad hip and his busted shoulder.

Heneberry looks at him, surprised. "Split the game up?

"Maybe I go three innings, you go four. Put the ginzu on them, the hoooooook."

Sweet nods. "John, that was the best pitching performance I've ever seen in my career."

Heneberry looks touched. "Really?"

"Ah, hell," says Shartzer. "Goose was great but want to know how we beat Lane Tech? They stayed out all night partying with the fans. They were so damn hungover and drunk, they couldn't play the next day. Ain't nobody told you that?"

There are startled looks. *How do you know?*

"Shit, I could tell by the way they played that they were partying all night," Shartzer says. "Plus, Miller and I sent a couple of girls over there to make sure they stayed up longer than they should. Those girls came back and said, 'Shark, they don't need any help. They're throwing down over there.' So the next day we're thinking we need to make them work in that hot sun, let that bastard beat on that drum, and get you some of Heneberry's curveball, which is about the worst pitch to have to hit when you're hungover."

Now Sweet is laughing. "That's a genius move, man, I like that," he says. "I didn't know you guys were so proactive."

Informed that the Lane Tech players had in fact been out drinking and Papciak had indeed benched his catcher for too much carousing, Sweet nods. "I don't blame him. Go have fun, but answer the bell, right Shark?"

"Yup, gotta stand tall, gotta man your post," Shartzer says. "Boys gotta know when to suck 'em and when to set 'em down."

There are sage nods all around. Sweet gets up and walks to the refrigerator to restock the beers. Jeanne comes over and joins in. Inevitably, the talk turns to the championship game against Waukegan.

"It came down to that throw," says Sweet. "It was on the money. Let's face it, I don't think he could do it three times in a row."

"I'm thinking he was playing in a little bit," says Heneberry, "knowing Jeff Glan wasn't going to hit it out of the park."

Sweet looks up, resolute. "I'd do it again."

Shartzer jumps in. "Hell, yes. Did I sit over there and think 'Fuck!'? No, I was pitching and I thought, 'What a play.' We didn't function like that. That was roll the dice, I'm letting everything ride on it and *that* was Macon at its best. One play."

Shartzer can only stay in the safety of Sweet's place out in the country so long. It's time to go back in to Macon.

The drive takes ten minutes, past hay bales and cornfields still green with newborn stalks. Shartzer sits in the passenger seat, slugging another Bud Light, as if the beer might provide a cloak of invisibility. He tries to work through why he's here, and why he's talking about this again. "When this started, Anna said, 'Dad, don't me and my children deserve some legacy?' It stopped me in my tracks. Children aren't supposed to be that wise." Shartzer pauses. "That and a couple other things set me on the quest. I gotta answer this before I die. Why did I take this so hard? I don't have any more answers today than I did yesterday, but I will someday."

They pull into town and park across from the one-story post office and the Masonic Lodge, its sign reading GET YOUR TICKET FOR THE FISH FRY 6/12/11. Shartzer takes one final swig, crumples up the can. "Ah fuck, might as well do this," he says. Then he gets out of the car and walks into Whit's End.

Over the next few hours, something unexpected happens: Shartzer comes to life. It begins at Whit's End and continues across the street at the Finish Line, which looks almost exactly as it did in 1971, when it was Claire's Place. Shartzer jokes with the waitress, hugs old friends, puts his arm around people who approach him, saying, "Sure, I remember you! Remind me your name again." A man in his fifties brings over his three children and stands there—he just wants them to meet the legendary Steve Shartzer.

What's left of the old town comes out: Jack Heneberry and Diane and Letha Tomlinson, the grown Jesse boys, and a bunch more. There is a woman here, too, one that Shartzer used to date in high school and whom he has started seeing again. Divorced, she lives in Philly now and flew in for the weekend. She's thin and pretty and when she looks at Steve there's warmth in her eyes. They make a good couple.

Here, in the Finish Line, Shartzer is different. He is funny and charming and the life of the party. There is no hint of that sad man from the Waffle House in Alabama. The pieces start to fall into place. The softball sweatshirt and hat he wears everywhere? They are not the remnants of his coaching days, some ex-jock trying to subsist on old glory, but rather from the University of West Alabama, where Anna plays softball. He has also brought a printout of her stats, and will spend much of the next day in his hotel room, following her game online. He talks about how he wants to support her without smothering her, of how much she means to him, of how most parents these days don't realize that the most important gift they can bestow upon their kids is the gift of time.

As the night wears on, Shartzer takes it all in. He buys a round for the bar, tells old stories, and then, in a quiet moment, surveys the crowd. "Look at all these people lined up, Jack and Jeanne and Lynn—these are the people I let down," he says, waving his Bud Light in a circle around the room. And in this moment, his regret about the Waukegan game takes on a different hue. Maybe this really is about all those people—about Macon. It makes one wonder: Is it sad that Steve Shartzer still cares so deeply about his hometown that he regrets one long-ago baseball game? Or is it in some ways heroic?

One also can't help but ask: What if the Ironmen had won? How different would Steve Shartzer's life be? Would one win, one game, change that much?

Down at the end of the room, leaning on a stool at the wooden bar where he was once recruited to be Macon's baseball coach, Lynn

Sweet only smiles when you ask this question. It's not that he doesn't know the answer. It's that he knows it isn't the right question.

Glancing over, Sweet watches Shartzer with a small grin. None of this is his doing, Sweet contends, even though of course it is. He's just an old English teacher, he says. What does he know?

Maybe that line once worked. But wherever Sweet goes on this night, his past follows him. Old and young, they brighten up. "Sweet!" they shout, and then they talk about how he changed their lives, how he changed the town. "Can we take your picture?" a blonde woman says upon spying him. She is with two friends, celebrating a fortieth birthday. All three took Sweet's English class in high school.

"I became a writer because of you," the blonde says. "You influenced me so much."

Sweet tries to brush it off. "Oh, hell, I was having more fun than you were."

She won't hear of it. "No, you inspired me, you had such an impact."

Again Sweet waves it off. Just as he waves off the ex-players who still come around, telling him how he changed their lives—how they became coaches because of him. "I was just a coach," he says. "You guys did all the heavy lifting." And if you didn't know better, you might believe him.

Talk to those who know him best, though, and the story changes.

Just a coach? Ask Cassie Mavis, Mark Miller's daughter, about that. In 2003, when Miller learned he had pancreatic cancer, the doctor told him he had three to six months to live. He lasted three years, during which Lynn and Jeanne regularly visited and took him out fishing. During the final months, a number of his old teammates came around to see him, but one man showed up every day. Arriving with a book or a magazine, Sweet sat with Miller for hours. They didn't even have to talk. Miller might sleep, and Sweet would read. It gave Mark's wife, Lou Ann, a chance to run errands, and the family a chance to regroup. "That's something Lynn would never tell you about himself," says

Cassie. "He liked to be there when the doctor brought the daily report. It was incredible."

When the end was near, Sweet pulled Cassie aside. "I love you, kid," he said, and then he hugged her, even though hugging was something Sweet never did. Later, she realized it was his way of reaching out to her, of saying, *I know this is bad*. "It always made me feel a little sad when he'd do it," she says. "Because I knew he was hurting, too."

Just a coach? When Miller's funeral was held in 2006, Shartzer didn't plan on attending. He still couldn't bear to face Macon. Even though Shartzer had been one of Miller's best friends, the family didn't expect him to show up. After all, Miller always said Shark would never come back to Macon again.

Then, not long before the funeral, Shartzer got a call. "Shark, I need your help on this one." It was Sweet. He didn't demand anything, didn't browbeat him. Rather, Sweet told Shartzer that people needed him—that his teammates and his coach needed him. Shartzer booked his flight. The Miller family says it was important to see him there.

Just a coach? Shartzer claims Sweet knows as much about baseball as anyone he met on his journey through the game—that the proof resides in Shartzer's own dominant coaching record and hundreds of victories. He says it was Sweet who taught him not to look at the forest for the trees but rather to say, "Fuck the forest, look outside all that, because it's a big world out there." Just talking about Sweet causes Shartzer to tear up. "If I die today, I'd just like to thank him," Shartzer says. "It was an honor."

Just a coach? Every February, when Brian Snitker drives to Braves' spring training he pulls out a CD and slips it into the car stereo as he rolls through Georgia. As the opening songs of *Jesus Christ Superstar* play he sings along. Listening to the album has become an annual rite. It's a way for Snitker to remember who he was and where he came from. Inevitably, it conjures memories: of Sammy Trusner playing air piano, of Shartzer warbling along, of Sweet dealing cards on the bus.

So much has happened since then. Snitker has been to dozens of cities, coached all manner of teams, and shared clubhouses with future Hall of Famers. And yet, forty years later, he continues to draw upon the lessons of his old coach back in Macon: Treat people well, believe in them, entrust them with responsibility. Lift them up.

If you go looking for Lynn Sweet today, the chances are good you'll find him out by his lake. He might be sitting there, in one of his lawn chairs, watching the birds. Sometimes, if the mood strikes him, he'll bring his fishing pole and send a line looping out into the water. He doesn't catch much, but that's OK. Life is not in the catching, as Sweet sees it. It's the process that he enjoys.

Once in a while, when the afternoon has turned to evening, Sweet will head up Route 51, headlights illuminating the H-A-W-K-S sign outside Macon, until he reaches the turnoff and pulls into the P&V. Walking to the refrigerated case in the back, he'll pick up a twelve-pack and carry it to the counter. Then he'll look up, past the clerk, to that small trophy on the top shelf, its batter forever frozen in midswing.

There are those among the Ironmen who want to see the trophy moved somewhere more prominent. Maybe the community center, where it could be properly preserved, in its own glass case. Sweet's not one of them. It is just a trophy, after all. The way sees it, that's not how the season survives. "It was a beautiful thing that happened, but it's over," he explains. Then he points to his chest. "It's in here now."

So Sweet will allow his gaze to linger for a moment, fixed on the piece of his life that remains up on that shelf. Then, without a word, he will turn and walk out into the cool Macon night.

Acknowledgments

This book wouldn't have been possible without the assistance of Lynn Sweet and the members of the 1970 and 1971 Macon Ironmen baseball teams.

Throughout, Sweet was humble, accommodating, and insightful. He was a gracious host, a lively conversationalist, and an excellent drinking buddy. I will be forever grateful to him and Jeanne Sweet for allowing me into their life for the better part of two years. They showed me around Macon and handled my never-ending questions, follow-ups, and fact-checks with amazing good humor. I can't thank the two of them enough.

Three other Ironmen were especially giving of their time. Steve Shartzer hosted me in Alabama, shot the shit in Macon, and opened up unconditionally. He was charming, thoughtful, and uncensored, and I couldn't have written the book without his keen insight and impressive recollection of people, places, and dialogue.

Dale Otta and John Heneberry provided the backbone of much of my reporting. Otta answered endless questions, sent me boxes of old mementos, took me into the dungeons of Meridian High, and drove me around central Illinois, all without complaint, even when I mixed up the dates of our appointments (sorry, Dale). It's not hard to envision him as the rock of the Macon baseball team.

Heneberry was the ultimate raconteur. When I talked with John I always made sure to run tape, because his stories were so well-told that I often forgot to take notes. He and his wife, Karen, hosted me on multiple occasions—the deer chili was awesome, Karen—and were giving of their time.

Others from the team who provided invaluable assistance include Sam Trusner, who possesses remarkable recall and a big heart; Jeff Glan, whose quiet intelligence shone through; Brian Snitker, who exemplifies many of the best qualities of the small-town experience; Dean Otta; Mike Atteberry; Doug Tomlinson; Jim Durbin; David Wells; and Barb Jesse Kingery. And, last but not least, Chris Collins, who first emailed me at *Sports Illustrated* in 2009 suggesting a story about some long-forgotten high school team. He provided essential background and assistance on the initial magazine story, and I thank him for that.

On the publishing side, I am indebted to Matt Inman, my indefatigable editor at Hyperion. Matt stepped into the project late yet caught up almost immediately. He provided sound advice on narrative matters, was unwavering in his advocacy for the book, and proved a deft line editor. I feel fortunate to have worked with him and won't be surprised if he is running the show somewhere in the not-too-distant future.

Others I'd like to thank at Hyperion include Christine Ragasa, Jon Bernstein, and Bryan Christian.

At *Sports Illustrated*, I need to thank two people in particular. Chris Hunt shaped and shepherded the magazine article on which this book was based. There's a reason he's considered one of the best magazine editors working today. The other is Terry McDonell, for granting me the time to work on this book and always encouraging the writer's voice.

As always, my agent, John Ware, was steadfast throughout the process, the best advocate a writer could hope for as well as a good friend and loyal San Francisco Giants fan. Next round at the Dive Bar on 96th is on me, John.

Attentive readers are crucial with a book like this, and I'm fortunate to have a core group who are both talented writers and skilled editors. Longtime friends Dan Zehr and Owen Good provided valuable feedback on the entire manuscript, often within days of being asked and even when not being plied with pints of Pliny the Elder at Bobby G's, though of course those didn't hurt. Dan Greenstone, whose first novel, *A Theory of Great Men*, was published last year, helped me look at the book through a narrative lens and was a gracious host during my trips to Illinois. Duffy Ballard, Pat Cottrell, and Eric Kneedler provided their usual sound counsel and moral support, in addition to their keen editing eyes. They also assisted in the drinking of many IPAs during "creative brainstorming" sessions. I consider myself blessed to have such good friends.

It would take multiple pages to thank everyone who assisted in my reporting, but there are a few who require special mention. Jane Metzger Nelson had the best recall of anyone I encountered from that period at Macon High and was extremely helpful in re-creating the sense of time and place. The Lane Tech players welcomed me into their reunion, buying me endless rounds of drinks and answering my questions. I'd particularly like to thank Wronk (who even answered further questions via email during a Bears game, a true sacrifice indeed), Jim Iwanski, Greg Walsh, and Rick Wachholder. If you guys ever do play that rematch, count me in to cover it. Matt Troha at the IHSA provided research assistance. Kurt Wagner, a promising young journalist, helped track down obscure facts. Others who were gracious with their time included Jack Heneberry, Leslie Sweet Myrick (a talented writer herself), John Jaggi, Linda Shonkwiler Allen, Dana Dale, Wes Weikle, Bill Weikle, Regina Ward and Michelle Mathias (for providing the school board minutes), Ed Aukamp (for the city council minutes), Joe Cook, Bob Fallstrom, Cassie Mavis, Scott Taylor, Fred Schooley, Andrew Petersen, Dave Britton, Boomer Britton, Mitch Arnold, Joe Mirretti, Lou Ann Warnick, Tom Jennings, Craig and Jeff Brueggemann, Ed Neighbors, Carol Smith, Lavonne Chaney, Carl

Poelker, Jack Stringer, Vi McClard, Merv Jacobs, Dennis Schley, John Rockwell, Sherrie Otta, Patty Shartzer, Diane Tomlinson, John Geisler, Ruth Hilvety, and Brad Friese.

Finally, I'd like to thank my support system, including my parents, who facilitated many a writer's retreat, and in particular my wise, thoughtful, and beautiful (did I mention beautiful?) wife, Alexandra, who offered both her editorial insight and, on those many days and nights I needed to hide away and write, her infinite patience. And, of course, I must thank Callie and Eliza, the best two research assistants a guy could ever hope to have.

Notes

A NOTE ON SOURCES

This is a work of nonfiction. It is based primarily on the accounts of those chronicled herein, particularly Lynn Sweet and the members of the Macon Ironmen baseball team. Where archival information was available, I relied on it to provide a foundation for the narrative. In particular, the coverage of the Decatur *Herald & Review* was instrumental, as well as the Macon *News* and the Peoria *Journal Star*. Other sources that proved invaluable included the school board minutes from Macon High; the Macon city council minutes; old copies of the *The Ironmen Scene* newspaper; Macon High yearbooks from the years 1965–72; and the collections of clippings, letters, and mementos provided by a number of people, in particular Jane (Metzger) Nelson, Chris Collins, Dale Otta, and Lynn and Jeanne Sweet.

One challenge of writing a book such as this one, which focuses on events four decades ago in a small town, is the necessary reliance upon oral history, especially when many of those who lived through the time period have passed away. As a result, the events and conversations in this book are detailed to the best recollection of those involved. In cases where recollections differed, I have noted such below.

While I relied upon hundreds of sources for this book, I spent the most time speaking with the main characters, in particular Sweet, Shartzer, Dale Otta, and Heneberry. In the end this is their story, and the narrative reflects that. Any mistakes herein are mine and mine alone.

In keeping with the spirit of the book, which intends to be both edifying and entertaining, the notes below combine traditional sourcing information with nuggets of information that didn't make the book, as well as reporting anecdotes I found interesting (such as Shartzer's text-message beer taunts from Part III). As a reporter, these are the tiny details I enjoy digging up, so please forgive this indulgence.

PROLOGUE

1—The opening scene is described as witnessed on my first trip to Macon, in April of 2010. Any subsequent current-day descriptions of Macon are based on my trips to the town over a period of two years.

PRELUDE

5—Bob Fallstrom had to read the sheet twice: This anecdote is based on the recollections of Fallstrom and Joe Cook, as well as a column Fallstrom later wrote for the *Herald & Review*.

So as not to lard down the endnotes with attributions, readers can assume henceforth that scenes described in the book are based on the recollections of those involved, unless otherwise noted.

CHAPTER 1

8—a soul-deadening experience: Though Sweet hated the Kraft job, it paled in comparison to the time he spent working as a union roofer in Illinois during college, an experience that clearly influenced his perspective. In the winter he shingled without gloves and in the summer he ran kettles of asphalt up and down ladders onto hot roofs in 100-degree weather. His fellow hot-tar roofers were in their thirties but looked much older. As Sweet remembers it, most were wrecks: divorced, drunk every night. They didn't read books and the daily conversation revolved around topics such as who screwed whom the night before. The highest level of discourse the men reached was when someone fell off the roof or into the kettle and died—a scarily frequent occurrence—and the workers all contributed to the widow. *There has got to be a better way for me to get through this life than this,* Sweet thought at the time.

8—seventh grade report card: this and a number of later artifacts come courtesy of the files of Lynn Sweet.

8—The background on and descriptions of Roger Britton, who is no longer alive, come from interviews with Lynn Sweet; Jeanne Sweet; David Britton; Boomer Britton; LaVonne (Jones) Chaney; Carl Poelker (who provided the great phone negotiation anecdote); Jack Stringer; and others. Macon High yearbooks also proved useful, as did family photos and clippings from Roger's high school days that were provided by the Britton family.

9—past the barber shop: The descriptions of Macon from 1965–72 in this and later chapters are based on Macon *News* archives, *Herald & Review* stories, and interviews with former and current residents. Jane Nelson was particularly helpful.

10—ran the grade school menus: The *News* at the time really was a catch-all for Macon, combining everything from gossip to civic business to spirituality to agricultural advice. For example, a story on how to guard against bagworms—an agricultural pest at the time—shared the same page with a religious column.

10—A good portion of the Macon town history in this section comes from the book *When Macon Was Not: Early History of the City of Macon* Vol. 1," Cecil Cook, Macon Community Association.

CHAPTER 2

14—This chapter about Shartzer's youth could have been much, much longer. The Shartzers are natural storytellers, with a great eye for detail and dialogue. I could print transcripts of my interviews with Steve and they'd probably be enjoyable to read. The majority of what's in this chapter comes from Steve and Pat Shartzer (who now goes by Patty), with contributions from Jeff Glan, Sweet, Heneberry, Scott Taylor, and others.

CHAPTER 3

20—The description of Sweet's classroom is based on yearbook photos and interviews with Sweet, Heneberry, Shartzer, and others.

21—"the most interesting part of the paper": Since no syllabus and few written records exist from Sweet's class during this time period, this and some of the other exercises described are based on the recollections of former students and a number of fellow teachers, as well as Sweet. The exact date of each exercise would be impossible to pinpoint. They are recreated here as faithfully as possible, with Sweet's best guess at the dialogue.

22—*Carpmaster Magazine*: The details are from copies that Sweet kept.

25—The background and descriptions of Bill McClard (who has since passed away) are based on interviews with Lynn Sweet, Carl Poelker, LaVonne (Jones) Chaney, Jack Stringer, Linda Shonkwiler, Jane Metzger, and others. For much of the information, the primary source was Bill's wife, Vi McClard. Yearbooks, news stories, and archival photos also helped.

26—$450 monthly take-home check: This and other dollar amounts in the book come from either Macon city council records—where all town expenditures were noted—or the school board minutes. In some cases I also referenced Sweet's old pay stubs, which Jeanne kept.

30—The itinerary for the St. Louis trip comes courtesy of Lynn Sweet.

CHAPTER 4

32—Claire's was the kind of small, smoky bar: Of all the places in Macon, Claire's appears to have changed the least. Other than a new name (The Finish Line, a nod to the Macon Speedway nearby) and a sign bearing pictures of race cars, the bar looks the same now as it did then, according to those who would know. Descriptions of the characters who populated Claire's are based primarily on the memory of Lynn and Jeanne Sweet.

33—managed only one win—and that came on a forfeit: from an interview with Doug Tomlinson in 2011.

34—The recruitment of Sweet was reconstructed based on accounts of Lynn Sweet, Steve Shartzer, Dale Otta, John Heneberry, Jack Heneberry, and Jeff Glan.

34—first conference title since 1962: Since there are no sports records kept at the school, I had to rely on newspaper accounts for much of the Macon sports history. This comes from the Macon *News,* "Macon Wins Meridian Baseball Title," May, 1969.

35—After two days of rain: This and other weather descriptions in the book come from one of a number of sources. Where possible I relied on reports from Weather Source, which pulls meterological readings from weather stations, or the National Climatic Data Center. I also used published information from the Macon *News*, the *Herald & Review*, and—for the postseason run described in Part II—the papers in Peoria and other playoff sites.

39—fond of ordering the boys: I ended up with a wealth of great Jack Burns anecdotes. My favorite that didn't make the book is that, when the going got tough during a game, Burns often turned to his players. "BOYS," he would shout. "IT ALL COMES DOWN TO WHO'S GOING TO BE THE FUCKEE AND WHO'S GOING TO BE THE FUCKOR. WHICH ONE DO YOU WANT TO BE?"

The stories about Burns as a teacher were also amusing. Apparently, at least once a month in Burns' chemistry class, a strange smell wafted out into the hallway. The smell was followed in short order by a stream of evacuating students. This shouldn't have been a surprise, as Burns had no chemistry training.

40—"World War II rejects": This is from a retrospective Decatur *Herald & Review* article by Joe Cook, March 25, 1972. The majority of media coverage of Macon prior to the tournament was based on the reporting of Cook. Fallstrom began writing more about the team once they made the state tourney.

CHAPTER 5

43—The description of the team's equipment is based on the impressive recollection of Sam Trusner. Shartzer, Sweet, Heneberry, and Dale Otta were also helpful.

43—most precious commodity: this was in the age before aluminum bats, so everything was wood and manufactured by Louisville Slugger. The first aluminum bat was introduced in the spring of 1970, made by Worth. It was years before they were widely adopted.

45—The description of the Pana game is from interviews with Sweet, Trusner, and the other Ironmen, as well as accounts by Larry Kehias in the Pana paper.

45—a parent walked into: The parent in question is deceased and could not answer to the charge of calling Sweet a communist. Since using his name didn't add to the narrative, I chose to refer to him only as "a parent."

45—The descriptions of the school board meetings, and the school board in general, are based on the school board minutes from 1965–72 as well as interviews with former board president Merv Jacobs and a number of teachers, including Poelker, Chaney, and Sweet.

CHAPTER 6

52—The description of the Maroa field is based on interviews with Maroa alum Wes Weikle, Maroa athletic director Dana Dale, and Maroa alum Bill Weikle, as well as a visit to the school.

55—"He ain't got shit": I loved this nickname so much that for a while I thought about trying to use it as the name of the book.

56—covered roughly one hundred schools: all Joe Cook background comes from Joe Cook. The background on the *Herald & Review* is from Cook, Fallstrom, and the current *Herald & Review* librarian and staff.

59—"They found that ball yet?": This story is oft-told and beloved by the Macon players and exists in a number of variations, though most are quite similar. The version I used comes from Mike Atteberry, who went on to room with Mike Ferrill in college.

62—That the Mt. Zion players left the field cursing: The Mt. Zion perspective here and elsewhere in the book comes from 2011 interviews with Mt. Zion players Craig Brueggemann and Jeff Brueggemann, as well as Mt. Zion coach Ed Neighbors.

62—headed to the regionals: Around this time, the Ironmen were fond of invoking a Sweet-concocted character called "King Siege," who served as a mythical mascot of sorts for the team. Mark Miller, a talented artist, drew posters of the King, muscle-bound and glory-bestrewn, that adorned Sweet's walls. After the disqualification, Sweet even wrote a poem about the death of King Siege, and how he never lost on the field but was "drug down by his detractors, and treachery."

62—Background on the Illinois high school baseball playoffs, including the number of schools involved and the history of the tournament, comes courtesy of Matt Troha, assistant executive director of the IHSA, who was kind enough to send me some imposing Excel spreadsheets in addition to archival information.

62—bereft of divisions and classifications: At the time there was already talk of the need to add them. That spring, in an editorial in the Decatur *Herald & Review* titled "It's Time for a Classy Meet," Bob Fallstrom argued that the "class system is desperately needed in the state track and field meet," citing the long dominance of Chicago schools that are "simply too powerful." Wrote Fallstrom: "As in basketball, the small school athletes can't begin to compete on an equal basis."

62—Lane Tech background: Based on information provided by Lane Tech and its Web site, as well as interviews with former Lane Tech players and visits to the campus.

63—finishing the season with a 5–0 record and a staggering fifty-one strikeouts: this and other Macon stats courtesy of Lynn Sweet's records.

63—"Steve, I want you to pitch against Stew-Stras": based on an interview with Steve Shartzer in 2011.

CHAPTER 7

65—The history and description of Fans Field is based on the recollections of players on both teams, in particular Sam Trusner and John Heneberry of the Ironmen and John Geisler and Brad Friese of Stew-Stras. Archival information from the Decatur Public Library, including photos of the park at the time, also proved useful.

66—brimming with confidence: this and other representations of the Stew-Stras players' perspective are based on interviews with John Geisler and Brad Friese

66—nearly 150 fans: The number of fans present is based on talking to multiple players and fans, whose estimates varied between 100 and 250.

68—"renowned for his resolve": Sweet tells stories of watching Roush get passed by more talented runners late in races only to struggle back and win.

68—another high heater: Geisler gave Roush another fastball because he and Friese believed that until a new hitter—especially a pinch hitter—proved he could hit the fastball there was no need to slow it up.

70—The description of the final inning is based on interviews with Sweet, Shartzer, Geisler, Friese, Heneberry, Trusner, Shartzer, Atteberry, Glan, Tomlinson, and Dale Otta, as well as photos in the 1970 Macon yearbook and articles in a number of newspapers.

70—The background on Mike Atteberry and his father is from interviews with Mike Atteberry and the obituary of Charles Atteberry in the Macon *News*.

72—customary postgame sheet: courtesy of the archives of Lynn Sweet.

74—All background on Jeanne Sweet and her relationship with Lynn is based on interviews with the couple and their friends, as well as photos, letters, and the Macon High yearbooks. One quote that didn't make the book comes from their daughter Leslie. She told me that when she was a young girl, she once asked her mom who her best friend was. Says Leslie: "We were in the kitchen and I remember my mom stopping what she was doing and really thinking about it. Then she said, 'Your father.' I know it sounds trite or corny now, but at the time people didn't say things like that."

CHAPTER 8

77—"report to the library": The re-creation of this scene is based on interviews with nearly a dozen people, including players, parents, and teachers. Some had only vague memories of the meeting while others remembered a detail here and there. Dale Otta remembers the meeting being in the junior high gymnasium, which doubled as the theater. Others remember it being in the school library. In this case, I've gone in large part with the recollection of John Heneberry, who had the clearest memory of the proceedings and dialogue. I then added in details taken from other interviews, especially Sweet.

78—"This," he said, "is absolute horseshit": This and rest of the reaction is from Lynn and Jeanne Sweet, Tomlinson, Shartzer, Dale Otta, and Heneberry.

CHAPTER 9

83—For the special board meeting on September 3, 1970, the details and context come from the school board minutes for that year and years prior. Additional dialogue, details, and information comes from interviews with Lynn Sweet, Merv Jacobs, John Heneberry, Vi McClard, Dennis Schley, and others.

84—wasn't fond of Ernie Miller: This is based on the recollections of a number of people, primarily Lynn Sweet.

87—the seventy-foot trailer: The trailer park had only recently opened, to some fanfare, after a lengthy approval process by the city council.

88—Wedding announcement: from *The Ironmen Scene*, courtesy of Jane Nelson's files.

CHAPTER 10

90—Homecoming details are from the files and recollections of Jane Nelson and John Heneberry.

91—Reaction to Sweet's firing: Recollections of this varied. Strangely, some people don't remember it at all, even though it was recorded in the school minutes. Others remember elements of it. Shartzer's reaction is based on what he remembers thinking he would have done.

91—Since Dick Snitker is deceased, the descriptions of him are based on interviews with Brian Snitker and Angela Snitker, as well as Sweet, Heneberry, and many others.

CHAPTER 11

101—A number of the boys provided their recollections of Vietnam. The stories about Whittington are from the Macon *News* in 1968 as well as Heneberry, Otta, and Jane Nelson (who heard the sniper story).

102—The story of Miller's grain elevator ascent is pieced together from interviews with John Heneberry, Lou Ann Warnick (Mark's wife), Dale Otta, Sweet, and others. There was some dispute as to exactly when it took place—whether it was during Mark's junior or senior year—and here I've gone with Heneberry's recollection of the timing, though it doesn't impact the narrative much either way. The description of the grain elevator is from interviews, old newspaper photos, and present-day examination (it's still going strong).

103—a long history of foolish endeavors: In choosing which anecdotes about the boys to put in the book, I had plenty of options. Shartzer in particular has a keen memory for such exploits. Many of them involved hunting, though there was also the time Shartzer knocked back a bottle of homemade wine before winning the 100-meter dash (a feat he backed up by showing me the news clipping documenting his victory).

In the case of the snake in the drawer, Poelker was sitting in a wheeled chair at the time and was apparently so shocked by the reptile's presence that he shot backward the length of the room.

106—knew the team wasn't as talented: To this day, many of the players on the team believe this, including Dale Otta, leading them to wonder just how far that 1970 team would have advanced

107—relics from three different eras: This can be seen in the photos included in the book (as well as in the cover shot), where the variety of uniforms and caps is evident.

CHAPTER 12

109—"going to be in the pros someday": This conviction is something Shartzer's friends and family members recall vividly. Glan says there was never a time when Steve didn't believe he'd be a star.

110—In a 13–1 win: Alas, the scorebook from the 1971 season has been lost to time. All box scores from the regular season that I reference are from newspaper clips, primarily those in the Decatur *Herald & Review*. Those stats in turn came from Sammy Trusner, who in turn got them from Barb Jesse, who it's worth keeping in mind was a freshman at the time (and known to be generous when it came to determining hits versus errors).

111—"Glan has to be the quarterback": Glan ended up being a successful quarterback, even though he rarely threw the ball. Burns entrusted him to call all the plays, and the boys had full faith in him. One downside was that Otta, who'd been an elite wide receiver early in his career at Macon High, rarely saw the ball as a senior because the team ran the ball so much (and when Glan did throw it, it was usually a short pass).

112—monopolized the attention: The actual quote from Heneberry was, "Stu and Steve basically passed around all the girls."

112—saw no shame in discussing one's feelings: Linda Shonkwiler Allen remembers riding the bus to school with Stu from Elwin every day and spending the whole time talking about love, life, and relationships.

112—"those damn buzzsaws": This Burns anecdote comes, as so many in this book do, from Shartzer, who grew to be very close with his coach. When Burns was on his deathbed many years later, he called Steve at his home. Steve was accustomed to his coach being gruff. On this occasion, all Burns said was, "You was the best I ever saw," then hung up the phone. Steve still tears up talking about it.

113—the Teacher: This is one of a handful of teaching mementos Sweet kept.

113—DEFICIENCY REPORT: This and the anecdote about the Steak 'n Shake come from Jane Nelson.

115—Mt. Zion dress code: Description of the school, dress code, and impressions of the Ironmen come from interviews with coach Ed Neighbors, Craig and Jeff Brueggemann, and others.

117—CAT DIESEL hats: Dick Jostes was the father of one of the reserves in 1970 and a big supporter of the team. No one remembers exactly when the hats were banned. Otta thinks it was during the 1971 run when the team hit the playoffs, but others think it was earlier.

117—$1.26 a month to buy supplies: This is according to the school board minutes, which kept track of all official school expenditures. Any other bats and balls purchased were donated by parents or Sweet himself.

117—everyone had his own nickname: The boys often went exclusively by these nicknames when with each other. Some, like "Ott" and "Dean-O" for the Otta brothers, were easy to understand. Others, like "Chip" for Stu Arnold, were more involved. (It derived from the lead character in the Chip Hilton books, who was good at most everything.)

117—"with a little air under it": To this day, Snitker blanches a bit at Shartzer's descriptions of his foot speed, while Heneberry revels in it. As John says with a laugh, "If it hadn't been for Snitker, I'd be the one they were all calling slow."

118—relied primarily on two pitchers: David Wells also pitched in three games during the 1971 season.

CHAPTER 13

120—The Stonington field, where the Mt. Zion game was played, may well have been the worst in the area. There was no fence or infield grass, just a backstop opening onto a big swath of rocky dirt. Since the field was originally an elementary school, the little grass that did exist in right field quickly gave way to the concrete of a basketball court. As a result, right fielders learned to pack tennis shoes rather than spikes.

120—arguably his team's third-best pitcher: The reason for "arguably" is because Neighbors remains resolute in stating that Gary Jones gave him the best chance to win, even if he wasn't the most talented pitcher on the team. Relevant to the situation: The last time Mt. Zion faced Shartzer they'd teed off on him. (The thirteen runs, allowed on a day when the wind was gusting out, were the most Shartzer gave up in any game in his high school career.)

In retrospect, the decision appears easy, however. Gary Jones was a decent high school pitcher, but Jeff Brueggemann went on to be drafted by the Minnesota Twins, played Double-A ball against Snitker, and rose as high as Triple-A with the Toledo Mud Hens. He then became a minor league general manager, followed by a big league scout, and now works as an MLB envoy.

Then again, Neighbors went on to success himself. In the years that followed, Neighbors would build Mt Zion into a dominant program. When he retired twenty-nine years later, it was as the eighth-winningest coach in Illinois high school history.

122—routing Decatur Eisenhower: This was a monumental upset at the time, especially considering Eisenhower had beaten MacArthur. Coming into that game, MacArthur was undefeated, having destroyed city competition all year. Knowing his team needed an advantage, the Eisenhower coach had employed a novel strategy. Before the game, he gathered his players. "Boys, we're going to do something different," he had said. "I want the first four of you to lay down bunts." To the players' surprise, it worked. Four drag bunts later Eisenhower was on the board. The bunts both set the tone for the game and provided the winning margin when Eisenhower pulled it out 6–5.

After besting a program like MacArthur, the Eisenhower players weren't worried about Macon. That week, starting shortstop Jack Zimmer ran into two players from the 1962 state champion team. One of them, Roe Skidmore, had been called up by the Cubs just the year before (and would finish his MLB career with one of the most unusual stat lines in baseball history: one at-bat, one hit). "Keep that Eisenhower tradition going," Skidmore told Zimmer. "Don't let that little school beat you." Not that the Eisenhower players were cowed. "Looks like we're playing a bunch of women today," Zimmer remembers a teammate saying on the day of the game. "They can't be as good as they're touted to be. They're probably smoking pot between innings"

124—the star catcher they came to see: The background on Mt. Pulaski comes from interviews with John Jaggi and news clippings

127—The stories about Scott Taylor and his father are from interviews with Scott Taylor, who still treasures those memories. As for Bob Taylor, he was so enamored of the Ironmen players that once, upon receiving World Series tickets, he chose to bring Steve Shartzer instead of his own son.

CHAPTER 14

129—this was the Macon High Prom: Jane Nelson kept an impressive scrapbook from the prom, and much of what is in the book comes from her. The Macon High yearbook was also helpful.

130—"Mod Squad Bids for State": the funny thing about this story is that the photo the *Herald & Review* chose to run to accompany it was of Dale Otta. Now, not only was Otta perhaps the least "mod" of the Ironmen but the photo the *Herald & Review* used was from the 1968 Macon High yearbook, when Otta was a freshman and sported short, well-combed hair and a buttoned-up shirt. He looked about as mod as Howdy Doody.

134—Champaign Central boasted: The description of the school comes from news clips and the current athletic director at Champaign Central.

134—The background on Lynn Sweet Senior comes from Lynn Junior, Jeanne Sweet, and their archives, which include photos, letters, and other mementos. The details of his military service come from the National Archives and Records Administration, based on information releasable under the Freedom of Information Act. The description of the Battle of the Bulge comes from Sweet's family and friends, including Fred Schooley, and may well have been embellished over time, as such tales are.

The story about playing snow football comes from interviews with Sweet and Schooley, the latter of whom has a particularly vivid memory of the experience. As he says, "Sarge came out and was running through fucking everybody."

138—The description of McClard, and his thought process, comes from his wife, Vi, who has very fond memories of Macon, and now considers their time in the town perhaps the happiest of their lives.

CHAPTER 15

140—The Bloomington game description comes from interviews with Sweet; the Ironmen players (especially John Heneberry, who tells delightful, drawn-out versions of the key plays); Jack Heneberry; and a surprising number of newspaper stories (Spahn slumping on the bench is from one, for example). There are different recollections about the exact timing and number of bats procured during the bat run to Bailey & Himes, but in this case I've relied primarily on Sam Trusner's recollection, as he was the one making the bat run.

150—*He'd forgotten to cover the base*: This oversight, coupled with a few others, were what inspired Sweet to have Fred Schooley come down to Macon the following weekend and provide a two-hour clinic for the boys on where to throw and which base to cover in a number of situations.

150—"You got any of more those heart pills?": This wonderful anecdote comes from Jack Heneberry.

151—fractured a bone: There are varying accounts of Steve's injury. Dislocation is what was reported in the *Herald & Review*, but I read and heard other descriptions—most commonly a fractured wrist. Shartzer clearly didn't bother himself much with the terminology; he says he assumed it was broken. Forty years later, he says the wrist still aches at times, no doubt in part because it was never properly treated.

CHAPTER 16

153—The description of Macon's reaction at the start of this chapter and the next is based on a number of recollections, including everyone from Jack Stringer to Diane Tomlinson to Carl Poelker. Those who were particularly helpful included Dale Otta (whose mom used to take him out to follow the fire trucks) and Jane Nelson. As for Schley's wife—the one with "diarrhea"—while attending the game she had her picture taken by one of the *Herald & Review* photographers, whereupon she leapt up and pleaded with the photographer not to run the photo, lest her cover be blown.

158—JUMER'S CASTLE LODGE: Descriptions of Jumer's are based on the memories of the players as well as media accounts, in particular those in the Peoria *Journal Star* and on the Bradley University website.

159—Seven baseball teams gathered: Media coverage of the state tournament was such that there were two stories about just the banquet alone. Most useful was John Peterson's "Lane Tech Heavy Favorite" in the Peoria *Journal Star* on June 2, 1971. This also provided the tournament poll numbers.

159—welcome banquet was only: This and subsequent descriptions of the tournament events and atmosphere are from numerous newspaper stories, as well as from Sweet and others who were there. One story that was particularly useful was "Lane Tech Will Tie Baseball Meet Mark" in the Peoria *Journal Star* on June 1, 1971, written by the Chicago Tribune News Service.

161—"Macon and Nashville, opponents this morning . . ." This excerpt is from "Macon Players Supremely Confident" by Joe Cook, which originally ran in the Decatur *Herald & Review* on Thursday, June 3, 1971.

162—1971 State Tournament Poll by Illinois Sports Writers: This poll originally ran in the Peoria *Journal Star* on Thursday, June 3, 1971, in an article by John Peterson entitled "Lane Tech Heavy Favorite in Pre-Tourney Poll."

162—official tournament program: Both Sweet and Otta were kind enough to share copies of the program.

164—twenty-two from major league teams: This and other descriptions of the scouts are from a pair of stories by Phil Theobald of the Peoria *Journal Star*.

166—Dick Snitker lay propped in his hospital bed: This scene was necessarily re-created, since Dick has passed away. It is based on Brian and Angela Snitker's recollection and best estimate of what happened at the hospital. The timing (11:30 A.M.) is based on the two-hour duration of the game recorded in box scores. Dick Snitker would go on to listen to the rest of the tournament games from the hospital.

167—"for a press conference": This description of the presser comes from Joe Cook and Fallstrom, as well as from Sweet and Trusner. The quotes are from the newspaper stories that ran in the wake of the interview session. One analogy I didn't include came from E. W. Hesee of the *News-Gazette*, who compared Sweet to "a youthful Mark Twain."

CHAPTER 17

171—The background on Lane Tech comes primarily from the school's impressive website. I also drew from interviews with members of the 1971 team, news stories, and a visit to the school. Descriptions of making the team are from the players, as are the Papciak anecdotes. Tom Jennings, the coach at Lakeview High, is one of those who was subjected to Papciak's griping. Jennings remembers how Papciak was "always complaining even though he'd suit up twenty guys for varsity and have another twenty-five up in the stands, any of which would have started for me." When Papciak would start in about Tech's practice conditions, Jennings wanted to tell him what it was like to have your players walk dozens of blocks to practice every day.

175—"Many high school coaches try to imitate Lombardi." This excerpt is from "Sweet Ignores Coaching Rules," which originally ran in Bob Fallstrom's "Once Over Lightly" column in the Decatur *Herald & Review* on June 4, 1971. Courtesy of the Decatur *Herald & Review*.

CHAPTER 18

179—The description of the Macon fans who traveled to the game comes from interviews with a number of those on hand, in particular Jane Nelson and Scott Taylor, as well as photos from the tournament. The official game count, as recorded in the papers, was 1,971. Those who stayed in Macon on that day describe it as a "ghost town."

180—senior named Cliff Brown: Brown was known as a superfan at Macon, and many spoke highly of him. He also appears to have been something of a class jester. Here is the senior statement he made in *The Ironmen*

Scene upon graduating: "After graduation I plan to grow my hair long and become a hippie. Then I will start on drugs and blow my mind. After I have done this I will fight the draft. This will be great, because everyone thinks I like the Army and I am a clean cut kid."

182—The description of the Lane Tech game is based on interviews with Sweet, the Ironmen players, the Lane Tech players, Joe Cook, Bob Fallstrom, and others, as well as numerous newspaper accounts.

CHAPTER 19

190—no one was better prepared: The subsequent description of the Waukegan team and its approach in general, as well as in the final, comes from interviews with Joe Mirretti and Mike Uremovich, as well as dozens of newspaper accounts. In the end, Uremovich was named the tournament MVP, but he struggled with the game just like Shartzer and Wronkiewicz. He was drafted in the second round of the MLB draft in 1971 by the Minnesota Twins but was eventually cut after six years in the minors. Uremovich never gave up, though—at one point he showed up unannounced in the office of Charlie Finley, the owner of the Oakland A's, intent on convincing him he could still play. Finley called security.

192—The description of the title game comes from interviews with those involved and the spectators, as well as newspaper accounts and a short, grainy video provided courtesy of Chris Collins. Of particular interest among the newspaper stories were the number of classic photos that ran in the Decatur *Herald & Review* that Saturday, including a wonderful one of the Lane Tech drummer in which he looks like he's at an Allman Brothers concert.

199—didn't have much time to grieve: The anecdote about Fitzhugh and "Coach Smith" comes from the Ironmen players, who were too upset at the time to find it funny but now find it hilarious. The Lakeland College coach anecdote comes from a story by Joe Cook that ran in the Decatur *Herald & Review* following the tournament.

CHAPTER 20

203—The description of McClard's reaction during graduation comes from a Joe Cook story entitled "They'll Remember Macon" in the *Herald & Review* on June 6 . The full quote: "We like to keep graduation as formal as possible," McClard said, "but it was impossible . . . We were sitting in the gym waiting for everyone to get back. And here comes a large mass of students carrying Sweet on their shoulders. I would have been trampled to death if I had tried to stop them."

203—Given a few days to ruminate upon the tourney, the media ending up deciding it absolutely loved Lynn Sweet. The *Herald & Review* ran an editorial entitled "When Losers Are Winners." Chamberlain, the AP writer, wrote a follow-up story entitled "Coaches Relieved When Unorthodox Macon Lost." It described the annoyance of the opposing coaches and included the following editorial passage (which was unusual for an AP story): "Actually Macon was an extremely well-disciplined team, gritty and determined. It was a group of high schoolers averaging close to B grades and eagerly pointing for college. In these days that is pretty unorthodox."

Joe Cook, in his "Press Box" column, wrote: "Baseball fans around the state now know that Macon is ten miles south of Decatur. The second place trophy is not quite as big as Waukegan's. It's silver, instead of gold. And it sits in a sandwich shop for all of Macon to admire."

Finally, in a piece titled "Buddy System Without a Pool?" that ran in his *Journal Star* "Prep Scene" column on June 5, Phil Theobald went in whole hog.

> *I am, to the everlasting consternation of my father, somewhat of a liberal. Not the flaming type, mind you, because it is rumored there are fire hoses reeled up somewhere to deal with this element.*
>
> *So it did the heart a good beat to witness L. C. Sweet, with a hairstyle more suitable to a party at Rennie Davis' pad, coach his Macon team to the thirty-second Illinois State High School baseball tournament title game.*
>
> *Check that. Sweet denies being a coach at all, in which case here are congratulations to the first career English teacher ever to accept the runner-up trophy.*
>
> *The Ironmen aren't really a baseball team. They're a Crusade. If your imagination will allow you to hear the farmer and the hardware dealer join in singing "Power To the People" in the top of the sixth, you get the idea.*
>
> *The day of blind obedience in athletics (COACH: "Walk through that wall." PLAYER: "Yes, sir. You are my coach and*

that is a great idea and I will most certainly enjoy doing that.") will not long be with us.

The Macons of this world will see to that. The Macons of this world, my friends, operate on a theory that doesn't include walking though walls just to prove a point.

CHAPTER 21

208—Class 1A: Even with the lower level of competition, it took forty years for the Macon/Meridian baseball team to win another sectional title. In 2011, the team beat Danville to become sectional champs.

208—the shelf where the Ironmen's second-place trophy: The irony of this is that while the Ironmen's trophy is gone, the case it resided in still bears the inscription "Given by student council 1984 in memory of F. Dwight Glan."

208—Sweet is not an easy man to find: All scenes and conversations in Part III of the book come from direct quotes or personal observation. I chose not to write it in the first person but, for attribution purposes, readers can assume I am in every scene henceforth.

210—lost to MacArthur: In losing that game, Sweet says, "Again they put the bunt down on us and we couldn't execute."

211—"the world made sense": An aside on this: When Sweet's father passed away in the late '80s, his politics had changed so radically that he was a Democrat.

212—he seems perplexed: When it came to the story of the team, Sweet felt like he had already "lived the movie."

215—Mitch Arnold: His band is called Wayland and Mitch's goal (which I love) is to "bring back the guitar solo to rock and roll." Growing up, his dad talked about Sweet often. Mitch remembers hearing about the "hippie, free-thinking coach who was a big reason why they won." Stu described Sweet's methodology as "order out of chaos." "I know he passed a lot of ideas on to my dad," Mitch says.

215—the old names come up: One I don't mention is Jane Metzger. She graduated from Illinois State, married in 1974 to become Jane Nelson, and went on to get a degree in physical education, just as she planned, and later a master's in business. Now she is an executive assistant and assistant director of research at an investment management company in Chicago.

215—doing exactly what you'd imagine: The award Trusner has been a finalist for is the Glenn Sharp Award, given to the Equipment Manager of the Year by the Athletic Equipment Manager's Association.

218—led SIU to a third-place finish: In accounts of Shartzer at the time, he was described as a "walking commercial for Red Man Chewing Tobacco." When interviewed by local papers, he often brought up the responsibility he felt to his hometown. "A lot of people in Macon have really supported me and I'm pleased that I can make them happy with my performance so far at SIU," he said. "The first thing I feel when I go hitless in a game is that I've let down my team and those back home who are rooting for me to do so well."

218—Shartzer headed to Rookie League Ball: For the people of Macon, this represented the culmination of the dreams Shartzer spoke of so often when he was a boy. Shartzer, who had always been close with the Glans, received this letter at the time:

> *Dear Steve,*
>
> *Glad for you that you have obtained your childhood goal—so few of us can do that. Hope you can make good at it, and as the Indian proverb is, "May the wind be always at your back."*
>
> *Love and Best Wishes*
> *Grand "mom" Glan*

219—Along the way: When his mom contracted cancer and it became clear she was dying, Steve brought her into his home. "It was very important that I took care of her like she took care of me," he says. She died in his home, in his bed. When Bob Shartzer was also hit by cancer a few years later, Steve says he again refused to let his father be taken anywhere else.

CHAPTER 22

222—while playing in the low minors: Curiously, I could find no record of Wronk's minor league career in the various baseball databases. When I mentioned this to him, he replied in an email: "Don't feel bad about not finding my minor league career. Friend and family (my children) have looked me up and can't find me. Oh, well, I have my memories."

223—Greg Walsh: Greg told a story about how his older brother, Terry, was in Vietnam during the 1971 state tournament. Forty years later, when my *Sports*

Illustrated article about the Ironmen came out, Terry called Greg. "What the fuck?" Terry said. "I thought you won." Which is when Greg broke the news: "Terry, we just told you we won because you were in Vietnam."

223—remains conflicted: In 2010, when the *Sports Illustrated* story came out, the Ironmen players loved it. Shartzer, however, couldn't bring himself to read it. He got phone calls, received emails, and heard from his daughter. It took six months until he finally sat down and read it.

223—bought a beach house in Alabama: Shartzer is still a teacher, now focusing on American history, from the Civil War to the modern era. In many regards, he is the sum of Burns and Sweet. He tries to make students think for themselves, to challenge them like Sweet did. But then a little Burns always comes out when kids complain about how and why they can't get something done. "I'm from a town of eighty people, what you gonna tell me you can't do?" Shartzer will say. "Piss in my ear and tell me it's rain—ain't gonna happen." And if the kid's still apathetic, Shartzer lets loose. "Go ahead, be stupid the rest of your life," he'll say. "But understand that somebody cared, somebody tried, and you're now making a choice."

224—"let down all those people": Even his sister, Patty Shartzer, can't understand it. "I hope someday he realizes all the positive feelings people have about that ball club. He might have let himself down, but he didn't let me down, or Mom or Dad, or anybody I know."

224—"the following Saturday afternoon": Shartzer was in fine form on this day. In returning to Macon, I think he was also perhaps trying to return to his former self. At the time, I was driving down from Chicago, with plans to meet the three of them at Sweet's place around 4:30 P.M. or so. At 3:30, I received a text from Shartzer. It read "Are you going to forfeit this beer match? Sweet, Goose, and I are way ahead."

That night, he kept an eye on my beer supply and, when I matched him most of the evening, gave me the quiet nod of approval. The following Monday, as he headed to the airport, he texted me again. It read "You past [sic] your consumption test with flying colors." Strangely enough, I felt a small sense of pride.

229—It was an honor: Another thing Shartzer said that struck me: "He loved us boys, godalmighty he loved us, and we loved him—and we still do."

230—trophy on the top shelf: When the trophy cases were emptied at Macon High, the trophy needed a home. The owner of the gas station agreed to display it.